News Grazers

For Karen and Matt, Christie, and Annie

News Grazers

Media, Politics, and Trust in an Information Age

Richard Forgette
University of Mississippi

Los Angeles | London | New Delhi
Singapore | Washington DC | Melbourne

FOR INFORMATION:

CQ Press

An Imprint of SAGE Publications, Inc.

2455 Teller Road

Thousand Oaks, California 91320

E-mail: order@sagepub.com

SAGE Publications Ltd.

1 Oliver's Yard

55 City Road

London, EC1Y 1SP

United Kingdom

SAGE Publications India Pvt. Ltd.

B 1/I 1 Mohan Cooperative Industrial Area

Mathura Road, New Delhi 110 044

India

SAGE Publications Asia-Pacific Pte. Ltd.

3 Church Street

#10-04 Samsung Hub

Singapore 049483

Executive Publisher: Monica Eckman

Editorial Assistant: Zachary Hoskins

Production Editor: Laureen Gleason

Copy Editor: Jared Leighton

Typesetter: Hurix Digital

Proofreader: Wendy Jo Dymond

Indexer: Molly Hall

Cover Designer: Gail Buschman

Marketing Manager: Erica DeLuca

Printed in the United States of America

Library of Congress Cataloging-in-Publication Data

Names: Forgette, Richard, author.
Title: News grazers : media, politics, and trust in an information age / Richard Forgette.

Description: First edition. | Los Angeles : CQ Press, 2018. | Includes bibliographical references and index.

Identifiers: LCCN 2017037812 | ISBN 9781933116884 (pbk. : alk. paper)

Subjects: LCSH: Mass media–Political aspects–United States–History–21st century. | Mass media–Political aspects–United States–History–20th century. | Journalism–Political aspects–United States–History–21st century. | Journalism–Political aspects–United States–History–20th century. | Press and politics–United States.

Classification: LCC P95.82.U6 F74 2018 | DDC 070.4/49320973--dc23 LC record available at https://lccn.loc.gov/2017037812

This book is printed on acid-free paper.

SUSTAINABLE FORESTRY INITIATIVE

Certified Sourcing
www.sfiprogram.org
SFI-01075

18 19 20 21 22 10 9 8 7 6 5 4 3 2 1

Contents

PART II. THE EFFECTS OF NEWS GRAZING

List of Figures and Tables

FIGURES

TABLES

Preface

Chomp . . . chomp . . . chomp. Hello, fellow news grazer. I see you. Like a cow chewing its cud, you stand alone with your attention directed elsewhere consuming information, perhaps news. I see you. I see you at the red light with your head dropped to your phone. The light is green now, but you are not moving. I see you at a restaurant. You are sitting with others, but you are really watching the television in the corner of your eye. There you are at the airport. You are busily walking while reading the small text on your phone. Chomp . . . chomp . . . chomp.

Always in proximity to our digital technologies, we are changing our news consumption habits. We have become news grazers. This book is for us, fellow news grazers. Our news grazing is habitual, and we need to take better control of it. Our communication technologies make us feel more electronically connected with the world even as we partly disconnect from our immediate one. But a subtler result of our changing news consumption habits, our news grazing, is that we are changing what we consume. News is adapting to our distracted state of consciousness. This book is about this subtler but profound change that is affecting our perceptions of the political world, notably Congress and the media. I argue that news grazing is affecting our emotional responses to and trust in political institutions.

Public trust in Congress and the media has declined from its already low rates, and a premise of this study is that trust in government is essential for civil society and meaningful democracy. Measuring public trust in institutions is an important gauge of democratic governance. This book makes use of the great studies conducted by the Pew Research Center documenting Americans' changing news consumption behaviors and our trust in government. I would like to thank Pew Research Center for enriching Americans' political dialogue with the center's objective, timely, and important public opinion research. These useful Pew Research studies present compelling evidence of changing public attitudes relating to news and public trust.

The 2016 presidential election only magnified these changing behaviors and attitudes. Our shifting news consumption habits and our attitudes toward politicians and the media were on public display during and after the 2016 election. In the aftermath, the quickly evolving story of the Trump administration and its broader implications further underscore the significance of our changing news habits and attitudes. This book is not specifically about the 2016 election and its consequences; however, it may present some theoretical context that offers greater meaning to the election and its aftermath.

This book will certainly not be the last book (and definitely not the first) written on changing news consumption habits. However, it does synthesize the current state of knowledge produced by committed, objective, and truly insightful academic researchers who study Congress, the media, and their intersection. I would like to thank them for their work. I want to thank particularly my colleague and friend, Professor Jay Morris, who coauthored early papers with me on this topic. His work and ideas set the stage for this book.

Beyond thanking my colleagues broadly, I want to thank my family and friends specifically. I express my heartfelt love and thanks to Karen, Matt, Christie, Annie, Sarah, and Dorothy. Of course, this book would not have happened without them. Just like news grazing, they both distracted (but in the best of ways) and informed me. I dedicate this book to them. Without their help and support, it would not have happened.

Publisher's Acknowledgments

CQ Press wishes to thank the following reviewers, from whom we received valuable feedback during the book's development: Tyler Johnson (University of Oklahoma), Jason Martin (DePaul University Chicago Loop), Michael Parkin (Oberlin College), Jeffrey Peake (Clemson University), Anne Pluta (Rowan University), and Travis Ridout (Washington State University).

The Making of a News Grazer

CHAPTER 1

Why Don't We Trust Congress and the Media?

This book investigates how changing news-gathering habits are affecting our public perceptions of politicians and the media broadly. Particularly, I argue that the sources and devices we use to access news have grown dramatically with the advent of new communications technologies, and these changes are affecting public perceptions of politics. The ultimate goal of this book is to understand better how public perceptions of Congress and the media are formed and to explain how these perceptions are shaped by our own media choices.

Politicians and journalists have never been trusted professional classes comparatively. Gallup Polls have tracked the public's trust of different professions over time. According to Gallup, members of Congress, as a professional class, are less trusted than car salespeople and telemarketers (Gallup 2016). Journalists, meanwhile, have declined in public standing. The percentage of Americans rating journalists as having "low" or "very low" honesty and ethical standards has doubled since the early 1990s. Hetherington and Rudolph (2015) argue how the contemporary decline in political trust is reaching unprecedented levels and contributing to a polarized Congress.

Of course, the American political system is largely based on public distrust of political elites. It is grounded in principles of popular sovereignty, checks and balances, separation of powers, and limited government. This constitutional design was partly an outgrowth of public distrust toward centralized authority. While it is part of our American political ethos to distrust centralized power, we also tend to distrust congressional compromise, denouncing it as unprincipled and political (Hibbing and Theiss-Morse 1995). Instead, most Americans prefer elected politicians who remain consistent with their base constituencies and core values.

For these reasons, Congress has remained unpopular over time, sometimes referenced as the "broken branch" of our federal government (Fenno 1975). Congress has generally been held in lower public esteem over time compared to the executive branch and Supreme Court. It is precisely because of its public transparency and conflicting voices compared with the other branches that Congress is disliked. Congress is on public display, exposing Americans to the wheeling and dealing, appeals to special interests, and partisan rhetoric of representative government. This public transparency is mediated through a television, computer, and smartphone screen increasingly, and this mediated communication is another thing this book is about.

Hibbing and Theiss-Morse (1995) find that Americans do not like partisan conflict, long debate, and crass bargaining, instead wishing for a quieter, more agreeable Congress. Of course, this public preference for a populist consensus—a democratic wish that we will all agree with a well-defined national interest—does not occur in practice (Marone 1998). It is at odds with a legislative process that reflects our national diversity. Most Americans prefer politicians who remain consistent with their base constituencies and core values. In practice, though, effective legislatures compel broad-minded leadership, dialogue, and conciliation among diverse interests to bring about collective action. Americans do not trust or like Congress in practice.

Acknowledging this long tradition of congressional disapproval, I argue that the level of public acrimony toward Congress has deepened in the past decade. According to Gallup Polls, public approval of Congress in 2001 stood at a high of 84 percent. This brief, transcendent point of congressional approval reflected a rally-around-the-flag effect after 9/11. Public approval of all government institutions—Congress, the presidency, Supreme Court, and the military—peaked after the 9/11 terror attacks. Since 2001, though, public approval of Congress has steadily declined more sharply than for other institutions. In fact, congressional public approval dipped to about 10 percent approval or even single digits in 2013 after Congress's government shutdown battle. By 2017, Gallup Polls measured that public approval of Congress increased after the 2016 presidential election to 28 percent and then regressed back to now routine low numbers for both Republicans and Democrats. Despite some variability and regardless of your partisan views, we do not like Congress.

Likewise, we increasingly distrust the media. Americans' trust in the news media was at its highest in the mid-1970s in the wake of investigative journalism regarding Watergate scandal and Vietnam. Americans' trust leveled to the low to mid-50s throughout the 1990s and early 2000s. However, since then, Americans' trust in the media has fallen slowly and steadily. By 2016, less than a third of Americans stated that they had "great deal" or "fair amount" of trust in mass media to "to report the news fully, accurately and fairly" (Gallup 2016).

There are many explanations for why we do not trust politicians and the media. Trust in government, generally, has declined from highs in the

1950s and 1960s, and congressional distrust is just part of this larger issue. My interest, though, is to point out a connection between media and congressional distrust. I argue that our practices and attitudes toward news media are driving the more recent depths and intensity of congressional distrust over the past two decades. By proposing and investigating a new media explanation for congressional distrust, I do not imply that other explanations should be discounted. For instance, I am *not* arguing that excessive partisanship, crass pork barreling, special-interests lobbying, incumbency advantages, or political scandal are not all possible sources of congressional disapproval. I am only suggesting that an explanation grounded in the role of media is less recognized and understood.

My thesis is that our changing news-gathering habits are contributing to recent public distrust of Congress. The media outlets in which we view, read, or hear about Congress have expanded as new media technologies have supplanted traditional news media. Additionally, the diffusion of media devices, like smartphones, DVRs, and tablets, has resulted in an increasingly fragmented and distracted news audience. Media choice is not only altering who accesses news and how they do it; more important, I argue that it is also changing the news itself. I posit a news-grazing explanation of how the public views Congress that I describe subsequently.

News Grazing

Today's media consumers are flooded by choice. We click a remote control, tap a computer keyboard, or touch a tablet screen. But consider for a moment a world without these media screening devices. Would we watch the same programs and access the same information without them? When watching television, would we still be apt to turn from channel to channel if we had to get out of our seats and stand in front of the TV while doing it? Maybe not. If people were less apt to click from channel to channel, would so many channels exist today? Maybe not. Beginning with the remote control, media-screening technology has facilitated media choice. The remote control facilitated greater levels of television watching and highly influenced the manner in which we watched TV. We can be more selective, making a split-second judgment in our viewing. If a program does not tickle our immediate fancy, it takes little to no effort to merely click to another channel . . . and another . . . and another.

The remote control, though, was merely one of the first communication technologies that allowed us to screen or manage media messages. (I would emphasize that the remote control is old technology.) Consider the explosive growth of communication technologies that increasingly allow us to be both more selective with information but also distract us from the moment. Just like the remote control, more recent media technologies—smartphones, tablets, DVRs, video games, and social networks—offer further media choices and distractions. News media now extends far beyond the bounds of its traditional sources.

Not surprisingly, this media gadgetry and choice consumes more of our time and often decreases our focus on other tasks. For some heavy media users, use of media technologies may even approach many disquieting characteristics of a psychological addiction: spending large amounts of time, using it more than one intends, thinking about and repeatedly failing to reduce use, giving up other social activities to use it, and reporting noticeable withdrawal symptoms when stopping the activity. Psychologists dispute whether media addiction is a valid clinical disorder; still, for some, media use can be a compulsive behavior (Widyanto and Griffiths 2006; Winkler et al. 2013). Perhaps you may check your e-mail, Facebook, or text messages more times during the day than you care to admit.

Even if it is not a compulsive behavior, however, media use can become a disruption to other activities. In many ways, media choice and surfing break our attention. Individuals' media practices are increasingly bumping into social norms of appropriateness—cell phones going off in class or church, texting while driving, or TV watching or web-surfing during meals. Media technology—and, correspondingly, media choice—has become pervasive in our work and lifestyle.

This book is about the effects of media choice on politics. Our focus is not on the media technologies themselves but rather on our behavioral responses to them. Particularly, how have our news-gathering habits changed in response to media choice and technologies? Additionally, have these changed habits led to different formats of news media coverage, and correspondingly, are these different news formats changing public attitudes toward politics? I track how citizens adapt to media choice by changing their habits for collecting news. I refer to these still emerging habits as *news grazing*—the decline in traditional routinized news-gathering habits and a corresponding reliance on alternative news sources and formats.

I am particularly interested in a set of public attitudes toward politics—our perceptions of Congress and the news media. Why Congress? The U.S. Congress exists as our political system's clearest laboratory of democracy, a bicameral legislature that reflects our vices and virtues as a culture. Congress has never been popular in terms of public opinion, but it remains a resilient and hopeful institution for our popular governance. Showing how our media consumption habits affect our perceptions of politicians and institutions could sensitize us to our own media choices. Perhaps it may lead some to be more thoughtful media consumers.

Our thesis in this research is that growing media choice is indirectly and unintentionally altering Americans' political perceptions of Congress. I argue media choice is altering how we collect news, resulting in an emerging class of news grazers. In response to news-grazing habits, news producers and makers have correspondingly altered the news itself. I argue that a rising proportion of what we call commentary news formats is affecting how we perceive our politicians and political system. I argue that Americans consume greater amounts of news commentary than in the past. Particularly, I assess whether this commentary news affects perceptions of conflict and polarization between parties and within Congress. Figure 1.1 reflects my news-grazing theory of how media contributes to distrust toward democratic institutions.

The goal of this analysis is to show how our simple, everyday decisions about how we collect news may have collective consequences for our politics, in ways that we perhaps do not fully recognize. By changing how we watch our news, we may be altering the news itself and, correspondingly, how we perceive our political world. Our growing perceptions of congressional conflict and polarization may partly be manifestations of the growing fragmentation of media audiences and our growing distractedness from any single media source. I do not argue that today's polarized parties and Congress are wholly or even mostly due to a fragmented media, only that news grazing and commentary news are contributing to congressional distrust.

Our specific focus is on how Americans collect *political news*—news stories relating to government officials, government institutions, elections, and public policy conflicts. Political news is an essential means for citizens to frame and evaluate issues of government performance. Whether we watch television news, read a daily newspaper, or scan online stories, our political news gathering helps us to understand and participate in a

Figure 1.1 A News-Grazing Theory of Media and Congressional Distrust

Media Choice ⇨ News Grazing ⇨ Commentary News ⇨ Congressional Distrust

Source: Created by the author.

democratic process. This news gathering leads us to think, update our beliefs, discuss politics with others, and participate in elections.

In later chapters, I argue that the growth of news media sources has affected the range and style of coverage. Particularly, I show that television political news is increasingly delivered in commentary formats and less in traditional news formats. These commentary news formats imbue the news with opinion, urgency, conflict, or satire. These engaging forms of commentary news elevate our interest and possibly keep us from clicking away. I evaluate whether these commentary formats affect our public attitudes toward Congress, legislators, and party leaders.

The organization of the book follows the stages of our argument. In Part I, I investigate whether and how changing news-gathering habits have affected news formats and production. After this introductory chapter, Chapter 2 investigates how Americans' news-gathering habits have evolved with media choice, investigating the first causal relationship posited in Figure 1.1. Chapter 3 explores the media and political elite response to these changing habits, analyzing the second causal relationship in Figure 1.1. I conclude from Part I that media choice has created an increasingly distracted and fragmented viewership in which news makers and producers must work harder to engage.

Part II of the book analyzes the attitudinal effects of commentary news formats, the final causal arrow in Figure 1.1. Chapter 4 evaluates whether programs that include a clear mix of opinion along with the news affect how we perceive Congress and its members. Chapter 5 explores the effects of news urgency—breaking news and debate formats in which the volume and tone of news delivery attract our attention. Finally, Chapter 6 investigates how perceptions may be altered by satirical news—formats that blend humor and news. The concluding Chapter 7 returns to our broad questions of low congressional trust and citizen perceptions, whether contemporary media merely reflects or rather conflates the congressional divide.

The rest of this chapter elaborates further on my news-grazing concept, as well as different theories of congressional disapproval. I first review the growth of media choice and news media formats. I then review different accounts of congressional disapproval, proposing a news-grazing explanation in which contemporary media promote perceptions of partisan distrust and institutional conflict. An engaging and sometimes divisive media may not be the primary means of congressional disapproval; still, media may contort rather than clarify public perceptions of Congress.

The Evolution of Media Choice
and Screening

In 1950, Zenith developed an electronic device called "Lazy Bones." This product was an accessory to the television, which was rapidly gaining popularity as an everyday communications medium. Lazy Bones was a motor that attached to the television's tuner. When activated, the motor would rotate the tuner, or "knob," and allow watchers to view another station. The motor was attached to a remote electronic controller by a cable. Thus, by pressing the button on the attached controller, a television watcher could change channels from across a room without having to get out of her seat.

As a product, Lazy Bones was a failure. There were only a few stations to choose from in the early 1950s, and given the limited programming, viewers only turned on the television when there was a specific program they wished to view. When the program was through, the television was turned off. In that environment, a product that allowed people to turn channels without getting up and walking over to the television did not offer much added benefit. Also, the long cable that stretched across the floor from the television to the controller was an eyesore and considered more of a domestic trip wire than a technological advancement.

Despite these humble beginnings, the idea of this electronic TV knob was revolutionary. Lazy Bones was the world's first commercial television remote control. And when Robert Adler invented the ultrasonic wireless TV remote control in 1956, the device was on its way to becoming more than just a luxurious accessory—but an integral component that would drastically influence how we interact with media generally.

The variety of ways Americans gather and screen political news has changed dramatically since the days of only network news and newspapers. Remote-control technology and more recent screening technologies have only become truly empowering with the expansion of media choice. In the early 1960s, television news overcame newspapers as the dominant news source for most Americans, and by 1990, 58 percent of Americans reported television as their sole source of news (Ansolabehere, Behr, and Iyengar 1993, 44). During most of this period, viewers only had a handful of channels to choose from prior to the advent of cable television in the late 1970s. Additionally, news options were completely homogenized. The three networks—CBS, NBC, and ABC—each had a loyal audience largely built around their news anchor. During this so-called "golden age of network news," the differences in news content and format between the network news options were marginal, leaving the viewer with little real choice in news.

Despite these apparent viewing limits, this golden age may have had its advantages. Since the public was dependent on the same news outlets, there may have been a stronger common perception of the news. Americans were reliant on the same broadcast news, and thus, there was a common basis for mass communication. Public opinion polls indicated that the citizens had much greater trust and confidence in the news media—and all public institutions for that matter—during the 1970s and 1980s (Cook 1998; Ladd 2011). Correspondingly, the reliance on the networks for national news may have allowed media and political elite to direct public attention toward public priorities. Television news journalists may have exercised greater journalistic control toward the news compared with today's news fragmented audience. Larger audiences and weaker competition led network executives to make greater private investments in news-reporting divisions.

Still, the lack of media choice presented many limits to popular democracy. Foremost, it severely restricted public information. The three networks' thirty-minute evening programs (expanded from fifteen minutes in 1963) offered anchor-read, scripted news. This network news format continues to this day, with anchor-read news stories intermittently mixed with reporters' prerecorded, edited video clips, with prerecorded news reports usually lasting from one to five minutes. The news reporter gathers and edits interview clips and video and then scripts and records a voice-over to explain the pictures and link the elements together. These news packages, along with anchor-read news, constitute the traditional network news format.

The Sunday morning public affairs programs—*Face the Nation*, *Meet the Press*, and *This Week*—offered some variation to this traditional network news format. News commentators and news makers would sometimes directly engage each other in a live format. Additionally, starting in 1968, the CBS investigative news program, *60 Minutes*, provided some blurring of traditional, commentary, and entertainment news formats. Overall, though, network newscasting during this so-called "golden age" was a bit bland and boring, despite its broad audience.

More than any other change perhaps, the advent of CNN in 1980 transformed television news and empowered the news consumer. CNN was the pioneer of the 24/7 all-news channel. Prior to the advent of cable news, the "breaking news" event required networks to interrupt their regular programming schedule. Since this was disruptive to viewers and local affiliates, most emerging stories were not covered until the evening news or morning newspapers. CNN changed this practice, providing breaking news coverage on a continuous basis (sometimes on a nauseatingly continuous basis).

The effect of cable news grew with the increasing number of cable television subscribers. While only one-tenth of Americans had cable access in 1980, 55 percent of U.S. households by 1990 were cable subscribers. This cable television effect was twofold. First, viewers had a news alternative to network news that was available on demand. Viewers were no longer dependent on the same news outlets. Second, half of cable subscribers now had about ten times as many channel choices compared to noncable subscribers. Entertainment choices expanded. By 1989, about 45 percent of American households received thirty or more channels (Ansolabehere, Behr, and Iyengar 1993). The rise of entertainment media choice and the consequent distraction from traditional news began to transform our news-gathering habits.

Throughout the 1980s and after, the remote control became both commonplace and empowering with the increasing number of media options. Specialized channels began to emerge beginning with Home Box Office in 1972, WTBS in 1976, and ESPN in 1979. The remote control gave viewers the tool to both seek and avoid news. Soon hundreds of channel options propelled a huge cable industry (Parsons 2008).

As we entered the twenty-first century, 98 percent of U.S. households had at least one television, and 75 percent had two or more. Over two-thirds of American households had cable television (Parsons 2008). The average American spent almost four hours a day watching television, and the average number of channels available per home increased dramatically, from 18.8 in 1985 to 100.4 in 2003. Because Americans spend more time watching TV and because there are more viewing options, the remote control has taken its place as one of the modern day's most useful entertainment inventions. Virtually all televisions, DVRs, stereo systems, and Blu-ray players are now sold with accompanying remote controls, and "universal" remote controls have become increasingly common for controlling all television-oriented entertainment on one remote device.

The success of other media-screening technologies followed the path of the remote control. The VCR (video cassette recorder) first allowed viewers to tape programming. More recently, DVRs have advanced the ease and convenience of media screening, and subscription services like TiVo offer further screening capabilities to those willing to pay. Sling, Roku, and other streaming media technologies allow TV screening online. Media services and technologies will continue to innovate to enable customers to access on-demand screening and to further control their media choices.

This growing prevalence of media-screening technologies has promoted two phenomena: time shifting and commercial avoidance. *Time shifting* refers to individuals' practice of recording and storing media to be viewed, read, or listened to at a time convenient to them. The long-established practice of "appointment viewing," watching a program at its regularly scheduled time, has been broken. Technology and media providers have fueled the time-shifting movement. Individuals may now listen to a podcast or watch a video clip on YouTube at any time or place of their choosing. *Commercial avoidance* is a second motive of media screening. Media technologies have further empowered individuals to pinpoint their media preferences. Commercial avoidance has led advertisers to consider other methods of reaching consumers, including product placement strategies, integrating commercial brands directly into the media programs.

The story of expanding media choice is more apparent to those who are more interested and equipped to adapt to changing communication technology. Individuals younger than the age of forty are more likely to adopt media-screening technologies and make full use of media choice than are people in older generations. This generational divide has declined over the last decade as our citizenry ages; still, the nature and breadth of media use differ across age groups.[1] Younger citizens are more likely to access news from social-networking sites, cell phones, and blogs; correspondingly, they are much less likely to subscribe to a daily newspaper compared with those over sixty.

The generational divide in changing news-gathering habits is most apparent with regard to newspapers. With the growing access to cable and Internet news, there has been a clear generational shift away from newspaper subscriptions. Daily newspaper circulation, which stood at 62.3 million in 1990, fell 30 percent to 43.4 million by 2010. Some Americans dropped the newspaper-reading habit, but even more pronounced was the decline among young adults who never socialized toward reading newspapers. According to the 2016 Pew Research Center analysis, 16 percent of eighteen- to twenty-four-year-olds read a newspaper on a daily basis compared with 50 percent of those over sixty-five years old (Pew Research Center 2016).

This declining newspaper audience has correspondingly led to a real decline in advertising revenues. According to the 2015 Pew's State of the Media, newspaper print advertising revenues overall plummeted in the past decade from $47.4 million in 2005 to $16.4 million by 2014. Some of that fall was offset by rising newspaper digital advertising revenues, but digital advertising still represents less than 20 percent of overall revenues. The most pronounced decline in readership and revenues occurred among afternoon newspapers that made up about a third of daily newspaper circulation in the 1990s. By 2009, afternoon newspapers were just over a tenth of total newspaper circulation.

Overall, the evolution toward media choice has occurred with the introduction of new media technologies, the prevalence of screening technologies, and generational replacement. This media choice, I argue, has led to steady and significant behavioral changes. I introduce the evolution and meaning of news-grazing behavior next.

The Birth of News Grazers

One manifestation of media choice that affects the majority of Americans is *news grazing*. The Pew Research Center conducted a 2008 poll and found that 60 percent of respondents agreed with the statement "I find that I often watch the news with my remote control in hand, flipping to other channels when I'm not interested in the topic." Along these same lines, almost half of Americans (48 percent) report "checking in on the news from time to time," instead of "watching or listening at regular times" (Pew Research Center 2008). More than a decade later, Pew reports that Americans more than ever have many pathways to the news and are less routinized in their news gathering. Pew (2016) reports that Americans increasingly gather news by watching a screen, still mostly via a television but increasingly online. Print news readers are a dying breed, gradually being supplanted by online news consumers. Overall, Pew finds that Americans are increasingly variable in the sources and practices of how we consume news (Pew Research Center 2016).

News grazing, in short, refers to these changes in public news-gathering habits resulting from growing media choice. News grazing includes (1) a tendency to collect news at irregular and shorter periods of time, often with a higher level of distraction; (2) an expectation that news is immediately available upon viewer demand, facilitated by the growing competition and number of media outlet choices; (3) a desire for news to be more visually or psychologically stimulating and engaging; and (4) a growing preference for niche viewing that allows the public to gain specialized news on a narrow range of topics and perspectives. The rise of these news-grazing behaviors conversely relates with the decline of routinized news-gathering habits, like reading a daily newspaper or regularly watching the evening news. As discussed, news grazing is tied to media-screening technologies, the growing media choices, and the evolution of alternative news formats.

The "news-grazing" phenomenon has greatly influenced not only *how* Americans collect news but also *what* they watch or read. Americans have greater entertainment choices, especially the television audience (Baum 2003). As discussed in the next chapter, part of news grazing is consumers' selective avoidance of media messages. If the news is uninteresting or threatening, viewers will move on within seconds. Maybe they will "graze" back to the news a few minutes later—but maybe not, depending on what other program options grab their interest. This situation creates a challenge for the news producers: How do you present the news in a way that can both capture the attention of news grazers and keep it?

History has illustrated that one aspect of the news that can potentially capture and maintain the attention of news grazers is the spectacle of politics. Presidential elections, war, impeachment, tragedy, and scandal have all taken center stage in the news and captivated the American public at one time or another in the last few decades. Electoral campaigns, more than other stories, capture the spectacle of politics. Political campaigns can sometimes create a perfect storm of drama, conflict, and the outrageous. For example, cable news viewership for the primetime schedules of CNN, Fox News, and MSNBC increased 55 percent in the 2016 election compared with 2015 viewership. Moreover, the spectacle of a real-life political story can be very compelling to a news audience, in a way that great fiction cannot. Historically, the first Gulf War, in 1991, saw an unprecedented increase in CNN's ratings as it presented the drama of the attack on Iraq in startling real-time detail. Enraptured by the dramatic images and hooked on the unfolding story, Americans were glued to their television sets for weeks. Likewise, the Monica Lewinsky scandal and subsequent impeachment of President Clinton had a similar effect, as did the government's response to the tragedy of September 11. The competitive drama surrounding the uncertain 2008 presidential election created a compelling story line with seemingly unending subplots and surprising twists. According to the Pew Project for Excellence in Journalism, cable news channels spent three out of every five minutes in 2008 on one news story, the 2008 election. This coverage was almost double the rate of network news.

In short, drama-laden political stories attract and retain news audiences. Recent news audiences have been drawn to President Trump's latest tweets or executive decrees. In the last decade, the prolonged legal cases involving George Zimmerman's killing of Trayvon Martin, Casey Anthony, and other criminal and civil rights conflicts have resulted in ongoing dramatized news coverage. Natural disasters and weather events also offer a basis of drama-laden coverage. Hurricanes Katrina and Sandy, for instance, included news reporters often placing themselves directly in a storm's path to elevate audience interest.

Additionally, news grazers wander from channel to channel with greater frequency during these times of crisis, scandal, war, or elections. During these times, the news provides a drama that keeps many glued to their TV sets as the story unfolds over the course of days, weeks, or even months. It is during these times that ratings for all television news skyrockets, particularly cable news programs. For example, the tragic events of September 11, 2001, resulted in a spike of news interest. In the week of September 3–9, 13 percent of Americans reported watching nightly network news. This rate doubled to 26 percent the week of September 10–16. Cable news providers also saw their ratings spike. The combined average audience per minute for the three major cable news channels (CNN, Fox News, and MSNBC) was approximately 800,000 people in August 2001. This number increased to 2.7 million for September 2001 (Althaus 2002). Evidently, the size of the news audience varies by potential viewers' perceptions of crises, drama, or conflict. Election night on November 8, 2016, resulted in a news audience spike, with a total 71 million viewers of live coverage across thirteen networks.

This tendency of news-rating spikes further intensifies the competition of electronic news outlets—cable, network, and online news media. Increasingly, news outlets compete for an erratic audience share, and news producers recognize that drama-laden news events present opportunities to capture a new audience share. During the fifteenth anniversary on-air celebration of Fox News, founders Rupert Murdoch and Roger Ailes described the growth of the Fox audience being tied closely with these news spikes. Reflecting on Fox's success, Ailes linked a series of high-drama stories, such as the Monica Lewinsky scandal, the 2000 election Florida recount, and 9/11, with their growing audience share. "Whenever there's a big news story, there's a big peak [in ratings], and then a decay factor of people moving away from the story. The other networks were going back down to where they were before the peak. We had a big peak and people that were exposed to us stayed with us. We had a much lower decay factor so I knew in time we would eventually beat them."[2]

Delivering news in an engaging, emotion-laden format during a time of a dramatic, emerging news event may increase a news channel's audience.

Political scientist Larry Sabato discusses in his book, *Feeding Frenzy*, the intense and sometimes excessive media attention resulting from an emerging and dramatic news story. The feeding frenzy phenomenon is brought upon by a singular event—such as an election, disaster, or scandal—that results in a surge of public interest in an event or news maker. Media compete for new and different angles for reporting on this event or news maker, sometimes resulting, at best, in redundant news commentary. At worst, the news-reporting frenzy may result in misinformation about the event or news maker. During the frenzy, the competing media may be unable to confirm emerging news leads faster than the public demand for these leads.

The feeding frenzy phenomena may have always been part of news journalism. However, the growth of media choice, social media, and the advent of the news grazer have interacted to fuel media feeding frenzy events. Online and cable television news have significantly shortened the news cycle—the amount of time that elapses between news-reporting periods. Additionally, the news audience increasingly expects immediacy and an engaging news format that not only reports but also comments on breaking news.

As discussed in Chapters 2 and 3, a news-grazing relationship among the public, news makers, and news media producers has emerged that has changed the rate and format of news media coverage. National and international news at least is now provided on-demand and in a format that mixes news content with entertainment. Media scholars have argued that this changing relationship we have with news has also altered public perceptions of political elites and government institutions (Cappella and Jamieson 1997; Mutz and Reeves 2005). Scholars have suggested an emerging public cynicism, or video malaise, resulting from this style of news coverage. I elaborate next on the connection between news grazing and these political attitudes.

News Grazing and Congressional Distrust

The news-grazing concept is interesting and important alone, particularly for mass communications and journalism scholars. Grazing may be a good description of how we relate to media generally, not just the news. Still, my interest in the grazing concept extends beyond describing and explaining changes in news gathering. I am interested in how grazing may have broader implications for the political world. Particularly, I want to know how changing news-gathering habits may be affecting evaluations of our politicians and political institutions, specifically Congress.

In later chapters, I present evidence that news grazing is fueling a growing movement toward commentary-style news formats. These commentary formats are more emotion-laden, mixing opinion, urgency, conflict, and satire with the news. News producers present news in formats that appeal to an increasingly distracted audience. These commentary cable news formats, I hypothesize, may affect how we perceive conflict among political actors and institutions broadly. In Part II, I directly assess these possible effects of commentary news formats on public attitudes toward Congress.

While these effects may broadly affect public perceptions of politics, our focus will be public attitudes toward the U.S. Congress, particularly its parties and leaders. Congress, as an institution, has rarely had high levels of public approval. Figure 1.2 reports congressional approval and House incumbents' reelection rates over time. Evidently, the American electorate has had a natural skepticism toward Congress, even though this is typically not reflected in incumbency reelection rates, which typically exceed 90 percent. This public suspicion toward Congress has existed throughout our political history and been reflected by our cultural critics. Mark Twain, the late-nineteenth-century humorist, famously penned, "It could probably be shown by facts and figures that there is no distinctly native

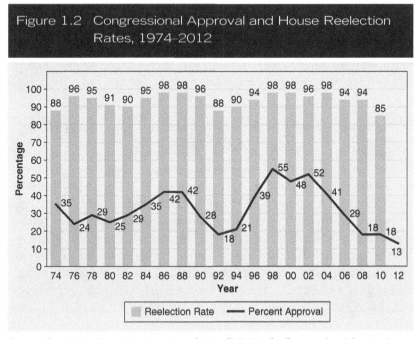

Figure 1.2 Congressional Approval and House Reelection Rates, 1974–2012

Source: Created by the author, based on Gallup Poll data for Congressional Approval.

American criminal class except Congress" (Twain 1897). Likewise, the early-twentieth-century humorist Will Rogers wrote, "This country has come to feel the same when Congress is in session as when the baby gets hold of a hammer" (Waldrop 2012). Twain's and Rogers's satiric comments toward Congress continue to strike a cultural chord among Americans. Congress has generally been held in lower public esteem than the executive branch and Supreme Court. Compared with the other branches, the more transparent and representative Congress probably suffers from its openness and diversity of opinion. For Congress, perhaps there is something for everyone to dislike.

Still, the nature and depth of public frustrations with Congress during the past decade transcend even the traditional low levels. According to Gallup Polls, public approval of Congress steadily declined and has ranged from 10 to 20 percent since 2008. This decline indicates a new level of pessimism about Congress. According to a 2011 *New York Times* survey, congressional job approval slipped to a new low of 9 percent, with Congress being more unpopular than "polygamy," "the U.S. going communist," and "the B.P. Oil Spill."[3] These new lows in institutional approval create uncertainty among current members who may fear that it will trigger an electoral wave of anti-incumbency. Of greater concern, though, is that historically low congressional approval may threaten public faith and popular legitimacy of the institution. Congress may cease to be followed by an interested public or may cede authority to a more popular executive. So why does the public dislike Congress? I discuss both Congress-centered explanations and media explanations for why the public disapproves of their Congress.

Congress-Based Theories of Institutional Disapproval

Perhaps an unpopular Congress is a self-inflicted wound. Shortly before the 2010 health care reform congressional vote, the Pew Research Center asked Americans for one word to describe the U.S. Congress. The most frequent survey responses were "dysfunctional," "selfish," "corrupt," and "incompetent." In fact, 86 percent of respondents gave a decidedly negative word, while only 4 percent gave a decidedly positive one (Auxier 2010).

The general public sentiment is that Congress, as an institution, does not work collectively to compromise and resolve public problems. Its members individually do better representing our public preferences than Congress collectively does governing. If this collective, institutional assessment drives our public disapproval toward Congress, what congressional actions fuel these institutional perceptions? Why do people dislike Congress *as an institution*?

Political scientists have crafted different answers to this question. These theories are not mutually exclusive; that is, you may agree with more than one, and one does not contradict another. Still, we may think that some theories of congressional disapproval are probably more determinative than others. Thus, researchers have argued over the weight or importance given to each over time.

One of the more compelling explanations for congressional disapproval has been the electoral theory dubbed "Fenno's paradox," the tendency for the public to approve of their own legislator's performance much more than Congress collectively. Richard Fenno's classic study, *Home-Style*, describes how U.S. House members behave back in their home district compared with their Washington "Hill-style" (Fenno 1978). He finds that Congress members communicate to constituents a view of Congress that contrasts sharply with how they project themselves. Particularly, members often present themselves to voters as hardworking, publicly minded representatives while portraying the collective membership as relatively slow, witless, and hopelessly gridlocked. In short, members sometimes run against Congress. This electoral explanation for congressional disapproval suggests that members use the institution as a foil back in their district to create favor with their constituents. The hometown representative is the protagonist with the collective Congress serving as the antagonist in the legislative drama.

A second explanation for congressional distrust is more policy based. Political scientists have explained congressional disapproval from member's Hill styles—their Washington behavior—rather than their home styles. Mayer and Canon (1999) discuss a "policy dilemma" explanation that individual members face within a large legislative assembly. For instance, members rationally pursue policy outcomes that serve their parochial interests but at a collective cost. *Pork barrel politics*, members' pursuit of localized interests and benefits but at a national cost, may contribute to a public perception of a parochial, self-serving legislature. Members' individual rationality leads to collectively irrational policy outcomes—notably, growing budget deficits, a lack of policy involvement in global affairs, and failed efforts at entitlement reform. According to congressional scholars, this policy dilemma is endemic to self-nominated, self-elected members representing single-member districts and states.

Former House Speaker Tip O'Neill's maxim, "All politics is local," suggests that members advance their reelection goal by addressing local needs rather than broader policy debates. Unresolved national and global problems may be blamed on or at least left to others—Congress collectively or the president. Members are better served electorally by serving their constituents. That is, constituency service rather than policy advocacy is a better use of limited staff and time resources. Solving local problems may allow incumbents to broaden their reelection coalition beyond just those who agree with them on the issues. Butler, Karpowitz, and Pope (2012) confirmed this finding that members prefer service to policy debate through a creative field experiment. They recruited over two hundred subjects to write a common letter to their hometown legislator. This letter either had an explicit service or policy request. They found that legislators respond to constituent (e-)mail when the request is for service rather than a policy position. Even in an era of partisan policy conflict, district service and legislative parochialism prevail.

A third explanation of congressional disapproval goes further than members' electoral and policy behaviors. An institutional explanation implies that the public's disfavor of Congress is tied to the very nature of legislative design. Members face an "institutional dilemma" in which no individual member has a strong, private incentive to engage in the often hidden, hard work of a legislature—organizing and attending often tedious committee meetings, engaging in independent policy research and bureaucratic oversight, and bringing together disparate political groups to frame compromises. Congressional scholars have referred to these largely hidden and thankless legislative tasks as *institutional maintenance*. Just like their policy dilemma, legislators are faced with an institutional dilemma not to privately contribute toward institutional maintenance. Members, instead, see a more immediate and personal benefit from engaging in activities that help their reelection or public reputation.

Institutional maintenance may be an even rarer commodity in a partisan age. The institutional incentive for members to shirk from legislative work may be even greater during a period of high party conflict. Members generally may defer to more senior legislative committee and party leaders to provide collective institutional maintenance. However, these legislative leaders are increasingly beholden to their fellow party members within a partisan Congress. Committees may increasingly produce bills favorable to the majority party rather than bills favored by bipartisan coalitions. Thus, legislators may engage in greater floor partisanship because the private work of bipartisan coalition building has not occurred at the committee stage.

To summarize, Congress-based theories of institutional approval include electoral, policy, and institutional explanations. All three of these explanations of congressional disapproval fit with a persisting trend in public opinion. This persisting trend is known by the political aphorism, "Love Your Congress Member, Hate Congress," which simply notes the consistent pattern over time in which citizens diverge in their individual and collective assessments of Congress. This same divergence holds in our individual and collective assessments for our doctors, teachers, and clergy. Still, it is a strong and consistent pattern in which we like our individual elected officials much more than Congress as a whole. Perhaps citizens see their own district's member as the only good apple in an otherwise rotten barrel.

Figure 1.3 reflects this aphorism by charting over time the percentage of registered voters who believe that "most members" should be reelected compared with whether "the U.S. Representative in your congressional district" should be reelected. Both trend lines evidently decline during the past decade; however, the decline was greater for voters' assessment of "most members." In other words, the gap between those supporting reelection of "your member" and "most members" widened throughout the past decade. A growing anti-incumbency mood among voters has had an unsettling effect on current members' electoral security. The 2010 elections

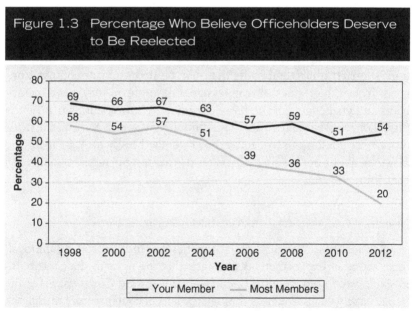

Figure 1.3 Percentage Who Believe Officeholders Deserve to Be Reelected

Source: Created by the author using Gallup Poll data for "most members" or "your member" deserves reelection.

resulted in fifty-four House incumbents losing, the most defeated incumbents since 1948.

Still, scholars studying congressional elections remain skeptical that that these intermittent waves of anti-incumbency will noticeably alter congressional politics. It is a constant point of partisan contention as to who or which party is accountable for voters' disapproval of congressional performance. Political scientist Alan Abramowitz notes that those exceptional election years with high numbers of incumbency defeats tend to be one-sided partisan affairs. That is, one party loses a disproportionate share of the incumbent-held seats. In 2010, for instance, fifty-two of the fifty-four incumbents who lost were Democrats. Abramowitz and Webster (2016) argue persuasively that congressional elections have become increasingly nationalized. Additionally, congressional election outcomes are more responsive to presidential approval than congressional approval. Congressional midterm elections, particularly, often operate as referendums of incumbent presidential performance. While voters may dislike Congress, they blame the president's party in elections. Incumbents have been at greatest electoral risk in midterm election years with an unpopular president of the same party.

In short, congressional disapproval, while worrisome for those who care about the institution, is not necessarily an electoral threat to all current members. Incumbents vary in electoral safety depending on the strength of district partisanship and loyalty of the member's primary and personal constituencies (Fenno 2010). Many members are well insulated from short-term electoral shifts that may be tied to an unpopular Congress. In fact, high rates of congressional disapproval may serve incumbents and challengers of the party opposing the president's party. As the three Congress-based theories of institutional disapproval show, the institution's reputation is a collective good—something which all members may care about but no single member has a strong personal incentive to contribute toward.

Media Theories of Institutional Disapproval

Besides these Congress-based theories for institutional disapproval, there are other explanations that suggest that the news media contributes in some way to our political disenchantment toward Congress. Since the public largely views Congress through the lens of contemporary media, the media may reflect, reinforce, and even distort our popular preconceptions of the institution.

In the 1970s, studies by Robinson (1974) and Miller, Goldenberg, and Erbring (1979) found that individuals with greater media exposure had lower levels of political trust in American political institutions and politicians. Robinson dubbed this phenomenon "video malaise." In essence, this "video malaise" theory suggested that watching television news contributed to a declining confidence in political actors and institutions. Proponents of the video malaise thesis argued that television news coverage gives viewers a negative and critical lens for observing political events. The argument proceeds as follows: Television news producers favor coverage of Congress with visual and conflict-oriented story lines. These news stories are often framed as intractable problems that reinforce viewers' negative impression of government's capacity to solve public problems. These intractable public problems—poor economic performance, social inequalities, or international conflict—communicate to many voters that government is unable to control events and social outcomes. As a result, news media coverage presumably contributed to changing beliefs of political trust among viewers during the 1970s and 1980s.

Of course, there are other explanations for the decline of political trust during this time. Still, the video malaise argument has lingered as a strong explanation for the public's dissatisfaction with Congress. Durr, Gilmour, and Wolbrecht (1997), in fact, found that congressional approval, in the aggregate, declined over time in the immediate aftermath of congressional actions, such as veto overrides or passage of major legislation. In other words, a more active Congress garnering more media attention may be less popular.

The video malaise theory may be conditional on viewers' predispositions to the media story. Vallone, Ross, and Lepper (1985) proposed a "hostile media effect" that suggests that video malaise extends to the media as well. The authors conducted an interesting experiment in which subjects were selected to include members from pro-Arab and pro-Israeli student organizations. Subjects were asked to watch network news stories relating to the Arab–Israeli conflict. Those subjects who had strong partisan predispositions on the issue prior to the experiment were found to view the media as biased against their side, regardless of which side they were on. In other words, media bias is in the eye of the beholder. This hostile media response has also been found for strong party and ideological identifiers (Dalton, Beck, and Huckfedt 1998). Perceptions of media bias are often greatest in those who have strong predispositions. Strong supporters of one side tend to view news as biased against their side. This is analogous to the tendency to find play-by-play announcers biased when your favorite college football team is losing.

This video malaise thesis has changed along with the changes in media technology. Notably, the growth of cable and online news brought about different format styles for newscasting. As discussed earlier, the traditional programming format for television news followed a "talking head" approach of anchor-read, scripted news with stories intermittently mixed with reporters' edited video clips. These edited video clips come in the form of short "packages" or prerecorded news reports. These news packages, along with anchor-read news, constitute the traditional television news format.

Cable and online news have moved away from strict adherence to this talking head and news package approach. Cable news established news formats that have altered the tone and content of newscasting. The general direction of these changes has been toward news commentary formats. Commentary news formats include opinion, debate, urgency, and entertainment intermixed with news. These formats are often delivered in real time, with less reliance on traditional norms of news reporting. The emphasis instead is news immediacy and commentary. Growing media choice has placed greater value on getting news stories out fast. Along with immediacy, news producers favor news formats that will allow viewers to understand and be interested in the news. Holding the attention of the viewer is essential to maintaining an increasingly distracted audience.

The public is increasingly watching commentary formats as a basis for understanding the news. A "new video malaise" literature has taken seed investigating the effects of these commentary news formats. Commentary news formats differ both in tone and content from traditional news formats. Media scholars have examined whether this changing news media contributes toward greater political cynicism and distrust of government actors (Cappella and Jamieson 1997; Elving 1996; Ladd 2011; Sabato 2000). Mutz and Reeves (2005), for instance, assess whether uncivil debate through television news—interrupting, raised voices, name-calling—affects viewers' perceptions of political actors. They find that individuals with a high aversion to conflict are more likely to negatively assess politics after viewing these uncivil media exchanges.

A paradox persists in that while uncivil television news may leave some viewers with a negative impression of government, these uncivil media formats may also attract and retain viewers' attention. Televised incivility may both attract and repulse. We are attracted by the drama and passion even though we claim to be turned off by the uncivil exchanges. This paradox may be similar to a car driver slowing down to sneak a peek at the roadside accident even though he or she may decry the resulting traffic jam. We may instinctively know that our individual choice to slow down comes at a collective cost, but we cannot help but look.

Or can we? Media choice and media-screening technologies empower viewers not to watch. They may merely click to something more entertaining, informative, or interesting. Selective perception theory in social psychology literature refers to individuals' tendency to favor information that reinforces preexisting views while avoiding contradictory information. This selective perception begins with selective exposure. Information-seeking viewers may privately choose news that they find engaging and confirmatory to their views. This information-seeking behavior continues with viewers' selective attention and selective retention of this news. Along with their selective exposure, viewers may be more attentive to or focused on news that fits with their prior beliefs. Additionally, they may be more likely to clear associations that link this new information with preexisting beliefs. These associations allow viewers to remember news that coincides with their predisposed attitudes.

The selective-exposure concept clearly relates to the "new video malaise" argument that expanding media choice and news formats are altering news media effects. With growing choice, viewers are exercising their judgment in what to watch and how much attention and how much importance to give to this information. The selective-exposure concept has links to popular debates of a "Fox News effect" voiced by political pundits. Brock and Rabin-Havt (2012) add to earlier popular accounts that the Fox News Network has promoted news media bias and media polarization. Filmmaker Robert Greenwald's 2004 documentary, *Outfoxed*, made a similar popular account against Fox News.

Sunstein (2001) was among the first to make the case that Internet news is greatly elevated this new video malaise. The reduction in cost and increase in sources available via online news permits greater ideological self-segregation. Baum and Groeling (2008) show that online news sources and blogs promote partisan filtering, attracting politically like-minded news gathers. These partisan online sites—like DailyKos.com, MoveOn.org, and HuffingtonPost.com on the left and FreeRepublic.com, RedState.com, and Townhall.com on the right—tend to present partisan polarization and negative stereotyping of the other side. The growth of cable and online news promotes partisan selective exposure.

The argument is a compelling one. An enterprising and partisan Fox News organization recognized viewers' propensity toward selective exposure. The eventual result has been an emerging red and blue media. That is, Fox News has intentionally grown its audience share among cable news channels by reporting on more stories appealing to conservatives and villainizing liberals. MSNBC, more recently, has also followed this strategy, appealing to a left-leaning ideological audience. The "effect" of this media polarization ultimately is presumably hardened ideological positions among preexisting partisans. In short, selective exposure, coincident with a Fox News effect, increases perceptions of political polarization. Online partisan media, in the form of Breitbart, Daily Caller, Huffington Post, and Daily Kos, extend the partisan selective-exposure thesis, even though they have relatively smaller audiences (Barthel and Mitchell 2017).

Academic studies of selective exposure have reached different conclusions. In her book *Niche News*, Natalie Stroud (2011) makes the case for "partisan selective exposure." She examines whether citizens prefer like-minded information and avoid information that conflicts with their beliefs. From an extensive analysis of survey and experiment data, she finds support for media polarization. Stroud concludes that partisans on opposing sides of the political spectrum tend to have different news-gathering preferences. Republicans and conservatives, generally, are more likely to listen to conservative talk radio, read newspapers endorsing Republican presidential candidates, watch Fox News, and surf conservative websites. Democrats and liberals, generally, also follow partisan selective exposure. She finds mixed evidence, though, regarding the effects of partisan selective exposure. Partisan news, in fact, may help encourage participation and help people make sense of politics more easily. Still, she also concludes that media polarization diminishes common conversation and disengagement among some viewers.

Other academic studies of the "new video malaise" also present well-reasoned conditions to broad selective-exposure effects. The popular claim among proponents of a "Fox News effect" is that partisan selective exposure intensifies partisanship. However, these popular accounts may mix association with causality since they typically cannot control for viewers' preexisting partisanship. Arceneaux, Johnson, and Murphy (2012) argue persuasively that media choice actually may diminish this new video malaise in some circumstances. They find that those most affected by polarizing conservative or liberal talk news programs are viewers whose political attitudes are counter to those of the host—for instance, a liberal viewer watching conservative news commentary. These counterattitudinal viewers are more likely to distrust media after watching the program. However, media choice and the remote control allow these viewers to merely click away from these programs. In fact, survey evidence, discussed in later Chapter 4, confirms that this is generally what happens.

In summary, the more alarming claims made by proponents of a Fox News effect are not always supported by academic research. In fact, Stroud's and other's works indicate that there may be some positive effects to partisan selective exposure, and other works indicate the negative effects may be muted by screening technologies. The causal relationship between viewers' partisanship, media choice, and partisan selective exposure is complex. Nonetheless, there is a case to be made that media, in some ways, contributes to perceptions of partisan polarization and congressional conflict.

The new video malaise may be another contributing factor to negative perceptions of Congress. News media, the lens through which most Americans view Congress, may present a slightly distorted reflection of the institution in order to attract and retain its audiences. Like the carnival mirror that distorts our bodies and faces, the commentary news format increasingly common with new media may present a more conflict-ridden, dysfunctional, and corrupting (if not corrupt) Congress than more objective accounts would communicate. The emergence of commentary news formats is a response to media choice and a 24/7 news hole. By promoting a more negative, critical frame for viewing Congress, these formats may partly confirm our predispositions in order to attract and retain an audience. Again, this media-based explanation of congressional distrust does not supplant other theories of congressional disapproval. Unfortunately for Congress, there are many reasons voters distrust it.

Conclusion

This introductory chapter has explored the main question driving this book: Why do we distrust politicians and the media? I argue that recent rise in public distrust of political institutions—notably, the U.S. Congress—is media driven. I introduced concepts of media choice and news grazing. Media choice and screening technologies have altered how we gather our political news. News grazing is the concept introduced to the distracted, intermittent news-gathering styles that a growing share of Americans today follow. The broader relevance of this news-grazing concept was discussed with context about emergence of media choice and the birth of the news grazer.

The causal connections posed in Figure 1.1 set the stage for a fuller investigation of news grazing in forthcoming Chapters 2 and 3. Chapter 2 explores who grazes and why. I argue that news grazing incorporates both intentional selective exposure and unintentional, accidental news media choices. Chapter 3 investigates the media elites' adaptations to news grazing. News makers—members of Congress and their various staff and spokespersons—must adapt by presenting a compelling media message to advance their political goals and policy agendas. News producers—the reporters and commentators of Congress—must adapt by communicating a more engaging news story for an increasingly distracted audience. The remaining chapters, Part II of this book, investigate the political consequences of news grazing, evaluating the behavioral effects of commentary news formats.

As discussed in the end of this chapter, academics and pundits have given multiple theories for why we distrust Congress. Of these theories, a media-based explanation is one that is less understood and is still emerging. The complexity of the new video malaise—who it affects, why it occurs, and what can be done—will be explored for its implications for politicians and the media. Particularly, why and how does media choice and news grazing affect public perceptions of Congress? Particularly, why do Americans increasingly see a distant and distrustful Congress? There is typically no single, right answer in social science, and my findings will not, by any stretch, resolve the debate about media polarization and congressional distrust. A media-based explanation of congressional distrust, though, reminds us that news media play an important mediating role in our politics, both informing and shaping our perceptions.

ENDNOTES

1. The Pew Internet and American Life Project provides excellent demographic information about media use. See http://www.pewinternet.org/topics/Generations.aspx.

2. The video of this interview can be viewed at http://video.foxnews.com/v/1205727600001/video-rupert-murdoch-roger-ailes-and-the-hosts-of-fox-and-friends-celebrate-fox-news-channels-15th-anniversary/?#sp=show-clips.

3. See Alana Horowitz, "Congress Approval Rating Lower Than Porn, Polygamy, B.P. Oil Spill, and U.S. Going Communist," *Huffington Post*, November 16, 2011, http://www.huffingtonpost.com/2011/11/16/congress-approval-rating-porn-polygamy_n_1098497.html.

The News Grazer

A gag gift called "the covert clicker" is a concealed, miniremote control that fixes onto the frequency of any television or media device. As the advertisement reads, the prankster waits until the victims are settling down to watch the Super Bowl or their favorite program only to maniacally switch the channel with their concealed remote control. Shocked by the interruption, the victims spring into an immediate panic. I do not recommend this annoying trick unless you enjoy causing distress to your family and friends. Still, the "covert clicker" does underscore an important, emerging cultural condition of our relationships with information technology. When individuals are denied control over media technologies, frustration ensues.

This frustration is elevated by media consumers' huge gains over recent decades in the number, range, and immediacy of media options. These gains have created expectations of media choice and control that are sometimes undermined when technologies fail or underperform. These perceived expectations drive consumers to search for faster, more reliable, and redundant technologies and services, all to minimize media interruptions. Likewise, it drives communication service providers to invest more in security and infrastructure, all to lessen the threat of media interruption. We are increasingly reliant on uninterrupted access to media for entertainment, communications, and work.

Applied to the news, our frustrations and expectations with media control are a function of growing media choice, a preference for immediate access, and the fixed hours in the day. There simply is not enough time and resources to view, read, or listen to everything. News consumers must make choices but are not reliant or loyal to any one media platform. The Pew Research Center's *Biennial Survey of News Consumption* confirms this emergence of an "on demand culture" of news consumers. According to the last Pew survey, 57 percent of Americans are news grazers, measured by Pew as "more the kind of person who checks in on the news from time to time" (Caumont 2013).[1] This percentage has steadily increased, over time. Fewer Americans have routine news-gathering habits. They are grazing—collecting news at different times and from different sources and platforms.

Additionally, there are significant generational differences in this news-grazing behavior. Seventy-four percent of those younger than thirty years of age identify themselves as news grazers, significantly higher than those in older generations (Rosenstiel 2008; see also Pew Research Center 2010). News consumption studies find that younger age cohorts routinely report fewer minutes spent consuming news (compared with older Americans). For instance, Pew Research longitudinal studies find that Americans between sixty-seven and eighty-four spend, on average, eighty-four minutes a day with news compared to "millennials" (eighteen to thirty-one year olds), who spend only forty-six minutes (Mitchell and Page 2015). Most troubling, Pew and others express concerns that this age difference is not decreasing as millennials get older, suggesting a long-term decreased appetite for hard news with generational replacement.[2] Perhaps media choice and political distrust will result in a persisting low rate of news interest. Journalism researchers at the American Press Institute (API) counter these concerns, though, arguing that younger citizens are hardly newsless. They argue, in a 2015 study, that younger citizens weave together news and other information gathering.[3] That is, they are more likely to access news via social media and entertainment sources. They are also more likely to seeking specific news for problem solving or social action. In short, news-gathering habits are changing but hardly disappearing.

Media choice and generational change, though, are subtly transforming the news-viewing public. Americans increasingly are acquiring their news when they want it, through their preferred medium, and on matters of interest to them. The 2015 API study shows that we are crafting unique habits keeping up with the news throughout the day and across different outlets, formats, devices, and technologies.[4] The traditional view of mass media being delivered to consumers from common sources and with the same news content is in decay.

In place of mass broadcast news, a media-rich public now expects broad choice and control over information. According to a recent study by Arbitron, a media and marketing research company, 61 percent of Americans are cable television subscribers. Still, 54 percent of these cable subscribers would prefer to only pay for the channels that they watch (Edwards and Williams 2006). These cable subscribers would prefer packages of channels or an à la carte approach in which they pay only for desired channels. Consumers increasingly want to customize their information access and content. These consumers routinely use their remote control or mouse to screen their news choices. They are increasingly investing in various screening technologies—digital video recorders, spam protection software,

Internet bookmarks, and search aggregators—to avoid undesired information or to create shortcuts to desired information. Increasingly, news consumers seek control over their media choices.

In this chapter and the next, I argue that news consumers, news makers, and news producers have each adapted to expanding media choice in ways that enable news grazing. In Chapter 3, I argue that news producers have adapted by offering shorter news stories, more engaging news formats, and more drama-laden stories with a greater sensitivity to retaining viewer attention among an increasingly distracted audience. Additionally, news makers—Congress, in particular—have adapted by making news that is more likely to interest news producers and, ultimately, a more fickle audience. In short, media choice has not only dramatically changed how Americans gather news; it has transformed the news itself.

In this chapter, our focus is on how the news consumer has adapted to media choice. Notably, I elaborate on the meaning and development of news-grazing habits. Our purpose is to explain what constitutes news grazing, who grazes, and why people graze. Specifically, what are the behavioral attributes and contextual triggers that lead people to click toward or away from the news? The answer to this question, I argue, is intrinsically interesting: Americans vary substantially in the amount and nature of their news viewing. More important, understanding why people graze has implications for what news is reported and what consequences emerging news formats have on our political perceptions. Related to Congress, news grazing potentially may contribute to perceptions of partisan conflict, institutional efficacy, and trust by altering how news is presented and which news is consumed.

We begin by contrasting the concepts of partisan selective exposure and news grazing, two related views of changing news-gathering habits. These similar but distinct concepts offer two explanations of contemporary news gathering. Partisan selective exposure states that news consumers largely prefer like-minded news, news that we are predisposed to agree with. In short, news consumers seek affirmation, not just information. Popular and academic works have argued that partisan selective exposure is an emerging trend in Americans' news media habits and is shaping our partisan evaluations and vote choices. News grazing is a concept that includes some elements of partisan selective exposure. I note these similarities of the news-grazing and selective-exposure concepts, suggesting that they have similar implications for our politics. Still, I argue that news grazing offers a broad explanation of news consumption that is inclusive of observed behaviors related to selective exposure. News grazing, though, explains other behaviors—namely, the unguided or inadvertent roaming that is another part of contemporary news gathering.

News grazing reflects a shift in the public's news-gathering habits in reaction to greater media choice. These shifting habits include a tendency to collect news at irregular and shorter periods of time often with a heightened level of distraction. The elements of news grazing relate to the both passive and purposive nature of news gathering with much greater media choice. That is, a news grazer is not always actively seeking news but may also passively or accidentally engage with it while broadly roaming the growing range of media options. The passive elements of news grazing relate to the heightened expectation that news can be accessed at any time and is immediately available upon viewer demand. Additionally, a less engaged media consumer may be more expectant that news be more visually or psychologically stimulating in order to hold his or her attention. Be it passive or purposive, though, the news-grazing concept relates to a growing share of the news audience. Additionally, it shares some related behaviors to a partisan selective-exposure view of news gathering.

Selective Exposure

The idea of *selective* exposure implies a purposive news gatherer. This purposive behavior includes a growing preference for niche viewing that allows the news gatherer to gain specialized news on a narrow range of topics and perspectives. For some news gatherers, this attraction to niche news includes a preference for like-minded stories, news reporting that implicitly reinforces the consumers' political predispositions. Partisan selective exposure is the tendency to choose news media that comport with an individual's own partisan orientation and/or ideological belief system.

Recent research has made the case that the growing news media choice promotes partisan selective exposure (Levendusky 2009, 2013; Prior 2007; Stroud 2008, 2011; Taber and Lodge 2006). Selective exposure, along with the notion of selective perception and selective retention of political information, are the primary elements of the minimal consequences theory of media effects, which posits that media have little to no influence on political attitudes (Lazarsfeld, Berelson, and Gaudet 1948; Patterson and McClure 1976). While a great deal of research challenged the notion of minimal consequence theory and demonstrated measurable media effects (see Iyengar and Kinder 1987; Zaller 1992), the notion of selective exposure has reemerged, especially in the context of the fragmented cable television news environment of the last few decades (Stroud 2008, 2011).

Media scholars have argued that the media fragmentation and partisan news outlets have enabled partisan voters to sort themselves ideologically, contributing to further political polarization (Jamieson and Cappella 2008; Sunstein 2001). The partisan selective-exposure concept implies this ideological sorting between cable news channels has promoted greater ideological homogeneity among news channel viewers. This "news with a view" notion implies that news gatherers fundamentally prefer like-minded news. News providers enable this consumer preference by matching news content that coincides with the views of their news audience. That is, fewer news stories cross-pressure, create dissonance with the public, if viewers purposefully access only news that fits with their predisposed political views.

As discussed earlier, the popular account of this partisan selective-exposure thesis is sometimes dubbed a "Fox News effect," named after the news channel that has been its driving force. This Fox News effect specifically refers to the growing audience share of political conservatives for Fox News. Writing in *The Nation*, media critic Marvin Kitman (2012), concluded the following after watching a steady diet of Fox News:

> Fox News is news with an attitude. It's proud to be American news with a lot of flag-waving. It's aimed at angry people who see good factory jobs disappearing overseas. It finds stories its audience didn't even know they should be angry about until Fox News called their attention to them. Fox News is aimed at people who feel left out. People who feel the left-wing media controlling TV news don't serve them the way talk-radio news does. It's only a niche, but Roger Ailes has driven an eighteen-wheel Mack truck through it. And it's all the Anointed One's fault. . . . If you don't like the attitude, the point of view, the opinion, you switch the channel. That's the way it is with newspapers or magazines. That's the American way.

Despite popular critics' concerns of possible media bias with a Fox News effect, though, partisan selective exposure suggests that self-selection minimizes the likelihood that news gatherers' attitudes are changed by partisan news. Viewers' preference for like-minded news implies that they seek to be confirmed rather than challenged. While like-minded news may harden preferences, it does not change these preferences.

Besides this partisan selective exposure, other selective-exposure studies have made the case that media fragmentation has also mitigated media effects among the less engaged and more passive audiences by allowing those passive viewers to avoid news altogether and seek more entertaining programming (Prior 2007). The related idea of *selective avoidance*—choosing entertainment over news, perhaps—subsequently increases the knowledge gap between the engaged and disengaged publics in America. Media choice has widened the divide in political knowledge between those who actively seek news and those who do not.

Ultimately, growing media fragmentation and corresponding selective exposure has led researchers to conclude that a new era of "minimal effects" may be unfolding (Bennett and Iyengar 2008). In short, news media messages have little or no effect on altering our attitudes or mobilizing us to act as media choice expands. Bennett and Iyengar (2008) write, "We anticipate that the fragmentation of the national audience reduces the likelihood of attitude change in response to particular patterns of news" (724). In short, partisan selective exposure reinforces (hardens) but does not alter preexisting behaviors and attitudes. This hardening of partisan ties presumably is affecting our political evaluations and ultimately vote choices. Gary Jacobson (2017) assesses the 2016 election, for instance, concluding that the Trump election represents "the triumph of polarized partisanship."[5]

News grazing, while sharing the idea of motivated or intentional media choices, presents a broader description of news-gathering behavior than selective exposure. Grazing implies that some news gathering may partly occur through unguided roaming, flipping, or surfing behaviors. Additionally, grazers' media choices may not be a decision for like-minded news but rather engaging news, news that is delivered in a form that invokes an emotional response. Thus, news grazing may not necessarily imply a clear ideological sorting among news gatherers. Additionally, grazing does not imply that viewers have a strong loyalty or preference for any single news source. Grazers may draw news from varying sources.

In fact, recent measures of Americans' news consumption habits do not indicate we have grazing tendencies. The Pew Research Center Biennial Media Consumption Survey asks respondents every two years to agree or disagree with the following statement: "I find that I often watch the news with my remote control in hand, flipping to other channels when I'm not interested in the topic." Pew asked this question from 1998 to 2006. (More recent data are not available, unfortunately.) The results do not paint a picture of a devoted, self-selected news audience. About 60 percent of all respondent agree with the survey statement, indicating news-grazing tendencies. Furthermore, it appears that this grazing behavior is even more prevalent among the younger adults (ages eighteen to thirty-five), compared with older individuals (ages sixty-five and over). About 70 percent of younger adults respond affirmatively that they news graze. Perhaps a younger audience is more likely to use screening technology to avoid certain types of political information and eschew older formats of news (Davis and Owen 1998; Prior 2007).

This tendency to "flip" from one channel to the next indicates a lack of selectivity that opens up the possibility of exposure to a different news sources or formats. The Pew data indicates that grazing behavior is typical among most Americans, especially among the younger news gatherers. With generational replacement, we may expect that grazing behaviors will only increase.

In addition to the Pew results, television news exposure from the Biennial Media Consumption Studies offer another indication of grazing behavior. For these measures, subjects were asked to list the frequency in which they followed various television news sources (regularly, sometimes, hardly ever, or never). Some accounts of the selective-exposure thesis may suggest that news viewers have become more desirous of—more loyal to—partisan news sources even as the number of news sources has increased. This, however, does not appear to be the case when respondents report their news exposure.

Table 2.1 illustrates the correlations between these exposure variables and demonstrates little evidence that individuals shun some sources while pursuing others. The results indicate all the television news exposure variables are positively correlated and statistically significant. That is, respondents indicate that viewing one news outlet increases the likelihood that they will access news from another source. This result challenges an account that news gatherers eschew other forms of news in favor of any specific source. Even Fox News and MSNBC, which are considered the quintessential partisan selective-exposure news channels, are positively correlated and statistically significant. While news gatherers may be attracted to like-minded news, they may also graze to news outlets that provide other engaging news stories. Generally, most news gatherers do not appear to be loyalists to any news media provider.

I further examine this tendency by reporting exposure correlations separately on self-identified Republicans (Table 2.2) and self-identified Democrats (Table 2.3). In these cases, we see weaker cross-exposure, particularly for Republicans, than with the overall sample. Among Republicans, Fox News exposure only significantly associates (positively) with NBC News and CNN usage ($p < .05$) and no other sources. Among Democrats, the significant positive overlap is almost uniform across all television news sources. Still, these measures do not indicate news audiences flock to a single source, even when we control partisan identification.

Table 2.1 Television News Exposure Correlations

	CBS News	ABC News	NBC News	CNN	Fox News	MSNBC	CNBC	Local News	C-SPAN
CBS News	—								
ABC News	.25*	—							
NBC News	.27*	.24*	—						
CNN	.16*	.25*	.22*	—					
Fox News	.14*	.11*	.12*	.16*	—				
MSNBC	.20*	.17*	.31*	.46*	.16*	—			
CNBC	.26*	.18*	.29*	.45*	.19*	.50*	—		
Local News	.21*	.27*	.26*	.14*	.17*	.07#	.10*	—	
C-SPAN	.12*	.11*	.13*	.31*	.09*	.34*	.35*	.08*	—

Source: Created by the author using data from Pew Research Center, Biannual Media Consumption Survey.
Note: All cell entries are bivariate correlation coefficients.
$*p < .01, \#p < .05.$

Table 2.2 Television News Exposure Correlations (Republicans Only)

	CBS News	ABC News	NBC News	CNN	Fox News	MSNBC	CNBC	Local News	C-SPAN
CBS News	—								
ABC News	.26*	—							
NBC News	.24*	.31*	—						
CNN	.10	.21*	.30*	—					
Fox News	.00	.11	.15#	.16#	—				
MSNBC	.12	.00	.32*	.45*	.07	—			

	CBS News	ABC News	NBC News	CNN	Fox News	MSNBC	CNBC	Local News	C-SPAN
CNBC	.22*	.16#	.33*	.53*	.06	.54*	—		
Local News	.17*	.24*	.24*	.04	.10	.02	.01	—	
C-SPAN	.00	.00	.11	.19*	.03	.38*	.28*	.11#	—

Source: Created by the author using data from Pew Research Center, Biannual Media Consumption Survey.
Note: All cell entries are bivariate correlation coefficients.
*p < .01, #p < .05.

Table 2.3 Television News Exposure Correlations (Democrats Only)

	CBS News	ABC News	NBC News	CNN	Fox News	MSNBC	CNBC	Local News	C-SPAN
CBS News	—								
ABC News	.22*	—							
NBC News	.25*	.18*	—						
CNN	.15*	.22*	.18*	—					
Fox News	.23*	.14*	.19*	.10	—				
MSNBC	.22*	.27*	.34*	.46*	.21*	—			
CNBC	.26*	.16*	.31*	.37*	.23*	.56*	—		
Local News	.23*	.22*	.20*	.13#	.19*	.06	.14#	—	
C-SPAN	.18*	.16*	.14#	.34*	.06	.33*	.31*	-.03	—

Source: Created by the author using data from Pew Research Center, Biannual Media Consumption Survey.
Note: All cell entries are bivariate correlation coefficients.
*p < .01, #p < .05.

Table 2.4 Americans' Preference for Like-Minded Political News

Year	Percentage who prefer news that shares their point of view	Percentage who prefer news that doesn't have a particular point of view
2004	25	67
2006	23	68
2007	23	67
2008	23	66
2010	25	62
2011	29	63

Source: Created by the author using data obtained from Pew Research Center, www.people-press.org.

The Pew survey evidence of news-grazing frequency and news cross-exposure suggests that strict selective-exposure news-gathering habits are not typical. Most news gatherers graze. Another measure of grazing relates to respondents' like-minded news preference. On several occasions, the Pew Research Center has administered a survey item that asks, "Thinking about the different kinds of political news available to you, what do you prefer . . . getting news from sources that share your political point of view or getting news from sources that don't have a particular political point of view?" Table 2.4 shows the responses to this question from six unique surveys taken from 2004 to 2011. Two out of three respondents state that they prefer news that doesn't have a particular point of view, and only one-quarter of the sample wants news from sources that share their political viewpoints. These numbers do not significantly change over time, signaling further that the vast majority of news consumers are not actively seeking like-minded minded news.

Overall, the Pew Research evidence illustrates the prevalence of news grazing among television, cable, and online news audiences. Digital news has steadily grown as a source for most Americans' news gathering, largely supplanting traditional print news. The growing number and variety of digital news sources is contributing to declining loyalty of news gatherers of any single news source. Additionally, the plethora of ways Americans access digital news—social media, search engines, news aggregators, or news websites—contributes to our increasing uncertainty of where we ultimately get our news. Our increasing access to digital news through social media and online links further contributes to the fracturing of Americans' attention spans while contributing to a shared and strong sense of news accuracy.

Once again, Pew Research has marked our movement toward digital news, further underscoring emerging news-grazing habits. Pew's 2016 study of online news consumption asked respondents twice a day whether they got news online within the last two hours and, if so, the source of that news. In their assessment of news gatherers' recall of news sources, Pew finds that online news consumers can recall the name of the news sources outlet 56 percent of the time. In other words, Americans almost half of the time are unable to recall the source of their online news. Younger news consumers (eighteen to twenty-nine years old) were much more likely to get online news via social media and were more likely not to know the ultimate source of the news content (Barthel and Mitchell 2017). Digital media, in short, is accelerating our behavioral tendencies toward news grazing, an ongoing but serendipitous gathering of news.

This section has noted that news grazing is a related—but distinct—concept to partisan selective exposure. Partisan selective exposure has become a more important part of the American news media landscape as media choice has grown, particularly in understanding media and electoral partisan polarization (Arceneaux, Johnson, and Murphy 2012; Levendusky 2013; Stroud 2010). News grazing emphasizes both purposive and passive parts of news gathering. Like this selective-exposure concept, news grazing suggests that ideological or partisan news stories may attract the attention of like-minded, distracted viewers. As explored in later chapters, news gatherers may be selectively drawn to not only ideological messages but also visual, audio, and production cues of news—elements of news format. I discuss in Chapter 5 the political consequences of opinion news, a news format that is clearly linked to partisan selective exposure. News grazing, though, includes other formats that emphasize urgency, conflict, or humor to engage relatively passive news gatherers. These formats may add to the proportion of negative messages and cues about Congress. The following section describes the practice of news grazing and poses different explanations of why we graze.

The News-Grazing Decision: Practices and Theories

The simple act of clicking a remote control, mouse, or screen seems at first to be an innocuous, universal, and largely random act. On the surface, it appears that one click is the same as another and that people do not vary much in their grazing practices. Digging deeper, though, we find this is not quite so. The practice of news grazing varies in meaningful ways. News consumers vary widely in their rate and nature of their grazing practices. Bellamy and Walker (1996) first outlined the initial uses of remote control to get more out of the television-viewing experience:

> They [grazers] sample a wider variety of program sources. They explicitly avoid certain content by zipping and zapping television commercials and other unpleasant stimuli (e.g., politicians, personalities, newscasters). They are more likely to select programs by first sampling many of the available options rather than reading a program guide. Once viewing begins, they are more likely to reevaluate the options at program breaks. (vii)

"Zipping" and "zapping" behaviors signal a viewer's attraction or avoidance of content, respectively. These behaviors suggest directed or intentional grazing by viewers. Zipping refers particularly to behaviors for information attraction. It is the fast-forward button, channel-specific button, or Internet bookmark that immediately takes the individual to the desired news source. "Zapping," on the other hand, refers to behaviors for information avoidance. The remote control's "on/off" button is the ultimate in zapping; however, the up/down channel change button, spam filters, or DVRs relate more to the practice of zapping.

This zapping behavior is most associated with advertising avoidance and has thus been the basis of considerable marketing research (Cho and Cheon 2004; Johnson 2013; Speck and Elliot 1997). Commercial advertising frequently triggers clicking behavior. The remote control and mouse have empowered consumers to avoid advertisers' efforts to force revenue-generating product information onto an ambivalent audience. Advertising research indicates that about 25 to 50 percent of commercials are zapped by a disinterested viewer (Heeter and Greenberg 1988; Napoli 2003, 2012). As viewers' media choices expand, so does this propensity to zap or avoid advertising.

Content providers and advertisers have devised inventive approaches to combat this pesky zapping problem. These strategies include product endorsements with star athletes or performers, eliminating commercial breaks between programs, and combining advertising with the programming (Bellamy and Walker 1996; Deery 2004; Ferguson 1994). The latter strategy, product placement, involves packaging or embedding advertising within the program itself. Reality television programs—*Celebrity Apprentice, The Amazing Race,* or *Extreme Makeover: Home Edition*—have particularly made use of the product placement strategy, combining their reality competitions with product advertising. Marketing research has shown that all of these strategies do significantly reduce advertising avoidance (Gupta and Lord 1998; LaFerle and Edwards 2006). Evidently, program providers and advertisers are adapting to intentional grazing.

Intentional grazing—zipping and zapping—is distinct, though, from the more random clicking that most viewers engage in. Unintentional grazing involves the roaming, flipping, or surfing behaviors that often occur at the start of a viewing or reading session. Individuals may survey the range of media choices before they select any one program, story, or site. Alternatively, they may sample a few media options, staying at each program for a short interval. Whether surveying or sampling, viewers' attention spans are closely tied to their grazing decisions. Communications scholars have recently shown the immediate physiological responses associated with channel clicking. Lang et al. (2005) report the effects of clicking on cognitive effort and physiological arousal. They find that cognitive effort and arousal decrease in the seconds leading up to the channel change and increase in the seconds following the channel change. Our minds and senses are highly alert in those few seconds requiring a quick judgment about whether to stay or click.

Political communications scholars have presented alternative theories for what triggers grazing. I discuss three of these theories or explanations for why we graze—a uses and gratification approach, a selective attention approach, and a new media approach. A uses and gratification explanation emphasizes the role of entertainment and our desire for personal satisfaction. A selective attention explanation suggests a more directed search to seek messages that are psychologically consistent with our predispositions. Finally, a new media approach implies that we respond to stimuli that trigger immediate emotional arousal, underscoring the indirect effects of media production. Each of these grazing explanations has implications for citizens' levels of political information, political attitudes, and voting.

A uses and gratification approach is the view that individuals' media choices are foremost motivated by their practical and immediate desires for personal satisfaction. Our desire for gratification leads us to seek entertainment, escapism, and relaxation when making media choices. Individuals, of course, vary in their preferences for gratification—sports, Hollywood, humor, or shopping. However, these entertainment preferences generally motivate individuals' media choices, particularly as media options grow. Entertainment attracts and retains an audience.

What is solely entertainment, though? The line between entertainment and news has been blurred considerably since the 1970s, when television viewers were limited to three network channels and newspapers. Several authors analyze this encroachment of entertainment on a traditional journalistic approach to broadcast journalism, distinguishing between hard news and soft news (Baum 2003, 2005; Patterson 2000; Prior 2007). Hard news is traditional news programming that largely centers on stories involving governmental and political events, actions, or issues. Soft news, in contrast, is an emerging programming that focuses on entertainment-based news stories that may appeal to viewers but have no lasting, compelling social importance. They may be celebrity news, sports news, or shock/scandalous news. Programs like *Entertainment Tonight, Hard Copy,* and ESPN *SportsCenter* present some type and level of soft news, but these programs are clearly distinct from a strictly hard-news approach.

The audiences for soft news have grown as traditional sources for hard news—newspapers and network news—have declined. Scholars debate whether and to what degree soft news affects viewers' news information, political attitudes, and voting. Baum (2005) argues that viewers do learn indirectly from soft news, and if the choice is soft news or no news, these viewers may benefit from these media choices. Soft news may also be a gateway to hard news, increasing viewers' interest and indirectly providing context for understanding hard news. This view follows the approach in which news gathering is a by-product of other entertainment-directed media decisions rather than an end to itself. Prior (2003, 2007) agrees that viewers are replacing soft news with hard news as media options expand. Ultimately, though, he argues that these growing media choices are promoting an increasingly fragmented audience in which some viewers are opting out of political news. His research does not show clear support that viewers learn about politics from soft news. Regardless, a uses and gratification approach suggests that viewers are ultimately guided by their entertainment preferences, not some other media stimulus.

A second approach to understanding news grazing may be called a selective attention explanation. Selective attention suggests that individuals have predisposed attitudes and information levels that shape their viewing habits and preferences. In other words, viewers self-select the news they wish to gather. As discussed earlier, scholars have demonstrated that viewers avoid and are less likely to recall news that conflicts with their preformed belief systems (Lodge and Hamill 1986; Luskin 1990). The social psychological concept of cognitive dissonance relates to this general tendency for people to ignore or reduce access to information or ideas that contradict their political predispositions. In this case, viewers "click" to find a news format that fits better their ideological or informational preferences.

Also consistent with this selective attention approach is the premise that news gathering is a habitual practice. Viewers have preferences for particular news channels, programs, and newscasters. Their news-gathering habits are framed by a desire to collect stories that they understand, that they believe are important, and that do not offend or challenge their underlying political values. Morris (2005) reports evidence indicating the growing partisan divide between Fox News and CNN audiences. Iyengar and Hahn (2009) show experimentally that many news consumers select news based on anticipated agreement, particularly politically engaged partisans.

Finally, political communication scholars have proposed a new media approach to understanding grazing decisions (Lang 2000; Lang et al. 1999). This new media approach is a view that the format and production practices of news programmers are increasingly important in viewers' decisions to click or stay. Emerging news formats that incorporate opinion, debate, urgency, conflict, or humor with news may offer a more engaging and dramatic media stimulus than a traditional format. Following this drama metaphor, the news host in this case serves more as a character or at least narrator to the news. The news story, in this case, is presented as involving some protagonists (the focus on the news) that may fit into an established script or repeated story line. For instance, Bill O'Reilly's program, the *O'Reilly Factor*, conforms to this drama metaphor, with O'Reilly as a character in revealing and challenging a politically liberal worldview. The guest on the news program serves as the protagonist in which the liberal–conservative story line is repeated on a nightly basis.

A new media approach also suggests that production techniques adopted by emerging news programs also suppress viewers' urge to click. These production techniques include shorter segments, faster-paced discussion, colorful graphics, and multiple speakers (again, compared with the traditional television news format). These production techniques promote emotional arousal among viewers (Fox et al. 2004; Lang et al. 2005). In their split-second decision to stay or go, viewers respond to the immediate arousal and are more likely to recall this news afterwards. Researchers have shown that this attraction is particularly strong among younger viewers. They perhaps have less engrained news habits and are attracted to understanding the source of this dramatic delivery of news.

In summary, the concept of news grazing includes different clicking practices and explanations. Some grazing practices are benign, undirected searches that satisfy an immediate impulse of viewers. Other grazing, though, is intentional and involves a greater level of cognitive involvement by the viewer. Building on these ideas, we also describe three alternative explanations for this grazing. Each of these explanations implies different motives of the viewing audience—a desire for gratification, a preference for avoiding conflicting or dissonant messages, or a desire to respond to immediate emotional stimulus. Regardless of which explanation is most in line with grazing behavior, the type of news we get depends increasingly on the news we seek. The news content and format received by viewers is a function of their media choices. In the next section, I describe some patterns of news-grazing behavior and analyze these patterns for evidence relating to our three grazing explanations.

News Grazing: Trends and Analysis

News grazing is an outgrowth of media choice. The expanding universe of television and online news media compels citizens to be more discriminating in what news they gather. I begin assessing why we graze by first describing trends in changing news consumption practices over time. Unfortunately, survey questions clearly identifying grazing behavior have not been systematically asked in surveys over time. The Pew Research Center's Biennial Media Consumption Survey, however, has posed some questions since 1998 about viewers' media practices. Examining these trends from Pew Center data offers some context for understanding individual grazing decisions (Pew Research Center 2012b; see also Pew Research Center 2008).

Trends in News Grazing

The general trend in these media consumption surveys over time is the sharp decline in audience share for traditional news—newspapers and network television news—and a corresponding rise of digital news consumption. In 1993, 58 percent of Americans read a daily newspaper. In Pew's 2008 study, only 34 percent of Americans reported "reading a newspaper yesterday." By 2012, the rate declined to 27 percent, with more Americans reading news online than in print newspapers. By 2016, it fell further to 20 percent. The precipitous drop in print news has more than halved the daily print newspaper reader population. This decline is even more pronounced among younger age cohorts, indicating a clear generational replacement.

Television network news has also declined over time, though not as sharply. Twenty-seven percent of Americans in 2012 regularly watched the nightly network news—down by over one-fourth since 1998. Correspondingly, social media and online news aggregators in the past decade have become a growing source of news, particularly for young age cohorts. Overall, we are drawing news from a greater variety of sources, and we are less reliant or trusting of any single source. There is some evidence Americans are spending slightly less time per day with the news. In 1994, the average American spent seventy-four minutes collecting news; by 2012, it was sixty-seven minutes. Most of this decline, most likely, is due to a growing share of Americans "going newsless," about a 35 percent increase since the early 1990s. According to the 2012 Pew study, 29 percent of eighteen- to twenty-four-year-olds said that they "go newsless." These disengaged citizens do not report any regular news-gathering practices. An optimistic account of this trend is that at least some of these news consumers seek news "on demand," only when interests or opportunities arise. They may not be fully disengaged but rather are episodic news gatherers.

Besides the growing media choices, what other values or demographic traits are driving this trend toward this intermittent news gathering? One value associated with this trend is individuals' expressed belief that they have interest in and enjoy accessing news. Not surprisingly, Americans' news consumption habits reflect their news interests and enjoyment of news as part of their daily life. In general, the public's news interests have changed little in the past decade. About half of Americans claim to have an interest in national news "most of the time," with about 40 percent interested "most of the time" in international news. There are significant gender differences in types of news interest. Males are significantly more interested than females in news on sports, science, business, and international affairs. Women correspondingly are more interested in celebrity, health, entertainment, and religion news.

The share of Americans over time who find keeping up with the news enjoyable has also remained about constant over time, with one-half of Americans finding news gathering "enjoyable." There are significant differences across age groups, though. Younger citizens, those eighteen to twenty-four years old, are over a third less likely to find regular news gathering enjoyable. Almost twice as many Americans over fifty enjoy the news (61 percent) compared with those Americans between eighteen to twenty-four years old (34 percent).

A second value affecting the trend toward irregular news gathering is individuals' perceived busyness. Americans' self-professed demand for their time affects news-gathering practices. The busier you think your life, the less you may have regular news-gathering habits. Americans' preference for news around the "dinner hour" has clearly declined relative to their increasing preferences for news in the morning or late night. Additionally, Americans who express a low news interest find that time and information demands are a particular challenge for following the news. Forty-two percent of these "low-attention" Americans agree that it is "pretty easy to keep up with the news" compared with 82 percent for high-attention Americans. Time constraints are less a burden for those who are naturally interested in news.

Finally, the perceived importance of the news is also associated with regular news habits. As we would expect, perceived importance to news events promotes more routinized news gathering. These three values—news interests, perceived busyness, and news importance—are interrelated. Individuals' perceptions of the importance of news are closely associated with whether they report enjoying the news. Most Americans prefer a broad overview of the news. However, a growing percentage of Americans, driven by younger age cohorts, are significantly more likely to prefer niche news, stories on "specific topics of interest." For Americans over fifty, 66 percent prefer an overview of the news, and 20 percent prefer news on specific topics of interest. For Americans eighteen to twenty-four years old, 48 percent prefer an overview of the news, and 44 percent prefer news on specific topics of interest.

Overall, the trend toward irregular news gathering is closely tied with Americans' preferences for whether they enjoy the news, their perceived value of time, and their perceptions of the importance of the news. The growing number of media options is evidently resulting in a wider range and a deeper intensity of individuals' media preferences. The trend toward irregular news gathering is most evident among young Americans, with a third of eighteen- to twenty-four-year-olds now reporting that they receive no news. Given the ubiquitous nature of communication technologies—cell phones, Internet, and satellites—perhaps young Americans are getting news indirectly through secondary sources, even if they are not watching, reading, or listening directly. Still, media choice, coupled with changing media values, has resulted in an increasingly fragmented audience. This audience fragmentation is increasingly diverse, representing the extremes in their levels of news gathering.

Figure 2.1 represents this audience fragmentation by classifying types of news gatherers by the source of their news (Pew Research Center 2008). Traditional news includes newspapers, local news, and network news programs; new media news comprises cable news and Internet news. The framework suggests four types of news gatherers that vary in size and composition. Traditionalists are still the largest class of news gatherers, though their numbers have declined as the other three types have all grown in size over the last decade. Traditionalists constituted about half of Americans in 2008 and are significantly older than other types of news gatherers.

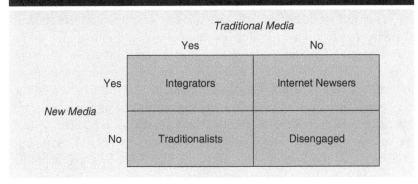

Figure 2.1 Types of News Audiences, Reliance on New and Traditional Media

	Traditional Media	
	Yes	No
New Media — Yes	Integrators	Internet Newsers
New Media — No	Traditionalists	Disengaged

Source: Created by the author, using Pew Research Center's "Key News Audiences Now Blend Online and Traditional News," August 17, 2008.

They are generally less educated and tend to prefer a general overview of news rather than pursue news specific to their interests. Integrators represent Americans who rely both on traditional and new media sources for news. They are a growing segment of Americans and include the most informed and interested in politics. Integrators are relatively younger and more affluent than the general population.

The other two news-gathering types do not regularly access traditional media sources, representing about a quarter of American adults. Internet newsers are Americans who rely on the Internet, mostly accessing online news at least three times a week. They are younger than the overall population, and they have irregular and less frequent news-gathering habits. They are more likely to read political blogs than watch a network news program. Finally, the disengaged is a growing cohort of Americans that do not rely on either new or traditional media for news. They are the least educated of any cohort and have lower incomes. These disengaged citizens are relatively uninterested in politics and are much less likely to profess any partisan or ideological attachments. At best, we can hope that the disengaged receive news indirectly from soft-news sources.

Evidently, growing news media choices are increasing the variation in how much news Americans routinely access. The nature and substance of news accessed is also increasingly varied. This growing variability in news gathering leads us back to our "Why graze?" question. Besides the demographic and attitudinal associations with news-gathering types, can we make more discerning causal connections with why Americans choose particular news?

Analyzing the Grazing Decision

One means of making these causal connections is through experiments. Experiments are artificial—that is, they are designed to occur outside of our real-world setting. Still, they allow researchers to isolate and test a causal relationship independent of external influences that often occur in a natural setting. This independence from external influences is a two-edged sword. On one hand, it strengthens our ability to draw conclusive findings from the experiment about the causality of a relationship; on the other hand, though, it may result in the experiment being unrealistic and experimental, with findings not really relating to real-world behavior. This is a careful balance. Increasingly, experiments can be helpful for understanding causal relationships and are increasingly used by social scientists (Druckman et al. 2006; Kinder and Palfrey 1993).

In this and subsequent chapters, I report results from various news-grazing experiments. The first of these experiments includes one designed simply to address the "Why graze?" question. The experiment was designed as follows: Subjects were instructed to visit an online site. They were asked to first complete a brief online survey that gauged their preexisting levels of entertainment interests (sports, movies), political interest, political trust, and political knowledge. The experiment then allowed them to view a simulated television in which they could choose to watch one of seven television clips that ran concurrently online via five minutes of streaming video. They were able to turn from one channel to the next with a virtual remote control that was provided for them on screen next to the simulated television. Next to the virtual remote control was a guide listing channels and corresponding programs. By simply clicking the "up" or "down" button on the virtual remote control with their mouse, the subjects were able to turn the channel. This approach was intended to re-create a normal television news experience.[6]

The benefit of conducting this experiment online was twofold. First, as mentioned previously, subjects were able to complete the online experiment on their own time and place without the unnatural confines of a laboratory setting. This gives an added boost of external validity, the degree to which any experimental results can be generalized to the external real-world phenomena. External validity is a typical limit with traditional experimental approaches. Second, we were able to embed a program within the online streaming video that recorded which channel the subjects were viewing at a given second of the experiment. Thus, we were able to know unobtrusively how often an individual "clicked" during the course of the experiment and how long each subject watched each channel. Within the approximate five minutes of experimental viewing, we were able to record what channel each subject was watching at a given second. This approach yielded a stream of click data to gauge news grazing.

The different channels in the experiment captured a range of different news and entertainment viewing programs and formats. We included entertainment news programs—ESPN and *Access Hollywood*—to assess the gratification view of grazing. Participants were asked a series of survey questions prior to the experiment about their entertainment preferences, news preferences and habits, and political attitudes. We would expect that individuals with a strong sports and movie preference and low political interest would be most likely to intentionally graze away from hard news and toward entertainment news. Generally, a gratification view suggests that the rise of news grazing behavior is due to declining political interest coupled with expanding media choice. Iyengar and McGrady (2007) refer to this gratification explanation by offering an "attentive public" theory that suggests that expanding media choice is making the "rich richer, and the poor poorer" (117). That is, individuals with low political interest opt out of news altogether while those with high interest collect more news. Greater media choice begets greater audience differentiation in rates of hard-news viewing and ultimately news informedness.

The grazing experiment also included news channels that were intended to appeal to program loyalists. Recall the selective-exposure view implies that grazing allows viewers to seek news consistent with their predispositions. We would expect higher rates of intentional grazing toward media messages that are consistent with individuals' memories and associations. These associations may be triggered by the viewers' partisan or ideological predispositions, interest in specific news content, or the viewers' long-standing program practices. For instance, viewers may engage in selective exposure by seeking partisan-consistent news—news that fits an existing political worldview or issue interest. Alternatively, viewers purposively seek out news channels that fit with their news-gathering routine. They may seek news from news networks that they find trustworthy and consistent.

The selective attention view suggests specific patterns in who grazes. For instance, we would expect higher rates of grazing toward preferred news channels for individuals with strong political attitudes—news interest and partisanship. Generally, the selective attention view suggests that grazing behavior is largely due to expanding media choice and triggered by individuals' behavioral preference to seek like-minded news.

Finally, we included two final news programs—*The O'Reilly Factor* and John Stewart's *Daily Show*—to assess a "new media" view. The new media view suggests that grazing is often an unintentional activity in which individuals are attracted by immediate emotional arousal or appeal. Like the uses and gratification view, the new media view is entertainment based. However, it is the format rather than the news content that engages viewers. News formats that emphasize a dramatic presentation—opinions, conflict, or humor—may affect news-grazing habits. The news content on these programs includes traditional news stories involving governmental and political events, actions, or issues.

This new media view suggests that individuals are increasingly distracted and perceive a sense of busyness. They have low to moderate political interest and a greater comfort with and interest in technology. The new media hypothesis suggests that screening technologies and greater media choices promote news grazing. Americans' attention spans are decreasing as they seek more engaging and immediate stimuli. The new media view of grazing suggests that political interest generally has not declined as much as an attitude that news gathering is a mundane task to be done in a set routine.

Our experimental analysis generated interesting findings. First and foremost, we found that "clicking" frequency was high among our respondents, which is not surprising given the average age of the participants was under twenty-five. Within this relatively short experiment (five minutes), we found that each subject changed channels an average of 13.33 times. This represents changing the channel two or three times per minute on average. Indeed, as we look within various age groups, we do find that younger subjects changed channels with greater frequency. However, contrary to popular perception, we did not find evidence that men were significantly more inclined to change channels than females. Women averaged thirteen channel changes, while men averaged 13.69.

Going beyond the overall measure of channel-changing frequency, I examined channels that were most frequently viewed. More important, I examined the respondent attitudes that were associated with an individual choosing to watch one form of news longer than another. As Table 2.5 shows, there is significant variation in the average length of time each channel was viewed. Clearly, the most popular program was The Daily Show With Jon Stewart. The popularity of The Daily Show has been well documented, particularly among young adults (see Baumgartner and Morris 2006; Baym 2005, 2008; Jones 2005; Young and Tisinger 2006).

Although The Daily Show falls under the heading of entertainment-based programming, our summary statistics do not necessarily support the notion that entertainment-based programming was more successful in attracting the

Table 2.5 Average Viewing Time, per Channel

Program	Average viewing time, in seconds (out of approximately 300 seconds)
Access Hollywood	33
The O'Reilly Factor	54
CBS Evening News	34
CNN News	31
The Daily Show	85
ESPN	26
Fox News	37

Source: Created by the author using original data.

attention of the experimental subjects than more traditional news sources. Other entertainment-based channels, particularly the television tabloid program, *Access Hollywood*, and ESPN's *SportsCenter*, did not draw more attention than other programs. Instead, the program that drew the second-largest level of interest was *The O'Reilly Factor*. Certainly, *The O'Reilly Factor* is not "traditional" news, and it is formatted in a manner to attract the attention of potential viewers, but the subject matter is more news-based than that of ESPN or *Access Hollywood*. Thus, we cannot firmly accept the premise that purely entertainment-based media are most effective in attracting the attention of news grazers. The picture is more nuanced and likely dependent upon certain attributes of the viewer.

What factors may be associated with program choice? From a demographic perspective, one might expect that gender plays some role in the process. While our general findings show that gender appears unrelated to the rate of channel changing within the confines of our experiment, programming choice may still depend on gender. As Table 2.6 illustrates, this is the case to a certain extent. We found a significant difference between males and females in multiple cases when we compared program preference across gender. Interestingly, this difference applies largely to the three entertainment-based programs. Women were much more likely to watch *Access Hollywood* than were men, and men were more likely to watch ESPN than were women ($p \leq .01$). Also, men appeared to be slightly more interested in watching coverage of *The Daily Show* than were women ($p \leq .10$). Among the programs that were more news based, only the coverage on

Table 2.6 Channel Preference by Gender

Program	Mean viewing time in seconds	
	Females	Males
Access Hollywood**	46	19
The O'Reilly Factor	56	52
CBS Evening News	32	36
CNN News	29	33
The Daily Show*	78	94
ESPN*	17	36
Fox News*	42	32

Source: Created by the author using primary data.
**Difference statistically significant ($p \leq .01$).
*Difference statistically significant ($p \leq .10$).

Fox News drew more interest from one gender more than the other. In our experiment, women were more likely to watch Fox News than men. We examined other possible demographic differences but found no significant trends.

We did, however, find attitudinal correlates with programming choice. Most notably, we see that partisanship is significantly associated with the tendency to watch The Daily Show and The O'Reilly Factor. As Figure 2.2 demonstrates, Republicans are more likely to watch O'Reilly and vice versa for Democrats. The trends are not modest and also not surprising. Among Republicans, O'Reilly was a more popular viewing choice. However, The Daily Show had a wider margin of popularity among Democrats and independents. This confirms preexisting notions that O'Reilly—a well-known conservative ideologue—attracts like-minded viewers. Likewise, Stewart has gained notoriety as a more liberal voice with a more liberal audience, and my findings confirm that Stewart attracts Democrats more than Republicans.

While O'Reilly and Stewart are clearly the most ideological news providers in our experiment, there were also three additional sources of news that are partisan stereotyped by many observers. Particularly, there is Fox News' standard news coverage versus CNN's coverage. Fox News leans toward the right side of the political spectrum while CNN is viewed as the opposite. Additionally, we have also included the more traditional network

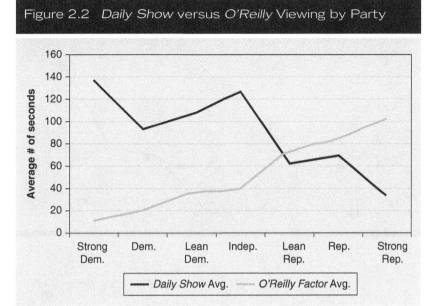

Figure 2.2 *Daily Show* versus *O'Reilly* Viewing by Party

Source: Created by the author using primary data.

television news source, *CBS Evening News*, in the experiment as well. Network news is now extremely unpopular among young viewers (Graber 2006), but it also has gained increased criticism as showing a bias toward the left (Goldberg 2002).

The findings displayed in Figure 2.3 illustrate the change in viewing frequency among each of the three channels discussed earlier. CNN and CBS follow very similar patterns. Interestingly, they are most unpopular among the strong partisans on both sides of the spectrum. Democrats and independents watched CNN and CBS slightly more than Republicans, but this difference was slight. I speculate that Jon Stewart's high popularity among strong Democrats was what lowered the frequency of those individuals viewing other channels.

Fox News, however, demonstrates a much more discernable trend. As an individual becomes more Republican, his or her frequency of Fox News viewing shoots through the roof. While independents watched only eighteen seconds of Fox News on average in our experiment, strong Republicans watched an average of seventy-eight seconds—over a 400 percent increase.

Beyond partisanship, I also uncovered some interesting trends within my experiment regarding general types of news preferences and specific

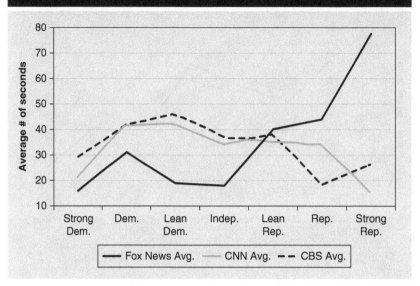

Figure 2.3   Fox News, CNN, and CBS Viewing by Party

Legend: Fox News Avg. — CNN Avg. — CBS Avg.

Source: Created by the author using primary data.

channel choice. As uses and gratification theory would predict, two of the most entertainment-based channels in the experiment increased in popularity among those who agreed that they lacked the background information necessary to follow the news (see Figure 2.4). By contrast, we can see that the trend is reversed for those who watched CNN with more frequency—which is a harder news program. Those who disagreed with the statement that "I don't have enough background information to follow the news" watched CNN an average of forty-eight seconds while those who agreed only watched an average of fourteen seconds.

Overall, the analysis offers some support for all three views of grazing explanations. As suggested by the new media account, grazers are attracted by programs that include some drama- or emotion-laden production format. The humor- and opinion-based news formats, particularly, were the most-watched programs among subjects in the experiment. This was true across all demographic groupings—age, gender, and race. However, the experiment confirmed that younger subjects were attracted in greater rates to the humor format. Generally, subjects were drawn to drama-laden formats that offer some entertainment along with news commentary. This is a finding that we will develop and analyze in later chapters.

The analysis also supports a selective attention view of grazing. Figures 2.2 and 2.3 show that individuals seek confirming news consistent with their

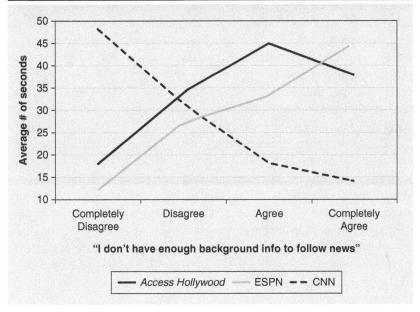

Figure 2.4 Soft versus Hard News by Perceived Background Information

"I don't have enough background info to follow news"

—— *Access Hollywood* ······ ESPN − − CNN

Source: Created by the author using primary data.

political predispositions and viewing preferences. The length of Fox News viewing, particularly, almost doubled for self-identified Republicans. Not all grazers have strong partisan identities; however, for those who strongly identify with one party, their likelihood to stay at a news channel appears to correspond with a preference for like-minded news.

Finally, we also saw evidence for the use and gratification view. Individuals who say they do not have enough background to follow the news tend to avoid traditional news formats for soft news. News avoidance appears to be another motivation for grazing decisions. This result reinforces the view that media choice is expanding the informational divide between those who are naturally interested in politics and those who are not.

Conclusion

The way most Americans get their news is changing from a routine practice relying on traditional sources to an increasingly episodic practice in which we access diverse media outlets. This chapter has given some background and evidence for assessing the fundamental questions of "What is grazing?" "Who grazes?" and "Why graze?" I began by first contrasting two views of changing news-gathering habits: partisan selective exposure and news grazing. These are interrelated concepts, and both have value in understanding changing news habits. The grazing concept, however, is relatively less discussed by academic literature. Compared with selective exposure, grazing implies a more passive explanation of why and how we gather news. Grazing suggests we collect news intermittently, often triggered by immediate impulses or emotional engagement. I reported several behavioral measures of grazing that indicated the utility of the concept for understanding contemporary news gathering.

The chapter then turned to evaluating explanations of who grazes, discussing different trends in news gathering. The emergence of news grazing is clearly a function of expanded media choice. However, Americans have altered news-gathering habits in varying rates and manner. Individuals' attitudes toward news and time significantly affect their news consumption habits over time. Individuals' expressed enjoyment of the news, their perceived value of time, and their perceptions of the importance of the news all impact how they consume news. Younger Americans have been most likely to form and adapt their news consumption habits around new media platforms and sources.

Finally, I offered and evaluated three alternative explanations for why we graze. Namely, I noted a uses and gratifications view, selective attention view, and new media view. The chapter discussed each explanation, and I presented some initial analytical evidence that supported each of these views. The experimental results offer a limited analysis, but they offer some insight into the various reasons for why we graze. The causes of news grazing are multifaceted and largely driven by our preferred mixes of news and entertainment.

Overall, media choice is enabling Americans to match their news with their political attitudes and to seek their preferred mix of news and entertainment. Evidently, the trend is increasingly for news to be less of a shared "mass" media phenomena for deciphering the political world. Media choice promotes greater variation in both the amount and nature of news accessed by Americans. While the proliferation of news sources and platforms enables individuals to access news, it is individuals themselves who choose what to view. News gatherers are increasingly varied in the amount and sources of news consumed. Consequently, news makers and producers have an incentive to target news that will appeal to an increasingly distracted audience. News formats that engage viewers rather than merely inform are increasingly evident. In Chapter 3, I assess how news makers and producers have altered the news to hold the attention of increasingly distracted audiences.

ENDNOTES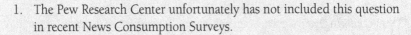

1. The Pew Research Center unfortunately has not included this question in recent News Consumption Surveys.

2. Several reports have noted younger Americans' news consumption patterns and the long-term implications. See Kohut (2013) and Mellman (2015).

3. The American Press Institute report can be read at https://www .americanpressinstitute.org/publications/reports/survey-research/ millennials-news/single-page.

4. Again, the 2015 American Press Institute presents a recent assessment of how we collect news at https://www.americanpressinstitute.org/ publications/reports/survey-research/how-americans-get-news.

5. Jacobson (2017) gives an excellent analysis of the 2016 election outcome. He explains how "the candidate with the much less elaborate and expensive campaign, the more divided party, the smaller convention bounce, and the worse debate performances, who was less popular and rated by more voters as unqualified for the office, won the presidency" (24).

6. The online streaming video program randomly assigned subjects to one of the seven channels as a starting point.

CHAPTER 3

News Makers and Producers

The Emergence of Commentary News

Our changing news-gathering habits are a product of expanding media choice, behavioral preferences, and institutional adaptations. The initial chapter explored the role of growing media choice and screening technologies, and the previous chapter introduced the behavioral tendencies that lead to news grazing. This chapter extends the argument by examining institutional adaptations—how news grazing is changing what and how news is reported and thus perceived by viewers. I argue that news grazing has subsequently pushed news makers and news producers to alter the content and style of news. The news has been transformed both to appeal to specific audiences and to better hold the attention of increasingly distracted news consumers.

I refer to this new style and content of information delivery as commentary news. Commentary news refers to a content and style of coverage that includes greater opinion, urgency, conflict, and entertainment integrated with straight or hard news. Compared with more journalistic news coverage, commentary news styles intentionally invoke stronger emotional responses for viewers. The purpose of this emotional response is to promote audience engagement and elevate attentiveness to news stories. Ultimately, commentary news keeps us from clicking, tapping, or turning away from news in an increasingly crowded media landscape. Commentary news formats are increasingly prevalent in how we view the politicians and institutions, particularly the U.S. Congress. This chapter focuses on the changing composition and strategies of congressional news makers—particularly those government communications officials in congressional party, committee, and member offices—and the news producers—the Washington press corps that report on Congress. It also discusses news makers are operating in election settings and the role of commentary news in the recent 2016 election.

The chapter begins by discussing the evolution of commentary news as a consequence of changing information economics. I present the news industry from this information economics perspective in which their journalistic government reporting role is likened to a public good, a good that many consumers value but few want to pay for if they can get it for free. As with most goods (but particularly public goods), we generally prefer to pay as little money as possible regardless of how much we personally value the news. Government information increasingly shares traits of other public goods, I argue, as news producers may provide it freely to consumers via the Internet or social media. We are less willing to pay for the news when it is increasingly accessible for free.

The information economics perspective helps to explain how news makers and producers have adapted to this increasingly competitive news media industry. This information economics perspective helps us understand our increasingly jaded views of Congress and the media generally. Following the information economics discussion, I describe the changing strategies of news makers and news producers to retain a news audience. News makers generally have invested more time and resources into strategic communications, tactics to advance the political message of a politician, party, government agency, or advocacy group through competing media sources. News producers, likewise, have adapted to media choice by altering the content and format of the news in order to attract and retain a less loyal audience. Broadly, news grazing has led news makers and producers to alter the news itself. One by-product of this altered news has been a shift in how much Americans trust Congress and the media.

Selling the News: Is News a Private or Public Good?

The traditional professional norms of journalists include a commitment to professional integrity, objectivity, fairness, and public service. While these journalistic values certainly persist, the realities of changing technology and market forces have compelled news providers to adapt how news is reported (Downie and Schudson 2009; McChesney and Nichols 2010). Viewers surf or click effortlessly—sometimes even subconsciously—from one media choice to another. The challenge to capturing public attention to political news seems to be an ever-shifting goal post. Ultimately, news—and information broadly—is an economic good.

We typically do not think of the "news" as an economic good, like a car or clothes. Public information is, after all, *public*. We may believe that government officials have a professional obligation to inform us about the state of public institutions and policies. Thus, we may optimistically think that public officials will regularly and voluntarily provide objective, timely updates of government performance. Additionally, from this public service lens, we may assert that journalists have a professional duty to objectively relate this news. Following this perspective, "news" would be distributed cooperatively and for the journalistic goal of advancing governmental accountability. This public service lens, though, is increasingly less common. A growing share of Americans are skeptical of journalistic standards guiding the news. The percentage of Americans who rate the honesty and ethical standards of journalists as "low" or "very low" has doubled (from 15 to 30 percent) since 1990.[1]

News as an economic good, one in which consumers and producers hold varying incentives and preferences, is an increasingly realistic view. News consumers have preferences for specific information or style of coverage; news producers, on the other hand, must attract and maintain an audience. Economists view "news" as a demand for information. Economic theories of information explain consumers' and producers' incentives to exchange information in a market economy (Hamilton 2004). Following this information economics framework, news is seen as having some qualities of both a private good, like food or clothing, and a public good, like clean air or national defense. Economists define public goods broadly as having two qualities: (1) nonrivalry and (2) exclusion of consumption.

The first property, nonrivalry, suggests that your consumption of the good does not limit the ability of another person to consume the good. For instance, food is rivalrous since your eating it (hopefully) precludes my consumption. Government or public information is not wholly rivalrous, though. Information is nonrivalrous because once it is provided to one person or group, it can be shared at a very small unit cost of production to others. As the costs to produce and reproduce information decrease, news becomes increasingly nonrivalrous.

Digital news media, particularly, reduces the costs of sharing the benefits of news without substantial production costs. Newsprint, printing presses, and access to professional journalists cease to be obstacles; the Internet has largely reduced these unit production costs. Increasingly, a political news story can be provided to one person without diminishing its meaning, access, or value for another. Online news aggregators and social media sites, according to Pew Research, are the preferred sources for political news among young news consumers.[2] Digital media has greatly reduced the rivalry of the news product and, as a result, altered the news media marketplace.

News is often nonrivalrous also because we value it as a "free" good. From a normative or democratic perspective, we value "free" or public information. Public information belongs to us as taxpaying citizens of a democracy, and we believe this evaluative information is necessary to hold government actors accountable. For example, C-SPAN (the Cable-Satellite Public Affairs Network) was established in 1979 by the cable industry as a public resource for delivering free (at least for cable subscribers, presumably as a by-product of your monthly cable bill) and uncensored coverage of Congress. The values of public information and democratic accountability affect government officials as well. Most government officials sense an obligation to provide citizens with information on our government's performance and needs, subject to legal and ethical constraints. Digital media extends the reach of elected officials to deliver public information. Esterling, Lazer, and Neblo (2013) look at the diffusion and effects of congressional websites on the nature representation, for instance. In short, a nonrivalrous news media product has social value for sustaining democratic accountability.

The second general condition of a public good, exclusion, implies that there is a means for limiting (or excluding) the benefits of an economic good to just those who paid for it. Tickets to an event or paid membership to a club exemplifies mechanisms for exclusion. Without a ticket, you are not able to go the event. To varying degrees, public information may allow exclusion. Access to news makers (elected officials) and enforcement of subscription fees may exclude news from being spread to those who do not have resources or commit to payment. Individuals may be excluded from public information either by the news makers (government source) or the news producers (a journalistic outlet). The news makers may want to affect public opinion by their decisions of who they release information to and how it is communicated. News producers, on the other hand, may exclude news to control access to their product and to ensure its profitability.

The means for exclusion, though, have significantly changed with broader media choice, particularly the growing influence of new media. News is provided through "free" television, online search engines, online news aggregators, social media, and subscription-free Internet news sources. News producers are less able to exclude nonpayers as the sources of news expand. For subscription print news, circulation and revenues have sharply declined over time. While there will likely always be a consumer demand for high-quality and niche news, traditional news media delivering national and headline news are increasingly facing an exclusion problem. Twitter, for instance, provides an instantaneous, direct, and free backdoor connecting news makers and citizens. President Trump's use of Twitter in the 2016 campaign illustrated its capacity to bypass news media gatekeepers. Trump independently and effectively framed the debate ("Build the Wall" and "Drain the Swamp") and labeled his opponents ("Crooked Hillary" and "Lyin' Ted") all in 140 characters or less.

There are countervailing trends, of course. Online news providers are increasingly using paywalls—online payment systems to restrict content digital access to only paying subscribers. Additionally, cable television installation and service fees function as a means of excluding public information available through cable news. Nonetheless, new information technologies have led to a proliferation of news media sources and methods for avoiding payments. Digital exclusion has its technical limits. Cable and Internet subscription fees still allow joint consumption in which one person's password may be used by others to access content. Additionally, web search engines, aggregators, and social media serve as ready means of accessing free news. Overall, the growth of and competition between media sectors—network news, print, cable, online, and social media—have made exclusion increasingly difficult.

Recognizing these trends toward nonrivalry and nonexclusion, I argue that national news, to varying degrees, is increasingly a public good. News producers are not always able to exclusively give their product (news) to only those paying for it. Furthermore, once it is provided, consumers can enjoy the benefits of news without incurring its costs or diminishing its value to others. Social scientists have a name for these nonpaying consumers of public goods: *free riders* (Hardin 2015; Olson 1965). The free-rider problem is endemic to public good provision, and it has its consequences. As economic theory implies, under free-riding conditions, both consumers and producers have weak incentives to engage in an efficient exchange; as a consequence, the public good will ultimately be underproduced.

Media choice, in fact, has also resulted in headline and national news increasingly taking on the characteristics of a commodity—a good in which quality differentiation between providers is slight. The consumer may not value whether the news story is from one source or another. This commoditization has made all news providers more vulnerable to aggregate market demand. Commodity markets characteristically result in economic competition driving down production costs and producer investments. One consequence of the problem has been local news providers relying more on wire services for national news, specifically news on Congress. The growing availability of national and headline news has many local television and newspaper providers to shift resources away from national coverage and toward their comparative advantage, local news.

Another response to this commoditization problem of national and headline news is branding. News providers have adapted economically by trying to differentiate their news service from other sources. The concept of "branding" was adopted to differentiate one person's cattle, a commodity, from another's by means of a distinctive symbol burned into the animal's skin. Applied to the news, branding refers to different strategies to define a news source's reputation and style of coverage in contrast to competitors. The objective is to develop a stronger audience loyalty, offsetting the forces of commoditization. Newspapers and magazines with strong brand reputations have been able to maintain their audience and economic standing.

However, news providers have had to work harder over time to avoid the economic forces of nonrivalry, nonexclusion, and commoditization as media choice has expanded. Online news, particularly, has transformed the economics of the traditional news industry. Ultimately, advertising, not the news product, is what generates profit for news providers. The "80–20 rule" of traditional print news media was the accepted principle that 80 percent of revenues would be generated through advertisement and 20 percent through subscription fees. Most newspapers adapted to the Internet by allowing access for free or at reduced cost for their online news. Their hope was to capture new advertising revenues while baiting future newspaper subscribers with online news.

The baiting strategy for print media over time, though, has not been good economically. Online news advertising revenues have been low compared with traditional print advertising revenues.[3] Print media, unfortunately, has swapped subscription dollars for advertising dimes over time while also experiencing a precipitous drop in their print subscriptions. These downward business trends are leveling off somewhat in recent years. Still, the competition for advertising revenues has exploded the "80–20 rule" of thumb. The economics of the news media industry are still evolving with the expansion of online sources. Paradoxically, Americans are spending more time consuming news even though we have fewer news reporters. The Pew Research Center finds that the average American spent seventy minutes in 2010 accessing news from various media sectors, a slight increase over the previous decade.[4] At the same time, the American Society of News Editors reports that the number of news reporters declined by a third between 2000 and 2013. This paradox is explained by our choice to consume less traditional print news and correspondingly increase online news.

These information economic forces do not bode well for democracy—and Congress particularly—in a world dependent on information exchanges among government elites, journalists, and citizens. Given the high fixed costs of gathering and reporting the news relative to consumers' willingness to pay, public information is not provided to the level and quality that some democratic advocates would prefer. James Hamilton (2004) elaborates on the state of information economics, explaining the growth of "soft" news over "hard" news. Soft news emphasizes a lighter fare of human interests, entertainment, or conflict-ridden news. It is different in format and content from a traditional, journalistic sense of public affairs. This traditional news format and content, "hard news," focuses on factual reporting of government actions or events with clear public policy implications.

Professional journalists have traditionally been schooled in the five W's of news reporting: *Who* is it about? *What* happened? *When* did it take place? *Where* did it take place? *Why* did it happen? Hamilton emphasizes that news is increasingly a function of a "new five W's": "*Who* cares about the information? *What* are they willing to pay, or others pay to reach them? *Where* can media outlets and advertisers reach them? *When* is this profitable? *Why* is it profitable?" (Hamilton 2004, 262). He argues that changing demographics and audience segmentation of the news marketplace—with the emergence of cable and Internet news—have shifted the demand toward soft news. Young viewers are more likely to prefer this style of news coverage, and the growing number of news outlets creates stronger market competition to retain this audience share.

Ultimately, the marketplace for public news applied to any mass democracy is further complicated by an individual's private incentive to remain "rationally ignorant" toward public affairs. Political scientists refer to rational ignorance as the condition of individuals not being willing to incur the informational and time costs of remaining informed about government when they are merely a single vote in a mass electorate. Each voter recognizes the cost of dutiful public citizenship, such as monitoring elected officials' actions or forming clear preferences on complex public policy matters, far exceeds the benefits of casting a single and ultimately inconsequential vote in a mass election. For nearly all voters, influence over electoral or governmental outcomes is dwarfed by the opportunity costs of active, informed citizenship. Perhaps for some citizens, rational ignorance is more prevalent as cable and online entertainment options have exploded. For citizens with low political interest, it has never been easier to avoid the news.

An information economics perspective, in summary, leads us to expect behaviors and outcomes resulting from media choice and news grazing. Particularly, I have discussed how the economics of news increasingly has public good features, struggles with commoditization of headline national news, and must combat the prevalence of rational ignorance among citizens with low political interest. New grazing is a behavioral response to growing media choice, but its growing prevalence compels an economic response by news makers and news producers. These institutional responses and changes in the nature of news are occurring in predictable ways. In the next sections, I first discuss adaptations among news makers, focusing particularly on how Congress makes news. The following section does the same for the news media industry, the news producers, with an emphasis on the emergence of digital news. Both news makers and producers have contributed to the trend of commentary news filling an increasingly larger share of the news hole, the amount of media space or time devoted to nonadvertising. The content and style of news are changing indirectly as a response to media choice and news grazing.

The News Makers

The news we receive ultimately is a function of decisions made by news consumers, news makers, and news media. News makers—elected officials and government elites—affect the news by their control and interpretation of public information. News makers are those political elites who possess or distribute government or political information. They include political staff of elected officials, public affairs officers of government agencies, and third-party press relations and media consultants. News makers act as political communications officers across all three branches of government, but we will focus on congressional news makers. The U.S. Congress has substantially increased the breadth of effort engaged in managing public communications across party, committee, and personal offices in recent decades (Frantzich 2015; Malecha and Reagan 2012; Vinson 2017). Along with news journalists, these congressional news makers try to advance their political goals by controlling access to and perceptions of information. To achieve their goals, they also have had to adapt to new information economics.

Academics have explained the relationship between news journalists and news makers as one of managed tension (Bennett 2016; Graber and Dunaway 2014; Leighley 2003). Each covets what the other provides. Journalists seek access to information; government officials seek access to a mass audience. Still, this is not a relationship of simple exchange. Despite a shared recognition for mutual accommodation, journalists and news makers often have conflicting goals. Journalists are interested in retaining access to sources of accurate, timely, and engaging news while also attracting a desired news audience. News makers, on the other hand, are interested in sound public information while also advancing political ideas and policy priorities.

Graber and Dunaway (2014) portray an adversarial relationship in which the media and political actors engage in a struggle for control. Similarly, Bennett (2016) and Leighley (2003) present an uneasy relationship in which political actors sometimes accommodate the work and informational demands of the media. These tensions occur both in information access and message control. While political actors may not control information access, they try to influence how information is communicated by journalists and ultimately perceived by the public. These messaging strategies are discussed later in the chapter. Government officials, at least prior to the Internet, lacked a great capacity to communicate independent from the media. Government officials thus recognize that most news must be mediated through journalists for it to reach an intended audience. Journalists have preferences, in most instances, for what information is publicly communicated and how the story is related.

Despite these tensions, news makers and the media coexist through mutual accommodation. Each needs the other to achieve its goals. The goals of political advocates and government officials are to advance a political or policy agenda. The media, on the other hand, has journalistic goals that value timely, relevant, and engaging stories. This mutual accommodation in recent decades has changed markedly with shifting information economics.

Historically, the role of public relations inside the national government was slow to evolve. Congress prohibited government public relations with the 1913 Gillett Amendment, which forbade the use of federal appropriations to pay for "publicity experts" (Martinelli 2012). Many members of Congress at that time did not deem public relations and interbranch communications to be appropriate function of government agencies. The amendment was renewed in 1931 and, because of its prohibition, was likely responsible for today's diverse set of job titles for government public relations. These job titles are often difficult to discern but include information officers, press officers, public affairs experts, communications specialists, and press secretaries.

The U.S. Office of Personnel Management today states that over fifteen thousand federal government officials work in public relations–related job. A major professional association estimates about forty thousand positions as "government communicators."[5] Public relations or public affairs officers exist in every branch and government agency today. The growth of the media relations community outside of federal government agencies has been even more dramatic. The number of public relations officers and consultants representing private interests on governmental affairs matters has grown in line with the growth in the lobbying industry. Baumgartner et al. (2009) provide an excellent analysis of how the Washington lobbying and government relations industry affects the policy process. Media relations work is often another service provided by government affairs firms separate from direct lobbying of government officials.

Today, government news makers have varying levels of control over how public news is released or understood. Political communications scholars refer to *agenda setting* as a capacity to affect what stories or events are (or are not) covered in the news. Iyengar, Peters, and Kinder's (1982) classic study of media effects found that agenda setting has significant effects on the public's perceptions of what is news and what is important when evaluating government officials. News makers vary in their capacity to exercise gatekeeping control over the media. The executive and judicial branches, particularly, are able to exercise considerably more information control than Congress or nongovernmental sources. White House press relations is able to limit information access often, allowing White House officials to have greater agenda power. In these cases, government information empowers news makers with opportunities to exercise discretion, if not outright exclusion, in how (or which) news is related to the public. This information control varies significantly across branches and agencies in government.

For Congress, though, news makers have less agenda-setting influence over what and how information is reported to the media. Instead, congressional news makers generally compete with each other to shape public perceptions of how the public responds to government actions and public events (Sellers 2009). Notably, congressional news makers attempt to shape politicians' reputations and define the public agenda by framing and priming the news. Framing and priming theory has developed through multidisciplinary efforts of psychologists, political scientists, and communications scholars.

Framing refers to the role that a speakers' symbols, words, and emphases may have on public attitudes of a public event, issue, or individual. Polling experts have long noted how a survey item's question wording can dramatically affect how people respond to a question. Survey outcomes on abortion rights, for instance, can be very sensitive to wording, particularly whether there is a "pro-life" or "pro-choice" slant to the question. Framing is similar to this question-wording problem. In this case, a media message can influence public perceptions of an event or person by how the message is related. Several studies have investigated public attitudes toward the U.S. military action in Iraq, specifically how words and phrases like "war on terrorism" and "weapons of mass destruction" had powerful effects on public perceptions (Baum 2003; Entman 2003). These media frames may have greatly affected public attitudes.

Likewise, news makers engage in media spinning by offering perspectives on how the public should understand a news story. *Priming* refers to the importance of news in structuring how the public evaluates or judges political candidates or institutions. In other words, the content and frequency of certain news stories may affect how we attribute blame or success to public officials. Priming influences public perceptions of the news. These media messages do not even need to be news stories. Holbrook and Hill (2005), for instance, find that watching entertainment crime dramas on television elevates ("primes") your likelihood of listing crime as an important issue and as an issue for assessing presidential performance.

News makers shape public perceptions through agenda setting, framing, and priming. These tools of news makers are essential to understanding how news is formed and how news shapes public opinion. How do news makers organize to achieve these ends, though? As noted earlier, news makers vary substantially in their abilities to control or at least shape perceptions of the news. Congress and nongovernmental public affairs officials do not exercise agenda-setting power to the degree of the White House. It is important to contrast executive branch and legislative branch communications in terms of their gatekeeping capacity.

Political scientists have shown that the Washington media agenda is formed mostly by White House press offices (Bennett 1990; Cook 1998). The prominence of White House news sources is a twentieth-century phenomenon; its growth, not coincidentally, has paralleled the growing prevalence of television as the public's primary news source (Pika, Maltese, and Rudalevige 2016). The gain of White House media agenda setting allows popular presidents at least to influence public opinion (Page, Shapiro, and Dempsey 1987). However, this gain comes at some loss in how news is shaped by commentary from an increasingly critical White House press and Congress.

Agenda-setting power comes at a trade-off to increasingly distrustful media. Patterson (1993) presents the case that media coverage of the presidency has become increasingly critical. Journalists increasingly interpret rather than merely report on the news. Similarly, Larry Sabato (2000) argues persuasively that media stories of presidents and presidential candidates tend to reinforce predefined images of these figures, contributing to the emerging media practice of "feeding frenzies." These feeding frenzies are fed by opposing partisan elites' increasing engagement with the media. Congressional party leadership offices, for instance, exercise a much weaker agenda-setting role but are often asked to respond to emerging stories and thus shape public perceptions.

The contemporary White House employs an elaborate media management and marketing enterprise on behalf of any administration. Over one-third of top-level White House staff members are engaged in media relations and policy in some form (Edwards and Wayne 2013). This media management and marketing effort is undertaken by two divisions of the White House staff. The White House Press Office, the first of these divisions, is charged with day-to-day press relations or media management. The management goal requires the White House media relations staff to react to journalists' inquires about emerging news by providing administration positions and policy. The president's *press secretary* is the primary spokesperson on behalf of the president and is in charge of day-to-day press briefings. There are two regular daily press briefings for journalists, as well as other on- and off-the-record sessions between White House officials and the press. The main task of the press secretary is to respond to media questions with an official administration position and to respond to emerging events. The press secretary must mediate a two-way conversation between reporters and White House officials. The press secretary must simultaneously preserve his or her journalistic credibility while still advancing the president's agenda.

The second team of the White House press corps is the White House Office of Communications. This staff is charged with planning a more long-term communications strategy. As Pika, Maltese, and Rudalevige (2016) note, the Office of Communications serves a more proactive, planning function relative to the reactive role of the Press Office. The Communications Office coordinates the president's media appearances, press events, and overall communications goals. These communications goals entail controlling administration press releases and coordinating executive branch media events to promote the president's media message.

Of course, the president and top political appointees are always the main voices and faces for any administration. The presidential press conference was a much more common practice during the 1960s and 1970s than for more recent presidents. Baum and Kernell (1999) refer to this period as the "golden age" of presidential television, in which presidents enjoyed much greater and less critical news media coverage. Presidential news management and marketing today occurs much more through intermediaries.

Congress, in contrast to the White House, has less gatekeeping capacity over news. Consequently, its media resources are more diffused and reactive to the executive's and media's news agenda. Nearly all members—but particularly senators—engage in efforts to shape the news. Members of

Congress began hiring press secretaries in the 1960s and 1970s to respond to the daily inquiries of reporters, mostly local and regional press. Members expanded their media relations efforts to include ongoing publicity strategies like newsletters, press releases, press conferences, and other planned media events. Since the 1990s, legislators have further expanded their media efforts to manage their online presence. Congressional communications officers have also become much more active in media efforts toward targeted constituencies via talk radio and online news outlets. The personal, committee, and party staff on Capitol Hill dedicated to media relations has grown over time. These communications staff seek out media through interviews, op-eds, and press releases. Compared with the White House, congressional media attention must often be sought out or "earned" by members and their staff.

Despite this group of congressional media entrepreneurs, most news making on Capitol Hill is centered on congressional leaders. Committee and party leaders have the dedicated staff support to have an ongoing and serious effort to affect the media agenda and alter public perceptions of media coverage. Party leaders, in particular, command a stage and bully pulpit as cheerleaders of their partisan agenda or critics of the opposition party. Party communications efforts occur both inside and outside Congress. Sellers (2009) explains the complex "cycle of spin" between congressional party communications offices and their copartisan, rank-and-file members' media strategies. Party communications strategies are both externally and internally directed. The external communications role acts to publicize some party position or achievement to a variety of media outlets. Internal communications serve to coordinate communications and planning among copartisan members with the goal of using similar phrases and media messages.

Party communications services have become a growing activity for building party cohesion. The party organizations produce a range of informational products from the basic—the upcoming week's floor schedule—to specific policy briefs and analyses. They invite outside speakers, coordinate media events, and maintain extensive informational online presences. Party organizations also engage in outreach efforts, planning meetings between members and outside groups. They serve members and their staff with a variety of informational services, training opportunities, and coordinated communications strategies. On the House side, most of the external and internal communications work falls with the Republican Conference and Democratic Caucus. Some of these communications services occur with the policy committees on the Senate side.

An aim of internal party communications is to plan a common political and policy agenda among copartisans. One way that parties work toward that end is by establishing at least a basic party agenda early in the legislative year. The *Contract With America*, the ten-point plan that served both as both a public relations plan and policy platform for House Republicans in the 104th Congress, represented the most visible version of a party agenda. As discussed earlier, Senate Republicans passed a Conference rule, partly in response to the House Republican experience with the *Contract*, mandating a party agenda at the start of each new Congress.

Another way the party leadership communicates legislative priorities inside Congress is by bill introduction. The majority party typically reserves the first ten bill numbers for party legislation. Bills are given a number when introduced. For instance, in the House, a bill may be designated H.R. (House resolution) 1 and the Senate may be S.1. In the 107th Congress, the top bill numbers were designated for the Bush administration's Education Reform Bill, the Social Security and Medicare surplus lockbox bill, and tax relief legislation. The prominence of the top bill numbers underscores to members that these are key party bills and votes.

Internal communications also occur in the various written and oral policy briefings circulated among copartisans and their staff. In the House, the party caucuses and the party whip's offices serve as clearinghouses for issue analyses, talking points, and legislative bill summaries that provide partisan analysis and spin to pending legislation. The Senate policy committees still provide longer analytic reports, although in recent Congresses they have also moved toward shorter summary reports. Party information is widely disseminated electronically through the party organizations' extensive and growing involvement in both a public Internet and private intranet presence. Members and their staff vary in their use of these materials. While many members and staff ignore or discard party communications, relying instead on their own press secretaries, others use these paper and electronic party briefing materials when writing floor speeches, talking points, or letters to constituents. The goal, presumably, is to coordinate members' understanding of pending issues by encouraging them to read common materials, as well as to write (speak) using common words, phrases, or arguments.

External communications is the other side of this informational, party-building role. In many circumstances, the media galleries, the television studios inside the Capitol Building, are the eyes and ears for Congress today. Members' floor statements and debate may be too ponderous for fifteen-second radio or television news clips, let alone an online blog or

Twitter feed. The media galleries afford an accessible television studio for Congress members to give a sound byte commenting on breaking news or announcing their congressional actions.

Party organizations dedicate substantial resources to affect the media's portrayal of congressional business. An increasingly important role of congressional party leaders is as principal spokespersons to the media (Evans and Oleszek 2001; Sellers 2009). House and Senate party caucuses operate as in-house, partisan press relations offices. Party leaders and party caucus press secretaries produce steady streams of press releases and statements to journalists. They schedule members to appear at press conferences, online chats, talk radio appearances, and personal interviews.

Adaptations and Strategies: Making Commentary News

The emergence of cable and Internet news has unleashed an entrepreneurial energy to news makers and producers affecting what news is covered and how we perceive the news. News makers have adapted strategies to make use of expanding media choice. The emergence of a permanent campaign, direct communications, and message coordination by news makers are all strategies employed by partisans, activists, and issue advocates to affect news coverage. As the diversity of news content and framing of news events grows with proliferating news outlets, these strategies generally are attempts by news makers to contain, if not control, public perceptions of the news.

The Permanent Campaign

News makers, first, have increasingly adopted a governing style in which the news media plays a permanent or ongoing role. Media campaigns are not just for electoral campaigns anymore. There has been a growing convergence of electoral and governing styles in American politics. The use of polls, press releases, news conferences, and other means of engaging media attention between elections has become the norm in Washington politics. Sidney Blumenthal (1982) introduced the concept of a "permanent campaign" into the American political vernacular to describe the growing use of media campaigns by political elites between elections seasons. Blumenthal views the permanent campaign as a destructive governing style, suggesting that it "remakes government into an instrument designed to sustain an elected official's popularity" (1982, 7). When every day is Election Day, partisans are less likely to engage in serious deliberation and compromise.

Similarly, Samuel Kernell (2006) describes the strategy of "going public" as an emerging and provocative presidential style. Kernell describes the pervasive use of communications, fund-raising, and interest group mobilization by presidents to bypass governing institutions and to make appeals directly to mass publics. Kernell concludes that going public has a corrosive effect on the capacity of political elites to deliberate and compromise outside of the public eye. Washington elites instead engage in public displays of preemptive issue statements and inflammatory rhetoric that polarizes positions and reduces prospects for a negotiated outcome.

At their core, these concepts of the permanent campaign and going public imply that politicians have, for better or worse, made use of emerging communication technologies to advance their political agendas. Washington political elites do not passively allow the news media or other interests to control communications technologies for benign or counterpurposes. Additionally, contending partisan elites compete with and incite each other with these media strategies, further fueling the flames.

The end result, according to Ornstein and Mann (2000), has been the blurring of campaigning and governing seasons among Washington elites. The authors contrast the current condition with an earlier political era, which they acknowledge may be partly fictionalized. Before the permanent campaign, "the day after the election, campaign materials were put away, as Christmas lights are boxed and returned to the attic after the holidays, and the tools and personnel for governing emerged" (Ornstein and Mann 2000, 222). Presumably, the permanent campaign is like a prolonged Christmas commercial season. Selling Christmas lights in August may devalue the public's attention to other holidays and promote crass commercialization of our holiday ritual. Likewise, the permanent campaign creates a sense that there is no governing season and that elections are ends to themselves.

So what created and sustains the permanent campaign? Why have elected officials doggedly pursued the news media coverage? Heclo (2002) offers six sources for this growing convergence of campaign and governing styles. The first set of explanations relate to the incentives and numbers of Washington political actors. Heclo suggests that weak party systems contribute to perpetual campaigning. The contemporary American style of electoral campaigns promote candidate-centered rather than party-centered vote choices. Consequently, American politicians are encouraged to be media entrepreneurs independent from their parties. Heclo also notes the dramatic growth in the number and resources of Washington organized interests. The growing activities of advocacy groups promote the permanent campaign.

The capacity for political elites to engage in media relations year-round has increased. Heclo notes three additional sources that have elevated the capacity for the permanent campaign. New communications technologies, improvements in political polling, and the growth of political fund-raising have all enabled news makers to engage in ongoing media operations. Political elites and parties engage private pollsters to track personal popularity, job performance, and issue priorities. Political elites claim that this polling during governing is not to allow public opinions to determine public agendas but rather to gauge how best to communicate or sell public policy initiatives to the public.

Finally, the stakes or payoff for the permanent campaign has increased. Campaigning has become big and permanent because government has become big and permanent (Heclo 2002, 27). The expansion in the federal budget and breadth of federal policy involvement over the last forty years has contributed to the growing number of organized, competing government claimants. More important, these organized interests represent a growing share of the American public who are in some way affected by current public policies. The permanent campaign is an outgrowth of the growing share of voters who have a personal or societal stake in public policy outcomes.

Direct Communications

Senator Daniel Patrick Moynihan, D-N.Y., famously identified an "iron law of emulation" in national politics stating that organizations in conflict become similar to one another. Moynihan coined this term to explain the growing parallels between the executive and legislative branches with regard to staffing and support agencies. Since the executive branch had an Office of Management and Budget, for instance, the Congress would need to establish its own Congressional Budget Office. Congress emulates—and perhaps covets—resources of the executive. This iron law of emulation implies that adversaries naturally conflict yet also converge in how they act. Applied to the adversarial world of news makers and producers, the emergence of cable and Internet news has enhanced conflict, challenging news makers' capacity to affect what news is reported and how news is framed. It has also, though, promoted convergence with the growth of direct communications.

Direct communications allow news makers to use new communication technologies to reach targeted audiences directly, effectively cutting out the news media. Direct communications are a second strategy employed by news makers to combat their loss of media control. We are accustomed to mediated news stories—ones initiated or controlled by the news media—as means of following public affairs. These mediated stories, though, do not allow news makers to control directly the nature and degree of news content. The oldest form of public relations, the press release, has long served news makers as a useful but limited tool to achieve some measure of control.

The press release is a news story written by a press officer of the news maker anticipating media requests for information or attempting to pre-empt or influence the eventual media coverage. This press release presents the news story in the words and slant of the news maker. Cook (1998) argues that news journalists have a long and entangled relationship with government. He discusses the evolution of government press officers offering news releases, briefings, and photo opportunities that subsidize and ultimately influence the work of journalists. This government subsidy, he argues, biases the press accounts toward official views of public problems and actions. News makers may acknowledge the benefits of the relationship but note it is limited since the news media may dismiss it in part or in whole. The press release may never reach its intended audience.

Given the changing media environment, direct communications has partly supplanted mediated reporting as a basis for the news maker "getting the message out." The press release has been supplemented by a long list of direct communications through web pages, multimedia video, blogs, podcasts, targeted e-mails, weekly radio addresses, cable news programs, or other means. These direct communications have expanded with technological capacity, and they afford many benefits to the news maker compared with traditional mediated approaches. In their edited book, Farrar-Myers and Vaughn (2015) give insight into how digital data and technologies are increasingly empowering political campaigns to control and target online communications to voters bypassing traditional media. Direct communications permit the news maker to present his or her own news accounting uninhibited by the page limits, editorial judgments, and possible press biases of the news media.

The decline of "hard" government news reported by television and print news, discussed earlier, may lead news makers to rely more heavily on unfiltered accounting of their new accounts through direct communication. While the amount of government news has declined, the tone of news reporting has also become more negative. Patterson (2000) presents evidence that news stories about the president have taken a more negative tone over time. Negative stories—scandals, misstatements, and responses to unfavorable events—now constitute a greater proportion of news stories than positive coverage (10). Political scientists have presented contending evidence about whether this negative news promotes political mistrust or, in fact, stimulates political interest and participation. Regardless, for the target of those negative stories, the news is definitely bad. Negative stories have priming and framing effects that are contrary to the political goals of a news maker.

Direct communication affords direct control over the tone of stories. Not surprisingly, news that is directly communicated is sharply divided between a positive tone supporting the news sponsor and a negative tone for her or his adversaries. For instance, the House Democratic Caucus and the Republican White House websites present two sharply contested versions of news reality. The Democratic Caucus presents a poorly performing economy as "the Bush recession" while lauding their support for protections against home foreclosure. The White House site makes only passing reference to unfavorable economic statistics and, rather, includes statistics that present a more upbeat perspective on economic growth. Direct communications allows news makers to control the content, amount, and tone of their news.

Direct communications may not supplant mediated news for most news grazers. Consumers' online access, news knowledge, and political interest may limit the current capacity of direct communications to replace traditional news. Still, there is an apparent trend toward news immediacy and away from the values of accuracy and independence more common of traditional news journalism. Around 2007, more Americans stated a preference for the Internet over print newspapers as a main source of news, and in 2013, about half of all Americans stated that the Internet as their main source of news.[6] Those individuals relying on Internet news tend to be younger and better educated than the public as a whole. Certainly, the audience has grown dramatically over time and will continue to grow with generational replacement. While not replacing news, direct communications at least promotes mobilization among partisans who are predisposed to support news makers' policy positions.

Message Politics

News makers have adopted a final strategy in response to a changing media environment. *Message politics* refers to news makers' organized efforts to develop, coordinate, and preserve their group's political message.

While direct communications bypass news providers, messaging strategies attempt to influence how news is told by altering the topics, words, or visuals tied to news reporting. Evans and Oleszek (2001) elaborate on message politics, particularly with regard to congressional leadership. They argue that media messages are a growing area of legislative conflict in which competing partisans fight outside of the confines of the legislative floor or committee for favorable media attention. The goal is to generate positive media coverage for a group, party, or official in ways that build mass support.

Message politics incorporates a set of tactics or activities that occur at different stages of media message development. An initial activity, positioning, occurs at a formative stage when news makers are still defining their policy agendas. Positioning refers to identifying issues, words, symbols, and explanations that evoke favorable public responses. News makers engage in polling and focus groups to select the rhetorical devices that resonate and connect with the public. News makers may work to uncover rhetorical positions in which there is widespread agreement among group members. These rhetorical positions become "owned" by their party or group and build a stronger group identity. Petrocik (1996) introduced the concept, issue ownership, to define the apparent strategy of partisans to maintain a consistent set of issue positions in order to preserve their "ownership" over an issue. For instance, Republicans have worked to maintain their rhetorical ownership of the "no new taxes" position despite the often complex, convoluted nature of legislative issue agenda.

A second tactic of message politics is coordination. Party communications staff and leaders attempt to coordinate all of these various press activities to communicate a coherent, central party message. Since all members have their own press secretaries and legislative agendas, though, party organizations struggle with coordinating a simple and common media strategy. This struggle has been complicated by turf battles between ambitious party leaders and staff. Who and which office is responsible for party communications? The lines of responsibilities are often blurry, and copartisans often complain about the absence of a clear, coordinated media campaign. House Republicans have tried to improve coordination of a media message among its rank-and-file members by distributing "boarding passes" and "recess kits," folders of press briefings and talking points in the hope that members are saying the same things when they go home to their districts. Members and party staff are as uncertain as congressional analysts whether any or which of these activities make any difference in how the media reports congressional news. It may, though, signal to members and the media that the legislative struggle is more party based.

The challenge of party leaders is to focus the public mind on a shared party agenda. Thus, news making has become a central part of their strategic effort. Patrick Sellers (2009) explains the sequence of stages in strategic communications on Capitol Hill. He refers to this sequence of strategic communications generally as the "cycle of spin." The first stage of strategic communications is message construction, a vital step in agenda setting, controlling the issues and arguments central to intraparty policy priorities. Issues are selected to unify the party and divide the opposition. The second stage is message promotion, work that aims to prime the media, affecting how news media reports on stories. The aim is to unify the party base and pressure cross-pressured copartisans to adopt party positions. The third stage is media coordination, trying to get news reporters to repeat party messages through a coordinated effort to discuss issues in the same words or ideas. The final stage is message influence, using these media messages in the legislative process to influence politicians who may be cross-pressured. Using the media message as feedback to legislators affords leaders an external means of influencing rank-and-file members.

Still another front of external communications is in building long-term relationships and trust among important interest groups and targeted constituencies. The Senate Republican Conference works on "long-term strategic planning," transcending any immediate legislative goal. Its members organize regular meetings and outreach events to create a dialogue between Republican leaders and interest group representatives, K Street lobbyists, trade or industry associations, and religious or ethnic group leaders. Presumably, these groups may then act as intermediaries to the media, propagating party messages and positions. The House Republican Conference also has engaged in cross-lobbying, lobbying the lobbyists to carry the party message to rank-and-file members. These outreach efforts create at least the appearance, if not the reality, of inviting organized interests (typically moneyed interests) to participate in very formative discussions of the legislative process. They may also be viewed as cynical ploys to promote party fundraising. The party organizations, though, perceive these strategies as party building, merely engaging and building their base of political allies.

What, if any, effects do these various internal and external communications efforts have in framing members' and the public's understanding of the legislative agenda? Certainly, members and their staff use the party materials to different degrees. As noted, in many offices, the party caucus issue briefs are routinely thrown away. The expansion of committee and personal staff, particularly in the Senate, has resulted in members having their own sources for policy information and analysis. Senior members holding committee leadership posts (and thus larger staff resources) and having established voting records are undoubtedly less reliant on party organizations to brief them on pending legislative matters. These senior members have developed their own preferences and policy alliances and thus are unlikely to be swayed by party analyses.

Still, party communications do help signal and justify to copartisans the party position on some pending issue. Even members who are ideologically predisposed to support the party position need to explain their vote to constituents, the media, and interest groups. In some cases, perhaps, members are ambivalent to the policy outcome. Party analyses are valued in these cases as informational cues to making and justifying policy decisions.

Overall, congressional news makers evidently have developed strategies—the permanent campaign, direct communications, and message politics—in response to media choice and changing information economics. Congressional news makers today spend more time and human resources toward these strategies to alter news coverage. Does it work? Certainly, from the vantage of their ongoing effort and expense, news makers *think* that they affect coverage positively. They continue trying to change news coverage to favor their issue agendas and perspectives. Additionally, there is both qualitative and quantitative evidence supporting the view that they do affect the content and style of news stories (Schaffner and Sellers 2009; Sellers 2009; Vinson 2017). Even if coverage is altered, it is unclear whether this favorable news content changes minds among swing voters and mobilizes latent partisans. An alternative view is that these frenetic efforts of congressional partisans to "spin" news coverage largely "cancel each other out," each providing a check on the media influence of the other while also promoting public cynicism toward a hyperpartisan Congress. I next turn to how information economics is transforming the news producers and how news producers are adopting strategies to adapt to media choice.

The News Producers

News producers—traditional, cable, and online new media—have also been transformed by changing information economics. It is one of America's founding principles that a free or independent press is essential to the maintenance of republican government. Still, the news—both in content and in format—is not truly "free" in terms of economics. In a private news media market, news producers cannot make journalistic decisions without considering their economic implications. Media choice and digital information technologies have altered the business model for the news industry by both increasing the number of providers competing for advertising revenues and dramatically cutting the costs of distributing the news. Digital news producers have expanded information access while also lessening the capacity for exclusion. News producers, particularly from traditional news sources, are less able to maintain a fee-paying, loyal, and large audience. In this section, I give an overview of how changing information economics has altered the news media industry in the past two decades.

The most dramatic change in the news industry during the last several decades has been the collapse of print newspapers. By any metric, the newspaper industry has declined sharply over several decades. The number of daily city and regional newspapers has declined over time, particularly the local afternoon newspapers. For example, New Orleans's newspaper, *The Times Picayune*, has existed since 1837 and managed to resume print edition in three days after Hurricane Katrina in 2005. In 2012, though, *The Times Picayune* could not withstand the storm of changing information economics. The newspaper shifted to a three-day-a-week publication, making New Orleans the largest U.S. city without a daily print newspaper. Many other newspapers have scaled back their news-gathering operations. Eighteen newspapers and two newspaper chains, according to the *American Journalism Review*, have closed all of their foreign bureaus since 1998. The Pew Research Center reports that newspaper readers declined in 2016 for the twenty-eighth consecutive year. Fewer traditional, newspaper journalists are working today than in 1978. The traditional production of news by beat reporters, editors, and news bureaus has scaled back with financial pressures.

The cause of the long-term decline has been the gradual erosion of newspaper subscribers and marked decline of advertising revenues brought on by media competition. Newspaper readership decline has occurred across the board regardless of readers' age, income, or education level. The clearest decline, though, has occurred among young and middle-aged audiences. News consumption, generally, is greater among older adults, and a marked decline of relatively younger readers indicates a weakening of a newspaper reading culture. According to General Social Survey data, about half of individuals born from 1943 to 1947 (the oldest class of baby boomers) continue to report that they read a daily newspaper. When these boomers were in their twenties in the late sixties and early seventies, their newspaper readership was about 57 percent, an evident decline in readership. However, the change in newspaper readership among today's twentysomethings is significantly greater. Only about a fifth of today's twentysomethings read a daily newspaper.

This generational decline portends a dark economic future for traditional newspapers as fewer younger citizens subscribe to newspapers.

Newspapers' advertising revenues have declined even more dramatically with new media competitors. According to the Newspaper Association of America, print advertising in 2016 was 36 percent of what it was in 2006. Classified advertising has also declined with the advent of Craigslist, eBay, and other free online classified sites. Changing revenues and information economics have been most unsettling, particularly to local news sources. Still, despite the decline in newspaper readership and revenues, there are reasons for assuming the worst is over. The rate of decline in newspaper subscriptions and revenues has decreased in recent years.

Declining audiences and advertising revenues have affected network and local television news, as well, though the changes have not been as severe. Local television news affiliates have responded to economic change by shifting content. More of the local news hole, over time, is filled with sports, weather, and traffic and less straight reporting. Stories on local crime and accidents continue to be most frequent local straight news stories (Pew Research Center 2012a). Comparatively, the economics of local television news broadcasting have been stable compared with other news outlets. In fact, political advertising has been a source of growing revenue for local channels as campaign finance spending has grown and legal restrictions weakened.[7]

Network news, comparatively, has not changed as much in its content or manner of coverage. Network news programs continue to rely on a series of edited and highly produced news packages. More human interest and lifestyle stories fill the network news hole, but compared with other news providers, network news' content has been fairly stable over time. The network news audience, though, has, over time, dramatically declined and aged. Audience size for network news has been halved over the past three decades. Most of this decline has been due to a clear generational decline, with younger viewers tuning out. Today's average network news viewer is fifty-three years old and has above-average income and education levels. This audience demographic is reflected in the steady stream of commercials targeted to older viewers—prescription drugs, insurance, and aging-related products.

Of course, the decline of these traditional news providers has occurred along with a rise of emerging online and cable news. A more competitive, diverse news media market offers greater choices and innovations for consumers. News consumers, presumably, can now find news that better fits their preferences. Competition between news providers also drives innovative news reporting and production. Commentary news has been among these innovations. Certainly, for those looking to use the news media to communicate their message, be it advertisers or political groups, media choice has greatly expanded opportunities. As noted earlier, news makers benefit from media choice by avoiding traditional journalistic gatekeepers. Media choice has elevated their ability to communicate their political messages directly or via a more agreeable media outlet.

The main beneficiaries among news producers of changing information economics have been cable and online news providers. U.S. cable news networks—CNN, Fox News, and MSNBC—have grown financially over time, despite intense competition and year-to-year variations. CNN established the twenty-four-hour news network model; however, Fox News has far surpassed its competitor in terms of profits and audience share. Fox News, in 2014, generated nearly $1.2 billion dollars in profit, almost four times the profit of CNN and almost six times MSNBC's profit.[8]

Part of cable news' economic strength is its capacity to generate revenues both from cable subscription license fees as well as advertising. Roughly 60 percent of cable news channels' revenues come from subscription fees, with 40 percent coming through advertising. Fox News, for example, generated, in 2014, about $800 million in advertising revenues and over $1.2 billion in license fee revenues. MSNBC, despite lower advertising and subscriber rates than Fox, has grown in profitability as well. Part of both networks' success has been "product branding," in which these cable networks have developed larger, more loyal, and more ideologically homogenous audiences. Fox and MSNBC have developed right-wing and left-wing news brands, respectively. This branding has occurred particularly through the hosts of their primetime news opinion and commentary shows.

CNN has changed its market strategy over time, sometimes in response to its competitors and in other times toward maintaining its strength in covering international news and providing more in-depth news analysis. CNN has a greater international news-gathering operation compared with its competitors. It is made up of forty-five news bureaus around the world, compared with seventeen news bureaus for Fox News and twenty-one for MSNBC. CNN has greater revenues from its international news channels that generate large international audiences.

Despite its growing profitability, cable news' audience has not substantially grown in recent years. Cable news audiences have grown only slightly over time and are still small compared with network news. The three main cable news channels averaged 3.7 million viewers in 2012 during their primetime hours. This average represents about half the average of network news audience. Still, cable news audiences are relatively difficult to measure, spiking in presidential election years and with breaking or high-interest news stories. The final two months of the 2012 presidential election saw the average cable news network audience almost double, approaching 7 million nightly viewers.

Generally, cable news channels have flourished under a pay TV model. This model, though, is becoming less certain as growing numbers of consumers choose to "cut their cable." The so-called "zero-TV" households are those that choose to forego cable and satellite television services, relying instead on news and entertainment from the Internet. Almost 85 percent of American households in 2012 had cable and satellite subscriptions. According to Nielsen, the number of these zero-TV households is still relatively small. The number is growing, though— about 5 million households in 2012, compared with 2 million in 2007. Wireless, online news providers are the fastest-growing and still-emerging competitor in a crowded news media industry. How is changing information economics affecting this sector?

The online news industry is still developing a sustainable business model. The initial wave of online news providers was mostly print news media extending services to the Internet. In effect, these multiple-platform news providers competed with themselves for advertising dollars, driving costs down. For most, the added revenues of online advertising have not offset their loss of print advertising. With more competitors and media sources, media advertising has become more complex and targeted. Online news providers are increasingly recognizing that digital advertising does not generate sufficient revenues alone to ensure profitability. News aggregators, search engine sites like Google and Yahoo, generate most of the online news traffic and advertising revenues.

As consumers shift toward mobile news—a growing reliance on smartphones or tablets and less toward desktop systems—technology firms like Google are increasingly dictating how online news providers link to their audience. According to Pew, in 2017, about 84 percent of American households have at least one smartphone. A growing majority of Americans use their mobile devices to collect news. As mobile technology continues to grow, the online news consumption will grow with generational and demographic change. Since 2010, more Americans already report getting news regularly from online sources compared with newspapers and other traditional news sources.

News coverage of Congress, particularly, has been altered with changing economics of news production. The Washington press corps, in the past, was composed heavily of local, regional, and national newspaper and television reporters. Examining registered membership over time of the

House and Senate Press Gallery, there are evident changes in who and how Congress is covered that are largely resulting from information economics. Foremost, there is significantly less coverage of local, regional, and original news stories. Instead, congressional news coverage is increasingly done by wire services, digital news providers, and industry-specialized reporters.

These news production changes alter how Congress is related to the public. Legislators—particularly House members—have fewer news stories in local and regional newspapers, which have traditionally printed congressional stories specific to local legislators and district activities. Between 1997 and 2015, the number of newspaper journalists as registered Press Gallery members was halved. By 2015, twenty-nine states had no local newspaper staff covering Capitol Hill.[9] The cost to local and regional newspapers of Washington reporting has become prohibitive, and they are increasingly reliant on general wire service stories rather than original, local content. Wire services like AP and Reuters are filling this role, resulting in fewer congressional stories about individual or local projects and more stories about Congress as a collective body. Pew Research Center's content analysis of congressional news coverage found that just 2 percent of wire stories made reference to the local impacts of congressional news, compared with 40 percent of news stories written by newspaper reporters (Mitchell et al. 2016).

As local and regional print journalists have declined in the House and Senate Press Galleries, they have been partly replaced with about a four-fold increase in digital-native news and niche news reporters over the past decade. These digital-native news sources—for example, the Huffington Post, Politico, or Buzzfeed—give exclusively digital coverage that attracts a national, not local, audience. Niche news sources—like *Kaiser Health News*, *American Banker*, and *Inside Higher Education*—cater to specialized news interests from a specific industry, professional association, or policy network. These digital and niche news providers are providing different congressional news to attract and retain their specific audiences.

Overall, the news media industry is still evolving with emerging technologies and consumer behavior, and the effects of information economics are still uncertain. Despite changing economics, the audience for online news will continue growing. According to Pew Research, the online news audience is younger, better educated, and wealthier than the general public. Online news gatherers are less likely to have routinized news habits and instead fit the quintessential news grazer profile. As generational replacement occurs, they are increasingly the norm rather than a unique subset of news consumers.

For news producers, media choice is transforming information economics and affecting the balance between types of news outlets. Cable and online news providers have expanded at the cost of traditional news providers. The number and diversity of news sources have greatly increased over time; however, the number of traditional news reporters and the investments made in news production have declined. News consumers have diversified their news sources and, on average, slightly increased the amount of time devoted to collecting news. All of these news industry market changes have led to emerging strategies to maintain an audience and viable business plan, which I turn to next.

New Media Strategies: Producing Commentary News

Hard news—the factual reporting of government actions or events—is increasingly a commodity given the changing economics of the news media industry. In other words, it matters less to news consumers about where or how they access headline news if this news content does not vary much from any source. In fact, with growing media choice, information economics have increasingly driven hard news toward the characteristics of a public good.

For news consumers, these changes have been generally good for news access. Choices have grown and fulfilled a consumer expectation of news on demand. Most news consumers do not rely on a single platform or source to receive news. They access news from online, cable, print, and network television platforms. They draw news from different news channels and online news sources. In fact, while entertainment options have also exploded along with news, committed news gatherers are able to access news more than ever on topics that fit their interests. For these citizens, media choice and transformed information economics have been democratizing and are contributing to an engaged, informed public. Ironically, this elevated news consumer access and fit parallel the growth in public distrust toward news media producers discussed earlier.

For news producers, the changing news market has had unsettling consequences, particularly for traditional news producers, whose audience share and revenues have declined in the wake of emerging new media. The changing economics, though, have led news producers to adapt their products. The growing competition for smaller audiences has driven news producers to adopt strategies to alter news format and content that attract and retain audiences. I analyze these news producers' strategies as a basis for under-standing the trend toward commenting on rather than reporting the news.

Niche and Opinion News

One adaptation that has broadened the breadth of news coverage has been the growth of niche and opinion news. Niche news outlets are media sources that focus on specific topics—for instance, an industrial sector, health, entertainment, the environment, or a political ideology. Niche news products have grown not only via the Internet but also through subscription television. Media technology has created opportunities for electronic communities with narrow but strong interests to take seed and share specific news relating to their interests. Revenue may come from advertising, subscriptions, or syndi-cating content. The sustaining power of niche news has been the capacity to attract a loyal, though sometimes small, following that can form a new digital community. Online news magazines have been one of the biggest benefi-ciaries of niche news. Political news websites like Huffington Post, Politico, Daily Kos, and Breitbart have grown regular, if niche, audiences. Niche news has swamped general news. *Time Magazine*, today, is the only remaining mass-market, general news weekly magazine in print. News magazines have are increasingly online and serving a niche interest.

The growing number of news choices has not necessarily resulted in head-to-head competition between opposing news outlets. Audience seg-mentation has led to greater *narrowcasting*—greater product differentiation in the news—at least with cable news. A Pew Research Center study found that nearly half of the public sees real differences among cable news chan-nels: CNN, the Fox News Channel, and MSNBC (Mitchell et al. 2014). In contrast, less than a quarter discern a difference among network news programs. Audience segmentation offers opportunities for news makers to deliver "their" news directly to a different base audience, those issue pub-lics or partisans that often act as opinion leaders. It also may allow news producers to offer news that interests a more defined and loyal audience.

The dark side of niche news and narrowcasting may be that it strength-ens social networks of like-minded groups instead of creating a general news audience. Mass news outlets may sometimes serve to bridge a politi-cally diverse news audience, to create a common space for consumption and debate of contentious issues. Citizens could become increasingly divided as a result of using niche media that coheres with their political beliefs. On the other hand, this niche news may also heighten these citi-zens' interest in news that encourages their participation. Natalie Stroud's concept of "partisan selective exposure," discussed earlier, relates to these effects of citizens seeking like-minded news. The so-called "Fox News effect" suggests that this media polarization is real. A Fox News effect refers to the presumed influence of Fox News in promoting a partisan divide in news preferences and perceptions, with Fox News attracting conservatives and CNN attracting left-leaning viewers. I evaluate, in Chapter 4, the evidence for the politicization of news—whether news grazing and audience segmentation promote political polarization and distrust.

Another related strategy has been to increase the amount of opinion as a share of the news hole. Opinions and editorials are long part of news reporting. The history of newspaper journalism in the nineteenth century partly took form from partisan presses, political newspapers that were controlled by political parties or by editors who used the paper as a means of sharing their views with elite stakeholders. Editorializing has a rich and valued history, and the news opinion format engages viewers by giving them greater context for understanding news events.

One strategy for adapting to information economics, though, has been to elevate the value of the opinion news format. A 2012 Pew Research Center study of news content concludes that 70 percent of the 6 to 11 p.m. cable news hole is filled with opinion/commentary news programs. The study also indicates a gradual drift away from factual news reporting during the daytime hours on cable news channels. Opinion news promotes audience loyalty, is less expensive to produce, and tailors its coverage to viewers' ideological niche.

Opinion programs may promote greater audience loyalty for the program host than straight news. The evening hour, or primetime, programming of cable news channels has long been dominated by the host-led opinion news format. Compared with other television audiences, opinion news commands a relatively small but loyal number of viewers. This audience loyalty is often built around the popularity of the program host, but it may spill over toward greater network brand loyalty. Opinion news hosts also promote a strong branding effect for their network, with MSNBC currently the liberal opinion news hosts providing a clear contrast to Fox News conservative hosts.

Besides audience loyalty, the costs of opinion news programs are also driving growth. The opinion news format is relatively less expensive to produce compared with traditional news. The production costs of opinion news do not entail paying reporters, their travel, and other news production expenses compared with factual news formats. The opinion news program tends to rely on other news sources to generate stories. These opinion format news stories are carefully selected and framed around viewer interests. Foremost, political stories dominate opinion programs' news agenda.

Cable news channels generally provide much greater coverage of national politics, particularly coverage of election campaigns.

The Pew Research Center devised measures of the news hole across different media sectors from 2007 to 2011. Figure 3.1 shows the percentage of the news hole filled with political coverage across news media sources over the five years of the Pew study. Cable news channels regularly fill their news hole with national politics; however, coverage spikes even more during campaign and election season. As Figure 3.1 shows, over 70 percent of cable news stories in the 2008 presidential election year were on politics. The opinion format news story further tends toward drama or ideological conflict, stories that can framed in ways that appeal to viewers.

Besides a heavier dose of politics and conflict, the opinion format attracts viewers' interests with its sharply different tone. The tone of a news format indicates the extent to which stories are clearly negative, neutral, or positive toward the subject of the news story. Opinion news formats have a significantly higher rate of negative tone. Often, the political news story is framed as an ideological drama, with the opinion news host playing the protagonists and the opposing "guest" playing the antagonist. Like-minded viewers typically are attracted to a clear ideological tone and are more likely to understand and recall the news story through this framing effect. The negative tone elicits emotional responses with viewers—anger, surprise, admiration, or contempt. The viewers' emotional response tends to affirm their political views and elevate their interest in the news story.

The amount of negative tone differs across opinion news programs. The Sunday morning news talk shows and newspaper editorial pages have long served as means of influencing public opinion and elites through news commentary. This traditional opinion news has often varied the nature of opinions by changing program guests or columnists. The news opinions help citizens understand the issue and form their own opinion. An emerging news opinion format, though, homogenizes opinions and elevates negative tone. Cable news opinion programs, online news magazines, the blogosphere, and social media have often injected greater negative tone along with the opinions. This greater negative tone both attracts and repels a potential news audience. The growing prevalence of the negative tone in opinion news has many media critics worried about partisan bias, whether news host's opinions polarize mass beliefs. The academic evidence is mixed and inconclusive (Prior 2013). What is known is that opinion news hosts largely preach to the converted; exposure to a one-sided media source, though, could have other behavioral effects short of ideological conversion. In Chapter 4, I investigate the effects of opinion on news grazers' broader political attitudes.

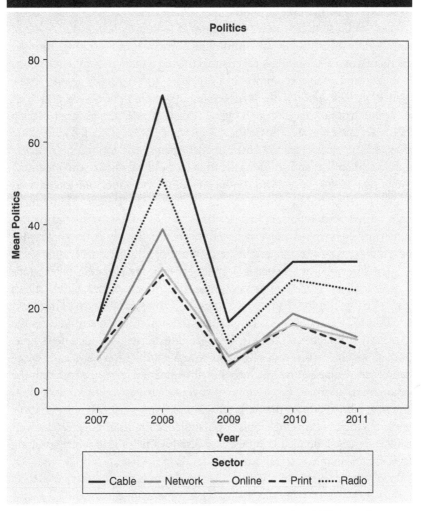

Figure 3.1 Percentage of News Hole Coverage on Politics, by Media Sector, 2007–2011

Politics

Sector

—— Cable ——— Network ～～～ Online – – Print ······ Radio

Source: Created by the author using Pew Excellence in Journalism (PEJ) News Coverage Index data.

News Urgency and Breaking News

Another strategy for adapting to new information economics has been elevating news urgency—reporting for extended periods on stories involving drama, scandal, or conflict. News producers recognize that news urgency keeps fickle news consumers from clicking. This urgency invokes emotional response with viewers and heightens their engagement with the story. News producers' choice of news stories allows them to elevate urgency. News stories that heighten urgency include criminal cases, political scandal, weather events, shootings, or disasters.

One of these urgent news story lines is foreign policy crises. A "CNN effect" refers to the policy and attitudinal consequences resulting from the emergence of a 24/7 cable news channel during a foreign or military policy crisis. Steven Livingston defines the CNN effect as "1) a *policy agenda-setting agent*, 2) an *impediment* to the achievement of desired policy goals, and 3) an *accelerant* to policy decision-making" (Livingston 1997, 2). He argues that a 24/7 news cycle elevates the political importance of emotionally compelling news video; complicates the government's operational control, particularly in military conflict; and shortens the time for political response to emerging events. This CNN effect affords both constraints and opportunities for news makers to affect public perceptions of the news. The Defense Department has required news reporters to be embedded into military units during foreign crises. This *embedded journalism* has concerned some critics that it may limit reporting and distort public perceptions of international conflicts.

The *breaking-news format* is another strategy for elevating perceptions of news urgency. Breaking-news coverage is an important part of 24/7 news channel programming. Figure 3.2 shows the average percentage of the news hole devoted to the top story. Pew defines the "top story" in any week as the news story that received the most coverage time during a defined news hole. Cable news channels repeat or extend coverage of the top news story more than other media sectors. Much of this this extended coverage comes in the breaking-news format. Breaking-news coverage creates spikes in news audience size, particularly for drama-laden stories, as news grazers tune into cable news for additional coverage. This larger audience size results in greater advertising revenues. Extended coverage may also fill a news void while lessening news organization costs. Political news tends to decline in summer months, and extended coverage of criminal cases or disasters may fill this news hole. For instance, the Trayvon Martin–George Zimmerman legal case filled a large share of the summer 2013 cable news hole. Extending the breaking-news coverage may lengthen audience spikes for hours, days, and even weeks.

It may even entail subsidizing the news story. ABC News, for instance, admitted that it paid accused murderer Casey Anthony $200,000 in exchange for exclusive rights to video and photographs while her case was being investigated. Casey was accused of murdering her two-year-old daughter, Caylee. The 2008 payment was used to finance investigative and legal expenses for her defense. In 2011, ABC News also paid $15,000 to Meagan Broussard for a sexually provocative photo exchanged with

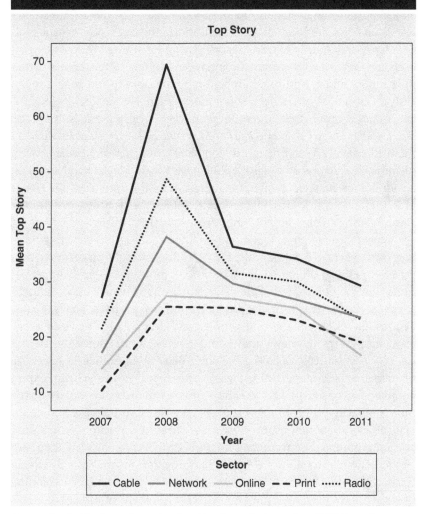

Figure 3.2 Percentage of News Hole Coverage on the Top Story, by Media Sector, 2007–2011

Top Story

Source: Created by the author using Pew Excellence in Journalism (PEJ) News Coverage Index data.

Congress member Anthony Weiner, D-N.Y. The photo led to extended coverage of Congress member Weiner during summer 2011. The drama was stretched out by Weiner's initial denial but culminated in his resignation from the House. Ultimately, television news networks profited from the lengthy coverage and audience of both the Anthony legal case and the Weiner scandal.

Extended breaking-news coverage may lead to some hard ethical questions for journalists. The practice of paying for news, *checkbook journalism*, is accepted in British and U.S. tabloids. It is not considered, though, the ethical norm for mainstream American journalism. To what extent should television news producers pay for or subsidize the news? Journalistic ethicists have traditionally advised against paying for stories. They worry that exchanging money for information may lead to questions about whether the source is being truthful or embellishing the story for the sake of more cash.[10] Checkbook journalism is not a new phenomenon, but its journalistic ethics continue to be questioned. At the height of President Clinton's sex scandal, Larry Flynt, the *Hustler Magazine* publisher, placed an ad in the *Washington Post* offering up to $1 million to anyone who could prove a member of Congress or a high-ranking government official had carried on an adulterous affair. Soon after, the designate for the Speaker of the House of Representatives, Robert Livingston, resigned after learning that *Hustler* was preparing an exposé on Livingston's extramarital affair.

Breaking-news coverage, intentionally extending and elevating news urgency to retain a news audience, may increasingly place news producers in ethical dilemmas like checkbook journalism. News organizations may be confronted with more situations in which news sources expect some benefits from sharing news and perspectives. News organizations have a financial incentive to extend drama-laden news coverage to retain a distracted news audience. Even if news organizations do not directly pay sources, does the breaking-news style indirectly subsidize or increase the commercial value of the sources' stories? Hiring expert commentators, subsidizing expenses of news sources, or merely giving more media attention to news sources may result in increased commercial value of these news sources' stories. These news sources—including alleged criminals, the victims, witnesses, or jurors—may alter their stories to heighten the stories' commercial value. Is it journalistically ethical for news organizations to subsidize this profitable coverage? Extending breaking news may have the same effect, ultimately, of direct payments in that it may increase the incentive of news sources to misrepresent their story for personal profit.

Regardless of the practice of checkbook journalism, are news organization professionals obligated to disclose if or how much they supported news sources? As private, for-profit organizations, news media may view any subsidies to news sources or stories as proprietary information that could weaken their standing relative to competitors. These news organizations, understandably, would resist any disclosure. Disclosure, though, may also bring criticism and greater scrutiny from fellow journalists. That scrutiny may place greater professional constraints on journalistic practices. These ethical questions are hard ones for journalists.

Elevating news urgency, generally, has been another strategy used by news media to attract and retain news grazers. Lengthy coverage of criminal court cases and political scandal news has increasingly become a norm, particularly of cable news. Does this breaking-news reporting affect our political attitudes? I address these questions in Chapter 5. For now, I note that regardless of its effects on how we see the political world, overreporting displaces other potential stories from "making the news." Lengthy breaking-news coverage of criminal cases or scandals results in less public attention to other news that may be more important but less visual and titillating.

Entertainment and Political Satire

A final media strategy in response to new information economics has been the growing prevalence of entertainment as an alternative to or mix with the news. Media choice and competition has had two effects with regard to entertainment. The first and foremost effect is that media choice has greatly expanded entertainment options. Blending entertainment and news is related to a broader phenomenon of media convergence. The media studies scholar Henry Jenkins introduces the concept of media convergence in his 2006 book *Convergence Culture: Where Old and New Media Collide*. Jenkins defines convergence as "the flow of content across multiple media platforms, the cooperation between multiple media industries, and the migratory behavior of media audiences" (2006, 2).

The traditional meaning of media convergence often describes the growing vertical integration of media companies subsuming media content providers across different platforms to create large media conglomerates. Media empires like Comcast, 21st Century Fox, Disney, and Time-Warner integrate the ownership of movie production studios, broadcast networks, cable news channels, sports franchises, theme parks, publishing houses, and music and digital media production companies. Jenkins's research extends this meaning of media convergence to include a cultural convergence as well. He argues that consumers are increasingly shaping media by engaging with others in disseminating and interpreting the news. Social media presents a new source of media convergence as we share and blend the news with each other.

The walls between news and entertainment have been breached. For some media consumers, expanded media choice allows them to almost avoid news altogether. Americans with low news interest have more alternatives when tuning out news; correspondingly, high-interest news gatherers may follow news more closely than in the past from different and specialized sources. While widening dissemination of political news, new media technologies have also promoted a mounting inequality in news gathering between those with high and low news interest. As discussed earlier, Markus Prior (2007) makes a compelling case that media choice results in an informational divide between news haves and have-nots. Americans with high news interest tend to be more ideological and partisan compared with those low-news-interest Americans. For partisan political news junkies, these are the best of times.

Combining news with entertainment attracts a more diverse audience of Americans, including those with less news interest and those who seek commentary with news. Upon taking the helm, CNN president Jonathan Klein noted, "I don't think of CNN as being up against Fox and MSNBC anymore than we're up against 500 choices on cable, millions of choices in iTunes, 10 million blogs, video games, DVDs. Our competition is every medium."[11] Media sources have expanded the level of competition for a less loyal and more distracted news audience.

A second effect of growing entertainment has been the expansion of "soft news," discussed also in Chapter 2. These programs may communicate news content along with entertainment. Entertainment shows like *Ellen* or the *Tonight Show* or news programs like *20/20* fit clearly as purveyors of soft news. They include news content sometimes and to varying degrees, but the news is mixed with entertainment. The case for soft news is that it may incidentally result in greater informedness and news interest for low-news-interest viewers.

The dominance of entertainment over news has followed by generational cohorts. That is, changes in the public's preference for news, preferred news formats and sources, and propensity for news grazing all conform to respondents' reported year of birth. Generally, technology diffusion is strongly affected by peer socialization. The acceptance of new communication technologies—e-mail, blogging, text messaging, and social-networking sites—have all conformed to a generational pattern. Anyone who has observed twenty-somethings' facility with text messaging compared with their parents will attest to this statement.

The Pew Research Center, for instance, finds that the Internet has now become a leading source of campaign news for young people. Candidate websites, blogs, and social networking sites are increasingly important to younger generations. Individuals between the ages of eighteen and twenty-nine choose the Internet more than any other news source as a basis for following political campaigns, and this percentage has more than doubled since 2004 (42 percent of respondents in 2008 compared with 20 percent in 2004). Emerging news habits affect younger generations at greater rates.

The political satire format has been a growth area for soft news. In other cases of soft news, entertainment far outweighs news value. The political satire format, however, presents the other extreme. Viewers of political satire tend to be younger, better educated, and *more* informed than typical viewers. The satire may not provide as much information as straight news, but the satire requires some degree of news informedness to "get the joke." Satirical news tends to elevate the importance of politicians' gaffes and the correspondence of political events with popular culture. What behavioral effects does the political satire—and entertainment news broadly—have on news grazers? Chapter 6 analyzes these behavioral effects of political satire while evaluating soft news broadly.

Conclusion

News reporting is ultimately a function of both events and choice—choices made by news makers, producers, and consumers as to what is important and how it is to be understood. Digital media technologies and media choice are transforming the news marketplace. The consequent new information economics have unleashed an entrepreneurial energy of news makers and producers. These changes are affecting what news is covered and how we perceive the news. In this chapter, I have analyzed some of these changes to explain the decline of traditional governmental news. A growing number and diversity of news outlets and an increasingly fragmented news audience are resulting in a growing amount of commentary news—news that offers opinion, urgency, or entertainment along with the facts.

Despite this growth and diversity of news, there is little evidence indicating that we are more informed. Despite this rise and diversity of news outlets, no evidence exists that Americans know more or care more about public affairs than before this change. A Pew Research Center study, for instance, compared Americans' levels of political knowledge between 1989 and 2007. Consistent with academic works, the Pew study finds that the public's political knowledge levels have not changed substantially over time (Delli Carpini and Keeter 1996; Prior 2005). Most Americans continue to have trouble recalling world leaders' names or correctly identifying congressional party leaders. Education levels and news interests remain the best predictors of political knowledge and engagement. Perhaps recall of political leaders' names is not the right measure of whether citizens can meaningfully evaluate political news and make defensible decisions about their interest. Still, access to more political information does not necessarily make us better citizens. Dimitrova et al. (2014) report that greater digital media use has very limited effects on political knowledge and political participation. Unfortunately, there is not compelling evidence that digital technologies and greater news access are empowering us to becoming more informed, engaged citizens. Rather, the growth in media technologies and choice is changing how we access news, not necessarily how much we learn. Correspondingly, these changes are affecting how news is made and reported.

Political news—specifically, coverage of Congress—has always been a mediated experience in which news producers present a lens for Americans to view events. I have argued that both news makers and producers have adapted to changing information economics in ways that have increased the move toward commentary news. I first discussed news makers. In a system of divided powers with increasingly polarized parties, government policy making has become a struggle over the public agenda, the battle over what Americans generally view as the most critical public policy problems facing the nation and how best to solve these problems. Congressional partisans battle for control of the public agenda, and media choice has expanded their battleground. A growing number and practices of news makers have evolved in Washington to affect the media: the permanent campaign, direct communications, and message politics. With the evolution of these strategies, news makers increasingly deem favorable new media coverage to be "earned." That is, news makers must actively seek and evaluate satisfying symbols, words, and phrases that engage the viewer. Pollsters and focus group experts seek policy explanations that broaden and intensify popular support for clients' desired agendas. Media choice—and the consequent change in information economics—is altering how news makers achieve their political goals.

I also analyzed how news producers assess these changes and adapt to new information economics. Traditional news media are struggling to keep up with new media choices. Many local and regional newspapers are struggling to maintain profitability as the competition for advertising revenues has intensified. Network news audiences are graying as younger generations opt for other news or entertainment sources. Comparatively, online and cable news are profiting from media choice. They are the innovators toward more commentary news formats that combine factual news with opinion, urgency, and entertainment. I analyzed each of these adaptive strategies and speculated on their likely consequences.

Part II examines the effects of these emerging commentary news formats on viewers' attitudes toward parties, political institutions, and the media. I focus more closely on how these media effects may be changing perceptions of the U.S. Congress. Is commentary news coverage making us less trusting of the opposition, more anxious of political events, and more cynical about politicians? As described in the first three chapters, news grazing is increasingly a norm of news gathering, and it has affected behaviors of news makers and producers. Part II investigates whether news grazing ultimately matters to how viewers themselves see the political world.

ENDNOTES

1. Gallup assesses public opinions of different professions over time. See http://www.gallup.com/poll/1654/honesty-ethics-professions.aspx.

2. The Pew Research Center reports news consumption preferences of eighteen- to thirty-three-year-olds in their report, "Millennials and Political News." See http://www.journalism.org/files/2015/06/Millennials-and-News-FINAL-7-27-15.pdf.

3. The main benefactors of digital advertising continue to be social media (Facebook) and technology companies (Google). The annual "State of the News Media" presents an accounting of news media economics over time. See http://www.journalism.org/2015/04/29/digital-news-revenue-fact-sheet.

4. See the Pew Research Center's study, "Americans Spending More Time Following the News" at http://www.people-press.org/2010/09/12/americans-spending-more-time-following-the-news.

5. The National Association of Government Communicators' website provides a history of the organization and a good overview of government public relations. See https://www.nagconline.org.

6. The Pew Research Center asks Americans annually about their main source of news. See http://www.people-press.org/2013/08/08/amid-criticism-support-for-medias-watchdog-role-stands-out.

7. Independent expenditure campaigns and super PAC funds have been a new source of campaign finance spending in recent election cycles. For the effects on local television channels, see http://www.wsj.com/articles/campaign-ads-even-more-than-before-bolster-tv-stations-1452475987.

8. Pew's 2015 State of the News Media presents different metrics of the news media industry. On cable news profits, see http://www.journalism.org/media-indicators/cable-news-channel-profits.

9. The Pew Research Center's report, "Today's Washington Press Corps More Digital, Specialized," includes a detailed breakdown of membership in the House and Senate Press Galleries. See the report at http://www.journalism.org/2015/12/03/todays-washington-press-corps-more-digital-specialized.

10. The Society of Professional Journalists' website discusses the value conflict of checkbook journalism at http://www.spj.org/ethics-papers-cbj.asp.

11. Klein served as president of CNN from 2004 until 2010. His comments are at http://usatoday30.usatoday.com/life/television/news/2005-06-06-cnn-hemmer_x.htm.

The Effects of News Grazing

Partisan News

N ews grazing is an outgrowth of expanding media choice, but it also has behavioral causes. Grazing is a function of a behavioral urge to click toward (or away from) news presented in formats and production practices that are drama laden and engaging. In Chapter 2, I called this a new media explanation of grazing, and these formats and practices have implications for the nature of our politics. In Chapter 3, I discussed how news producers and news makers have adapted to changing news-gathering habits by altering news content and formats. These adaptations aim to intentionally attract and retain an increasingly distracted news audience. I broadly refer to these more engaging, drama-laden news formats as commentary news.

Commentary news formats diverge from the traditional journalistic approaches of fact-checked, objective reporting. For television news, the traditional format involves the *talking head* approach of anchor-read, scripted news in which stories are a mixture of reporters' news summary and edited video clips. These edited video clips typically are framed into short *packages*, or prerecorded news reports usually lasting from one to five minutes. The television news reporter gathers and edits interview clips, pictures, and quotes. She or he then scripts and records a voice-over to explain the pictures and link the other elements together. News packages, along with anchor-read news, constitute this traditional format for relaying television news.

Commentary news formats are different. In contrast to the anchor format, commentary news is communicated in an often unscripted, live coverage. The primary purpose of commentary news is audience engagement, attracting and holding audience attention. Commentary formats thus integrate some form of emotional stimulus—opinion, urgency, conflict, or satire—along with the news content. In many cases, this news content—the stories that are reported—is selected precisely because of its capacity to deliver the emotional stimulus. In this way, commentary formats are changing news agendas.

I presented evidence earlier that showed that emerging news commentary formats attract and retain news grazers' attention and, consequently,

are a greater share of our news diet over time. Grazers increasingly consume commentary news since it engages them and resists their clicking
urge. Commentary news formats, though, are more likely to challenge traditional journalistic norms of objectivity, accuracy, and factual verifiabil-
ity. As noted, these live and unscripted formats elevate the importance of
immediacy in news reporting. This immediacy runs the risk of sacrificing
these traditional journalistic standards.

The next three chapters investigate the behavioral *effects* of these commentary formats on grazers. We begin by assessing the effects of a partisan
news (or, synonymously, opinion news) format on viewers' assessments of
political trust. Particularly, I try to answer whether partisan opinion news
results in more negative assessments of Congress, opposing partisans,
and the media. In the next chapters, I analyze the attitudinal effects of
watching breaking news (urgent or conflict ridden) and fake news (inac-
curate, exaggerated, and satire based) on perceptions of Congress and the
media. A common thread across these chapters is that commentary news
formats contribute further to an increasingly fragmented news audience.
More important, though, I conclude that commentary news is marginally
contributing toward Americans' more negative and jaded view of political
institutions and actors.

The debate about political debate—contentious political rhetoric and
commentary news formats—presents two contrasting views of how political news functions in a mass democracy. These two views are a deliberative
democracy view and a participatory democracy view. On one side, deliberative democracy theorists extol the potential civilizing effects of active political deliberation—hearing the other side's views. Gutmann and Thompson
(1996) present an eloquent, critical account of the benefits of civil, reasoned
political deliberation between democratic citizens, particularly as political
communities become more diverse and issues become more contentious.
Commentary news formats, in theory at least, could offer the prospects that
an electronic, mediated exchange of opposing ideas could enlighten viewers. While they may not talk directly with others who disagree with them,
individuals may at least view or read a mediated exchange that exposes
them to views counter to their own. Proponents of deliberative democracy,
though, generally agree that the current practice of commentary news falls
far short of deliberative ideals.

On the other side, though, other democratic theorists remain skeptical
that hearing or seeing opposing political viewpoints is essential to or even
improves democracy. Does a person really need to know someone else's
views to express his or her own political preferences? The purpose of news
in participatory democracy is to inform and activate like-minded citizens

so they participate in mass elections. Their reason for their participation is simple: to win the election, not necessarily to inform citizen judgment. Some advocates for participatory democracy are dubious of political deliberation claims that it builds toward a shared empathy. Direct political deliberation between individuals with contending views may possibly increase one's empathy for the other side. However, it may also leave individuals with an exaggerated and negative impression of opposing positions if the ideological exchange is largely rhetorical attacks. Additionally, is any empathy for the other side achieved when viewers are merely watching television news program rather than participating in face-to-face exchanges? Does a bystander or witness to political deliberation gain the same presumed benefits of deliberative democracy as an active participant? Opinion news may inform; then again, it may merely leave viewers with extreme impressions of one side of a political debate.

Diana Mutz (2006, 2015) analyzes the evolving role of media toward uncivil political discourse and political polarization. She presents a compelling contrast between these theories of deliberative democracy versus participatory democracy. Advocates of deliberative democracy emphasize the value of a civil exchange among politically different individuals. Exposure to dissimilar political views is important to citizens' capacity to understand the complexity of political conflicts and their tolerance toward legitimate political differences. These democratic values of political sophistication and tolerance are essential to maintaining an active, informed citizenry. Exposure to differing political views, however, may actually discourage political participation. This effect is most likely among individuals who are averse to conflict that may put social relationships at risk. Your parents may have instructed you to follow the maxim, for instance, never to discuss politics or religion in mixed company. The effect of this shared censorship is to silence all political dialogue. Additionally, exposure to opposing views may create greater ambivalence toward political options, and consequently, this uncertainty may lead to greater withdrawal from political participation (Mutz and Reeves 2005).

A participatory democracy view suggests that individuals naturally gravitate toward like-minded communities or social networks. These similar-minded networks tend to reinforce dominant political views. This may foster participation among a devoted base, but it undercuts the possibility of open deliberation and, thus, civility. Furthermore, the televised format for these ideologically based interactions—camera close-ups and incivility—may bring about an emotive responses—anger, fear, and cynicism—among viewers of political elites and Congress. These emotive responses serve to not only foster lower levels of trust in elites and institutions; they may also diminish the perceived legitimacy of opposing points of view (Mutz 2015).

This tension between deliberative and participatory views of democracy is central to our interest in commentary news formats, specifically partisan news in this chapter. Mutz argues that television news is a primary means by which citizens obtain opposing viewpoints, in contrast to face-to-face encounters. However, the audience makeup and practice of partisan news has important implications for the effects it may have on viewers. For instance, mediated opinions may merely be "singing to the choir," crafting news to a narrowly targeted audience predisposed to agree. A politically homogenous message and audience limits the prospects of opinion news of hearing the other side. Furthermore, incivility can occur in the context of opinion news even if the opposition perspective is not representative. Sean Hannity, for example, does not need a liberal guest on his program to show distain for the liberal ideology and the perspectives of liberals in general. In this case, opinion news may reinforce and legitimize fellow conservatives' opinions, thus encouraging them to political action. Additionally, the production practices of opinion news formats may also polarize perceptions of politics.

It has been pointed out, however, that many of the social science experiments that have examined the possible negative effects of exposure to opinion-based news fail to mimic the realities of television news viewership. Arceneaux and Johnson (2013), for example, point out that opinion news has more detrimental effects on subjects that are not given programming choices. Most particularly, the negative effects of partisan news exposure in some "forced" viewing experiments is partly due to partisan viewers watching cross-cutting partisan news—Democrat viewers watching Fox News, for instance. These negative effects are mitigated by the ability of viewers to simply turn the channel. In reality, if not in media experiments, news consumers are given significantly more choice than the limits imposed by news effect experiments. Arceneaux and Johnson (2013) argue that the possible effects of opinion and conflict-ridden news formats generally are lessened by media choice. Through self-selection, news consumers simply avoid stories and formats that are contrary to their interests.

My analysis of commentary news effects—news opinion, news urgency, and news satire—incorporates media choice as both a driving but also mediating force in how these formats affect perceptions of Congress. The analysis assesses cable and online news, though commentary cable news is tested more directly. Television continues to be a primary news source for most Americans despite the growth of online news, particularly among younger Americans (Pew Research Center 2016). Generally, television news has a more significant influence on the public's emotional reactions to politicians, institutions, and the issues compared with newspapers (Graber 2001; Hart 1994; Hibbing and Theiss-Morse 1998). Reading—as opposed to watching—the news facilitates more cognitive responses. That is, readers are more likely to collect and retain detailed information and analysis. The drama and imagery of televised news, though, has the greatest potential to stir our emotions—empathy, anger, fear, distrust, and even disdain. Consider television coverage of a natural disaster, for example. The visual reports of a natural disaster evoke a much stronger emotional impression than print coverage (Newhagen and Reeves 1992). These emotional impressions can often stay with people for extended periods of time and therefore color impressions of other political issues (Graber 2001).

Cable news programming, particularly, has led the way in this transformation toward commentary news formats. According to the Pew Research Center's *State of the News Media*, cable news stories have steadily moved toward live, in-house interviews or live stand-ups by correspondents as a means of news delivery. By 2008, only 30 percent of cable news stories were edited news packages, compared with 82 percent for network news. According to Pew Research, cable news "has all but abandoned what was once the primary element of television news, the written and edited story."[1] In its place, cable news increasingly provides a brand of live, unscripted news coverage that engages viewers with interviews, commentaries, and debate. This unedited and unrehearsed commentary format is less expensive than traditional news formats and addresses cable news' ongoing demand to fill a 24/7 news hole.

This chapter focuses on a partisan or opinion news format. The next section elaborates on the meaning and emergence of the opinion news format. I argue that opinion news programs typically have different news content and attract a different news audience than other news programs. The following section reports results from experiments testing the effects of media choice and opinion news exposure on attitudes toward Congress. Opinion engages viewers and may motivate viewers to participate; however, it comes at a collective cost toward declining institutional trust.

Understanding News Opinion

Opinion news—partisan or ideologically slanted news commentary—has become a more apparent part of the news media landscape over time. Generally, cable and online media outlets have contributed to the overall amount of opinion commentary available to most Americans. Compared with traditional news reporting, opinion commentary is less expensive to produce and can command a loyal audience built around a charismatic host. Thus, opinion news appeals to news producers working to fill a growing news hole. More important, opinion news appeals to citizens who want more than just an objective accounting of news; these citizens also want commentators to interpret and contextualize news events.

Opinion news broadly is a news commentary format framed around a program host's political perspective. This format presents "news with a view," with the program host becoming closely linked to the selection and interpretation of news stories. There is a long list of former and current cable opinion news programs, including *The O'Reilly Factor*, *Countdown With Keith Olbermann*, *The Rachel Maddow Show*, *Glenn Beck*, *Hannity*, *Hardball With Chris Matthews*, and *Lou Dobbs Tonight*; again, while our main focus is the cable news genre, talk radio and Internet partisan blogs serve as alternative mediums for this commentary format. As discussed later, the radio talk show is a long precursor to the cable opinion news program format. Internet partisan news websites like Breitbart and the Daily Kos significantly increased their audience size during the 2016 presidential campaign.

The opinion news format is most evident perhaps in the nightly, primetime cable programs that project American politics as a contentious ideological battle to a small (about a fifth the size of the network news audience) but politically active news audience. Fox News' *O'Reilly Factor* and MSNBC's *Countdown With Keith Olbermann* defined this ideological war of words for about a decade before Olbermann's 2011 departure. Since then, MSNBC's *Rachel Maddow Show* and others have sustained the liberal news commentary audience. Fox News' *The O'Reilly Factor* went off the air in April 2017 after more than twenty years as a singular force in the opinion news commentary genre. O'Reilly commanded the largest cable news program ratings during most of those twenty years. The audience success in the late 1990s resulted in his program being rebranded from the *O'Reilly Report* to the *O'Reilly Factor* to underscore the effect of his forceful persona.

In his 2006 book, *Culture Warrior*, O'Reilly writes that the United States is in the midst of a culture war between "traditionalists" and "secular-progressives." O'Reilly asserts that traditionalists believe in the family unit and place emphasis on spirituality, personal sacrifice, and responsibility. In contrast, he believes secular-progressives are socialists who are hostile to Christianity, disdainful of the military, and distrustful of free markets. O'Reilly says that the secular-progressive social movement is funded by a few far-left billionaires, and it dominates the news and entertainment industry, as well as higher education. While traditionalists and secular-progressives are not restricted to any one political ideology, he believes that the Democratic Party leadership has been largely captured by secular-progressives. The resulting culture war is the philosophical underpinning of his nightly commentary. As O'Reilly explains, "the *Factor* concept is very simple: watch all of those in power, including and especially the media, so they don't injure or exploit the folks, everyday Americans" (O'Reilly 2006, 3).

Opinion news programs that continue in *The O'Reilly Factor* genre present carefully scripted news commentaries and interviews about events and stories that project the host's ideological framing of the news. This opinion news is increasingly delivered via Internet news magazines and partisan political websites that use microtargeting strategies to market partisan news stories. Our web-surfing leaves a wake of browser history that allows marketing companies to glean insight into our personal interests, including our political preferences. The growing wave of opinion news is, with Internet news sources, aggressively seeking a partisan audience. Academic researchers have examined how partisan news contributes to political polarization or media bias effects. Stroud (2011) and Levendusky (2013) provide persuasive accounts of the effects of partisan news on political polarization. Particularly, they examine whether the increasingly evident partisan polarization between cable news network audiences—Fox News and MSNBC—tends to further reinforce and strengthen ideological polarization.

Today's partisan news, though, is far different from older questions of systematic news media bias. The opinion news concept may evoke, for some, the long-standing debate of media bias that has been hotly contended by both conservative and liberal activists. The media bias debate relates to critics' perceptions of pervasive, if immeasurable, incidences of news reporting that slight some group or interest, deviating from the traditional, objective, even-handed standards of news journalists. Conservative Reed Irvine waged a thirty-five-year battle against a liberal media bias with his watchdog group, Accuracy in Media. The Media Research Center continues this conservative watchdog role.

Conservatives' claims of slanted news coverage are empirically validated to the extent that a vast majority of national journalists are self-identified liberals and/or Democrats (Dautrich and Hartley 1999; Lichter and Noyes 1996; Patterson and Donsbach 1996). Still, critics' claims of a *systematic* liberal or conservative slant to news seem increasingly less credible.

A great deal of empirical research into the actual content of coverage finds little evidence to support this perception in past television news, as well as recent news (Niven 2002, 2003; Watts et al. 1999). As discussed earlier, the expansion in the number of news media outlets has contributed to the trend of *narrowcasting*—news programming that is directed to smaller and less loyal audiences. These market forces undermine these claims that viewers are *systematically* subjected to a liberal news bias. The growth of news outlets has led to more news media choices. News media outlets must compete for a loyal audience base. More broadly, screening technologies and news-grazing phenomena challenge the traditional "media bias" claim that news is imposed on a passive, unsuspecting audience. Traditional claim of "media bias" presumes that an objective journalistic news approach is subverted by the media elites' inclusion or exclusion of information unbeknownst to the audience. The anecdotes and rhetoric of media bias claimants, however, belie systematic evidence supporting their claims.

Be it liberal or conservative bias, though, this conception of media bias as subtly tilting stories to influence an unsuspecting, politically diverse news audience is quite different from partisan opinion news format. Opinion news, in fact, attracts a partisan audience. Do viewers choosing to watch Sean Hannity or Rachel Maddow really expect the host to give a truly objective accounting of the news? Probably not. More likely, most viewers are interested in the host's opinions, not a balanced accounting of news. Opinion news is intentional media bias to attract and retain an audience like-minded to the host's opinions.

Having defined opinion news, the remainder of this section now describes the opinion news format—its evolution, audience makeup, and typical news content. My argument is that partisan opinion news is a well-defined news genre that has recognizable structure, audience makeup, and news content. The case for well-defined partisan opinion news is important because it addresses whether opinion news exists as a class of commentary news. It also clarifies the causal mechanism—how opinion news affects perceptions of institutional trust. I argue that opinion news intentionally frames news stories to attract like-minded partisans and to create negative emotional responses of opposing elite partisans. For Congress, these negative emotional responses weaken popular perceptions that Congress can achieve shared, collective responsibility and bipartisanship toward legislative outcomes. After making this case, I next present experimental evidence assessing the behavioral effects of the opinion news format. Particularly, I answer how and to what extent does opinion news affect viewers' attitudes toward Congress and congressional actors.

Evolution of Opinion News

Opinion news has proliferated in various forms, evolving from conservative talk radio to cable news channels and the Internet. In recent decades, the genre has expanded greatly with online political blogs, ideological websites, and social media. This evolution of the opinion news format, though, has followed from various paths—our historical partisan press, interpretative or investigative news, and talk radio. I elaborate on each of these merging paths, noting how economics and audience preferences have interacted to firmly establish the opinion news format today.

The origins of party-based political campaigns were a result of opinionated newspaper editors allied with Federalists or Jeffersonian Democrats in the 1800 election. A *partisan press*, in which newspapers were aligned with a party and/or an individual political leader, was the norm throughout the nineteenth century (Sheppard 2007). Political communications and voter mobilization were largely directed by these partisan newspapers through negative and emotional appeals. This was also a very fragmented news environment. Hundreds of partisan press papers existed at any given time, and circulation was quite small. Even as a whole, these partisan papers reached only a small percentage of the American public due to a lack of literacy and the expensive nature of a subscription. (Newspapers were not typically sold on a single-copy basis.)

As printing technology evolved, so did the ability to produce larger-scale publications. Printers and editors soon realized that publications could be sold on a larger scale and with a larger profit margin. It was also determined that partisan and ideological devotions were not as profitable as creating news that was more accessible and more entertaining. These two notions brought in two new eras of journalism—the penny press and the era of yellow journalism. Penny press newspapers were grounded in producing inexpensive and accessible news while yellow journalism was oriented around the idea of altering the face of news in order to create a more entertaining product. Together, these two notions of cheap and entertaining news dominated the face of political journalism until the ethics and norms of the institution were altered by the idea of professional and objective journalism—but this was not until the 1940s in America.

A second path of opinion-based news, however, was established by the middle of the twentieth century. The call-in or listener participation talk radio format took form with the earliest radio stations, though it became more common after World War II. Early practitioners of the format in the 1950s and 1960s included radio hosts Barry Gray, Jean Shephard, Joe Pyne, and Long John Nebel.[2] Talk radio appealed to a late-night audience.

Production costs were low and audience loyalty high. Political talk radio evolved over time and grew most dramatically in the 1990s after the 1987 repeal of the fairness doctrine, which was a Federal Communication Commission (FCC) rule that required licensed radio and television broadcasters to provide airtime to contrasting viewpoints when presenting controversial public matters. After its repeal, broadcasters were free to air ideologically based programs without concern of endangering their license. Talk radio programming over time captured a loyal audience and expanded from four hundred channels in 1990 to fourteen hundred by 2006.[3]

Syndicated radio host Rush Limbaugh, particularly, began his assent in the late 1980s to the pinnacle of political talk radio. Joining Limbaugh has been a range of other conservative or libertarian talk radio hosts. Why conservative political talk has been so popular among talk radio audiences rather than liberal or nonideological talk remains puzzling. Perhaps this imbalance is random, even though progressive or liberal hosts to date have had only limited success. The ideological imbalance of talk radio may stem partly from the demographics of listeners who tend to be younger, more independent, and more male-dominated than the television news audience. Barker (2002) investigates the Limbaugh phenomenon and finds that Limbaugh's conservative messages persuade his listeners. His listeners, self-expressed "ditto-heads," share largely Limbaugh's political worldview and are more likely to express his positions after listening. Other recent research suggests this phenomenon applies to those who follow opinion-based talk shows on television from recent sources such as Sean Hannity on the right and Keith Olbermann on the left (Jamieson and Cappella 2008; Morris 2007).

A final path toward opinion news was the prevalence of interpretative or investigative television news programs during the second half of the twentieth century. Newspaper editorials, Sunday morning news interview programs, and television news magazines throughout this period have provided outlets for a style of news coverage that emphasizes deep reporting with the intent of revealing, not merely reporting, the news. The investigative and interpretative journalism styles are part of a muckraking journalism tradition that envisions news reporters as exposing crimes, political corruption, or corporate wrongdoing. Along with this vision, the 1949 FCC fairness doctrine functioned to balance news coverage by requiring television and radio stations holding FCC-issued broadcast licenses to devote some of their programming to controversial issues of public importance and to allow the airing of opposing views on those issues.

The CBS news program *60 Minutes* has defined this news style on television for about sixty years. For most of the 1970s, the *60 Minutes* program included a point/counterpoint segment in which a liberal and conservative commentator debated a particular issue. The segment originally featured conservative journalist James Kilpatrick facing off with the liberal Shana Alexander. The segment acted as a live version of competing editorials and was partly an outgrowth of the FCC fairness doctrine. The point/counterpoint segment was famously lampooned by NBC's *Saturday Night Live* with Jane Curtin and Dan Aykroyd as debaters and Aykroyd beginning his remarks with "Jane, you ignorant slut." In 1989, the FCC chairman Mark Fowler argued that the growing number of media outlets and the rise of cable television meant the fairness doctrine was obsolete. The public increasingly had access to different news media formats and a wide range of political viewpoints. Critics of the fairness doctrine long felt it also violated the First Amendment.

In summary, opinion news has a long history, evolving from the partisan press, political talk radio, and interpretative television news programs. In fact, many of the most popular hosts of opinion news programs began their careers in investigative news or talk radio. Thus, the opinion news format is an extension of traditional news; still, there are important differences. Compared with a traditional news format, opinion-based news is less costly to produce, and the program brand can attract a relatively loyal audience. More important, the opinion news program is a part of a news cable network, and audiences between the more traditional news and opinion news shows often are intermixed. Perhaps these intermixed audiences may not always distinguish straight news generally intended to inform and news opinion intended to persuade. Also, the format, production, and news content of news opinion programs tend to tap into the emotions of viewers (Graber 2001; Hibbing and Thiess-Morse 1998; Mutz 2015). These contrasts open up the possibility of behavioral effects on opinion news audiences.

Audience Composition of Opinion News

The opinion news format is also distinguished from traditional news by its audience makeup. The so-called Fox News effect—the growth of party-based media polarization between Fox News and other cable networks—has been noted earlier. Survey data and news media ratings have measured the growing partisan divide across networks (Barthel and Mitchell 2017; Iyengar and Hahn 2009; Mitchell, Gottfried, Kiley, and Matsa 2014). These network audience differences are magnified further when examining audience makeup across specific cable news opinion programs. According to recent Pew Research data, 60 percent of regular Fox News viewers consider themselves conservative, twenty-five percentage points higher than the population as a whole (Pew Research Center 2012b).

Partisan differences between cable news channel audiences have grown over time. The partisan divide began with Fox News. The proportion of Republicans that are regular Fox News viewers rose beginning in the late 1990s and began leveling out around 2010. Concurrently, the percentage of Republicans that are regular CNN and MSNBC viewers dropped somewhat over time. Among Democrats, the percentage of regular CNN and MSNBC viewers rose, albeit much less sharply than Fox News usage has increased among Republicans. Since 2008, MSNBC has followed a similar path toward a more partisan news audience. By 2014, 48 percent of the MSNBC news audience self-identified as political liberals.

Separate from network audience, cable news opinion tends to be closely tied to a host, and their audiences elevate the partisan and ideological homogeneity. Political opinion program audiences tend to be more partisan, more ideological, and have greater political interest compared with general cable news audiences (Mitchell et al. 2014). Pew's 2014 study of media habits arrays survey respondents on a twenty-point ideological spectrum. According to this measure, conservative opinion news audiences are significantly and consistently more to the ideological right compared with the other Fox News viewers. Generally, over eight in ten viewers of conservative opinion news audiences self-identify themselves as conservatives. This ideological slant for the Fox News opinion news audience is greater than other cable news networks. For a period, media critics suggested the opinion news format was distinct to Fox News viewers, implying that a left-leaning ideological audience was less interested in the opinion news. For most of the past twenty years, Fox News' opinion news audience did not have clearly left-leaning counterparts. Cable news, through its primetime programs, has redefined opinion news, and Fox News has simply had more immediate success in attracting viewers with its primetime genre than its peers. By 2014, though, MSNBC showcased different liberal-leaning opinion-based news programs during its weeknight, 6 p.m. until 10 p.m. ET primetime. Twenty-six percent of the MSNBC audience classify themselves as liberal or very liberal, which is seven percentage points higher than the population.

The opinion news audience also diverges from general cable news network viewers in their perceived level of trust in media. Pew Research's 2017 study of news media trust documented the deep partisan divide that widened in the wake of the 2016 presidential election. Trump's rhetorical attacks on news media routinely labeled them as sources of "biased," "corrupt," and "fake" news. These attacks resonated with Republican voters, as only 11 percent of self-identified Republicans in 2017 expressed a lot of trust in national news organizations. This compares with 34 percent of Democrats who trust national news, according to the Pew Research survey. The growing media trust partisan gap also reflects a marked decline in Republicans' support for the national media's watchdog role and their perceived fairness (Barthel and Mitchell 2017). The opinion news audience is even more distrusting (compared with copartisans) of news media beyond partisan news sources. In a 2014 Pew study, Americans collectively responded that opinion news, from the Sean Hannity show and online opinion news blogs like Drudge Report and Daily Kos, was among the least trusted news sources. However, among respondents who self-identify as "consistently conservative," though, conservative opinion programs are among their most trusted news sources. These consistently conservative respondents express trust in only a few partisan news sources while consistently liberal voters express trust in a broader range of news outlets. Generally, opinion news programs attract largely like-minded viewers (more so than cable news networks generally), and this opinion news audience reflects and breeds higher rates of media distrust.

Since partisan opinion news audiences are relatively ideological and distrustful, they serve as an important political force in mobilizing primary election constituencies and issue-specific social movements. Partisan opinion news presents a means of communication and mobilization for like-minded voters. The rise of the Republican Tea Party in 2010 midterm elections was fueled by conservative opinion news. Leading up to the 2010 midterm elections, 76 percent of those watching Glenn Beck identified themselves as Tea Party supporters, understandably making Glenn Beck a communication leader of that grassroots movement. On the other ideological end, regular viewers of liberal opinion news programs typically self-described themselves as "environmentalists" (78 percent), "progressives" (57 percent), and "gay rights supporters" (62 percent). These issue identifications among left-leaning opinion news viewers underscore the potential that these programs share for mobilizing like-minded ideologues. Clinton and Enamorado (2014) and Arceneaux et al. (2016) make the case that the geographically incremental rollout of the conservative Fox News Channel in the late 1990s corresponded with congressional Republicans casting more ideological roll call votes.

The opinion format draws a specific and loyal, though small audience relative to traditional news. This opinion news audience is growing at a faster rate than audiences for network news or daytime or early evening cable news. This was particularly true for viewers of Fox News. By 2010, the Fox News opinion programs had about three times the audience of its closest competitors at MSNBC (Project for Excellence in Journalism [PEJ] 2012). Despite the relative growth, the opinion news audience is still small compared with cable and network news. The opinion news program audience is only a third to half the size of the cable news headline news programs. Fox News, for instance, commands a much larger audience for its headline news programs than its individual opinion programs. Twenty-three percent of adults regularly watch Fox News, compared with 10 percent for the *O'Reilly Factor* and 7 percent for *Glenn Beck* (PEJ 2012).

Finally, opinion news audiences diverge from general news-grazing patterns in their audience loyalty. Relative to episodic viewers of 24/7 cable news, these "appointment" opinion news viewers are drawn by the opinionated persona of the host rather than the news itself. That is, the opinion news audience is more likely to be regular viewers regardless of "breaking-news" events or the news of the day, generally. The audience is drawn to the opinions and format of the host. This audience loyalty, coupled with each program's distinct audience profile, results in opinion news programs generating higher advertisement revenues compared with traditional news.

Despite their political differences, contending opinion news audiences do share similarities. Particularly, the audience composition of opinion news is demographically similar to each other and distinct from traditional news. Not surprisingly, the audiences for opinion news programs diverge politically and coincide with the political profile of their hosts. Demographically, though, both conservative and liberal opinion news programs tend to attract an older, more educated, affluent, male, and politically engaged audience. Both the *O'Reilly Factor* and *Rachel Maddow* audiences are disproportionately older, for instance. Sixty-four percent of *O'Reilly Factor* viewers and 57 percent of the *Rachel Maddow* audience are fifty or older compared with 43 percent across all news programs. Conservative opinion news programs particularly attract a senior audience. While 17 percent of the Americans were sixty-five and older, 42 percent of regular Sean Hannity viewers and 40 percent of regular O'Reilly viewers are in the senior age category (Pew Research Center 2012b).

The similar demographic profile across opinion news programs follows for income and education characteristics, as well. Opinion news audiences attract a greater share of upper-income and well-educated Americans, particularly the liberal opinion news programs. Both conservative and liberal media critics blog and tweet about the rhetorical excesses or inaccuracies of opposing opinion news hosts. These ideological critics of opposing opinion news programs host online boycott campaigns listing the opposing network's advertisers. Given the demographic similarities of MSNBC's and Fox News' opinion news audiences, though, there is a substantial overlap between the channels' advertisers. Ironically, opinion news programs share advertising of luxury cars, retirement and investment service companies, and pharmaceuticals that are common to their audience demographics.

Opinion News Content

The public aspirations of private journalism are often high-minded, though difficult to measure and assess. The 2010 Knight Commission Report, a recent commission assessing the state of news access and journalism, wrote, "Information is as vital to the healthy functioning of communities as clean air, safe streets, good schools, and public health."[4] It is hard to know how well news producers have achieved a journalistic goal over time of bridging communities and lessening political conflict. Media choice and emerging news platforms have resulted in a different mix of news formats, audience, and content. The opinion news format, though, clearly does not present news stories intended to bridge communities and mediate conflict. Instead, opinion news stories attract, engage, and mobilize politically like-minded viewers.

The news content of the opinion news format differs from traditional news content in its range, framing, and tone of coverage. Opinion news stories are selected to confirm and engage a program's partisan audience. Topics of opinion news stories are more likely to be on overtly ideological issues, actions or statements of national leaders, and domestic and election-related news stories that relate to the audience's interests. Some of these opinion news stories—such as commentary on opposing politicians' statements—receive much less attention by traditional news programs. Opinion news programs may cover a significantly smaller number of news stories in any given program compared with traditional news, with one or two stories covered at length. Opinion news content also gives greater attention to other news media and media actors, particularly opposing opinion news hosts. This preoccupation with news about the news is a unique feature of the opinion format.

In order to look for elements of opinion news content coverage, I conducted a content analysis of news transcripts accessed through LexisNexis Academic Universe. Specifically, I sampled transcripts from six different television newscasts between 2006 and 2010: *The O'Reilly Factor, Countdown With Keith Olbermann, Hannity, Hardball With Chris Matthews, CNN Newsroom,* and *CBS Evening News.* These sources were selected for the five years because they offer a good sample of the most common forms of television news on cable and broadcast. For cable, I sampled news coverage from a partisan, conservative commentator (Hannity), a self-described independent who leans toward conservatism (O'Reilly), a partisan moderate (Matthews), and a partisan liberal (Olbermann). Two of these programs, O'Reilly and Hannity, air on the Fox News Network, which is the highest-rated cable news station and considered to be more popular among Republicans and conservatives. Two other programs, Olbermann and Matthews, air on MSNBC, which is thought to be more popular among Democrats and liberals (Stroud 2011). The last two programs represent less opinion-oriented programming and air on television stations considered to be more objective, CNN and CBS.

For each of the five years examined, I selected all published transcripts for two months: June and December. This gave a sample of ten months in total. The unit of analysis was the coverage between commercials for the cable news stations and the individual topics for *CBS Evening News*. In total, this selection process created a sample of 7,083 unique television news stories. Table 4.1 shows the distribution of the number of stories collected from each source. Although *CBS Evening News* is slightly oversampled due to the shorter length of the news stories (not separated by commercial breaks, as is the case with cable news), it can be seen that each program is fairly evenly represented.

Within the sample, I coded for several elements of each news story. The first is the topic covered in the story. Some topics carry a greater degree of polarizing rhetoric than others. For instance, topics of war, scandals, and elections would carry more ideological debate than stories of less salient government affairs, such as state politics, health and science, and civil liberties. Table 4.2 shows the findings of my content analysis of story

Table 4.1 Content Analysis Sample		
News Program	**Number of Stories**	**Percentage of Sample**
O'Reilly Factor	1,304	18.41
Countdown	837	11.81
Hannity	944	13.32
Hardball	880	12.42
CNN Newsroom	1,139	16.08
CBS Evening News	1,979	27.93

Source: Created by the author using data from LexisNexis Academic Universe.

Table 4.2 News Topic by Television News Source

Topic	News Source (Percentage)*						
	O'Reilly	*Countdown*	*Hannity*	*Hardball*	*CNN*	*CBS*	*Total*
Crime	16	4	15	2	9	8	9
Legal Dispute	11	4	2	2	3	2	4
War	16	17	15	22	33	21	21
Congress	6	20	17	20	10	7	11
President	14	18	18	22	15	5	14
Supreme Court	1	1	2	1	2	2	2
Campaign	14	25	35	50	18	9	23
Economy	6	7	9	7	11	19	14
Political Scandal	3	7	6	10	3	2	4
Media	37	29	12	13	2	14	18
Civil Liberties	4	3	3	2	2	1	2
Gov't. Affairs	2	7	4	2	6	6	4
Immigration	6	0	4	2	2	1	2
Scandal	9	7	10	6	3	2	6
International	8	8	9	10	39	19	15
Natural Disaster	4	13	7	10	18	22	13
Human Interest	28	17	24	3	12	31	21
Science/ Health	4	7	4	3	9	18	9
State Politics	3	3	4	3	4	1	3
Undefined	10	5	2	3	0	0	3

Source: Created by the author using data from LexisNexis Academic Universe.
*Column totals do not line up to 100 because each story was coded for primary topic and secondary topic.

topic by television news source (each story was coded for two primary topics). As the results demonstrate, there is a good deal of variation in the topics covered. However, primetime cable opinion programs during this period—*O'Reilly, Hannity, Countdown*, and *Hardball*—tend to focus on more election campaigns and human interest news topics compared with mainstream news sources—CNN and CBS—which are more straight-news oriented. The source coverage on some topics is fairly well distributed, but the coverage on media and campaign-related stories is more prevalent on cable opinion news shows than on network news programs.

Partisan opinion news content is distinct and intended to engage its viewers. The agenda-setting influence of the partisan opinion news format is to select stories that attract like-minded viewers and to discourage grazing to other sources. The framing of opinion news content is also distinct. Levendusky (2013) persuasively concludes from content analysis and case studies that partisan news programs frame their stories around opposing party or leader actions or statements. Story topics and wording are more likely to produce an emotional response of anger, empathy, or aversion among opinion program viewers. For instance, while federal health care reform was a major topic during the spring and summer of 2009 for all media sources, opinion news coverage was more likely to focus on ideological extremes of the debate. From the *O'Reilly Factor* program, the health care story was framed as the excesses of "Obamacare," the "far left," and the outrage of Tea Party activists. From the left, *Countdown With Keith Olbermann* framed health care reform with stories on the "greed" of the insurance industry and obstruction of Senate Republicans. Throughout this period, Olbermann would frequently highlight O'Reilly in his regular "Worst Person in the World" segment.

A final element of partisan opinion news can be found in the tone of the coverage. While less urgent news situations should be expected to contain calm, civil discussion that reflects a more mundane environment, the opposite would be expected in an urgent news environment. That is, raised voices and heated exchanges would give a sense of urgency that may attract the attention of news grazers. In order to code for this type of news tone, I analyzed transcripts for "crosstalk" and incivility. Crosstalk is when news hosts and guests engage in the process of speaking over one another. This is identified in television news transcripts because words being spoken over each other become inaudible to the transcribing computer programs, and the note of [CROSSTALK] appears on the transcript. Of course, this is not a perfect method of detecting heightened disagreement that would indicate news urgency, so I also coded for the nature of the crosstalk. Specifically, I examined whether or not it was civil. Civil crosstalk examples would include apologies for interruption, technical difficulties, or cutting a guest short to go to a commercial break. Uncivil crosstalk examples included repeated crosstalk with strong disagreement, notations of shouting within the transcript, name-calling, or clear insults.

Overall, the content analysis of opinion news programs did uncover a fair bit of crosstalk, which indicates a more confrontational, drama-laden format. In total, 10.4 percent of the sample contained at least one instance of people talking over one another ($N = 737$). Of this 10 percent, it was clear in one-third of the stories (31 percent) that the exchanges were uncivil, while only 17 percent were clearly civil. Almost half of the crosstalk (53 percent) was not clearly civil or uncivil and thus coded as neither. Not surprisingly, the distribution of crosstalk was not constant across television stations. Out of the 737 instances of crosstalk, only three occurred on CNN or CBS while the other 734 occurred on the cable news talk shows. Most of these occurred on *Hannity* (42 percent) and *Hardball* (50 percent) while *O'Reilly* and *Countdown* had much fewer crosstalk instances (6 percent and 1.5 percent, respectively). This is not surprising considering that *Hannity* and *Hardball* are more guest-driven debate programs while *O'Reilly* and *Countdown* are oriented more toward a single-host commentary format. Along these same lines, it is also important to note that the uncivil crosstalk also occurred with more frequency on *Hannity* and *Hardball* (36 percent and 51 percent, respectively).

In summary, I find that partisan opinion news content is distinct from other news sources. These opinion news agenda and framing effects may be an outgrowth of what researchers have called a "hostile media" phenomena. The hostile media effect states that people with strong attitudes toward an issue (partisans) perceive news coverage as biased against their opinions, regardless of objectivity of the news. Vallone, Ross, and Lepper (1985) found that viewers with strong, extreme positions on *both sides* of an issue may watch the same neutral news story but claim that the news story was biased against their side and in favor of the opposing side. These "partisans" selectively perceive the slant of a news story to be contrary to their view, even though they are watching the same news (Vallone, Ross, and Lepper 1985). This hostile media effect has been supported by social scientists in different experimental conditions and different issue areas (Feldman 2011; Perloff 2015; Schmitt, Gunther, and Liebhart 2004). Opinion news content, particularly stories on opposing partisans and media reports, may have a priming effect by invoking a hostile response against this opposition. Applied to Congress, opinion news content may trigger hostility—and consequently distrust—toward opposing congressional party leaders and media. I explore these effects on congressional trust in the next section.

Evaluating the Effects of Opinion News

The increasing partisan divide across cable news channels has led researchers to investigate whether partisan—and sometimes uncivil—opinion news contributes to Americans' partisan divide. Is partisan polarization partly due to the news media? Several empirical studies have assessed this question—whether partisan news affects Americans' perceptions of political polarization (Arceneaux and Johnson 2013; Levendusky 2013; Stroud 2011). These studies propose different measures, explanations, and conditions for how media might affect mass partisan polarization. There is some agreement that partisan or opinion news exposure has an experimental (or treatment) effect in controlled settings; however, there is less understanding of how these controlled results relate to the real-world media choice environment.

I then describe a quasiexperiment that tries to evaluate whether the negative effects of opinion news are independent from viewers' self-selection and grazing. Like the earlier results, the research design here provides participants with news media choices—six to be exact. Participants are invited to engage in news grazing. I include not only opinion news options from different cable news networks but also other traditional news and entertainment options.

Similar to the research design discussed in Chapter 2, my opinion news experiment asked participants to watch television news with a remote control at the ready and a guide to the different channels. As with the earlier experiment, the remote control was a virtual one as part of an online experiment. The media choice experiment tracks how often a participant "clicked" during the course of the experiment, when they clicked, and how long a subject watched each channel by recording what channel each subject was watching at a given second during the five-minute viewing period. These data allow me to gauge how the viewers' news-grazing decisions—particularly, how long they chose to view opinion news—affected their perceptions of congressional trust. I had 441 participants participating in the opinion news experiment. This was a convenience sample in which subjects chose to participate rather than being randomly selected and assigned to treatments. This limits our ability to reliably generalize any findings back to a defined population, but it does provide some suggestive findings about the effects of grazing and opinion news.

Participants were asked about their political ideology, partisanship, political interest, and news preferences before the simulated television experiment began. With the simulated remote control activated with their computer mouse, subjects viewed television programming that included different opinion news formats, traditional news, and entertainment programs. They could choose to watch opinion news (*Countdown With Keith Olberman* or the *O'Reilly Factor*), traditional news (the *CBS Evening News* or the *Lehrer News Hour*), or entertainment (an ESPN sports clip or the NBC reality show *The Apprentice*). All these videos programs were taken from the same time period.

After grazing and watching television news during the experiment, participants were next asked to respond to a series of survey questions assessing their attitude toward parties, elites, and ideologies. For instance, respondents were asked whether they agreed or disagreed with whether "liberals and conservatives in Washington can put aside their differences to do what is best for America." They were asked whether they agreed or disagreed with whether "Republicans were too conservative," whether "Democrats were too liberal," whether "Democrats don't care about traditional values," and whether "Republicans fear change." A list of survey questions posed in the opinion news experiment is in Appendix II.

The partisan news research design allows subjects to make their own media choices within the constraints of select programs. However, this approach has clear limits. Foremost, the benefits of randomly assigning subjects to a prescribed condition is lost. In this case, subjects are, in effect, choosing their specific treatment with the media choices, and in this regard, the research is not a true experiment. Randomization aims to ensure that subjects with different media-viewing preferences are equally (randomly) spread out among the different viewing options in order to isolate the test or treatment effect. Despite the benefits of this approach for isolating the effects of a particular media treatment, it does not match up with real media consumption behavior. Particularly, it cannot address the possible effects of participants' media preferences and how these preferences condition behavioral outcomes. This design of allowing participants to make their own media choices corresponds more closely with the real-world news-grazing habits.

Still, the media choice design does not entirely match real conditions of media consumption. Reality permits even more media choice than viewing only six news and entertainment options. We may think that a greater range and number of media choices would only increase audience fragmentation and the influence of emotive appeals to retain that audience. Still, the proposed design achieves only a very limited degree of media choice. Furthermore, the design forces participants to watch some mix of viewing options. In reality, we may always choose not to watch anything at all or to turn the media device off. In this respect, the design is another form of "forced" viewing. Third, the proposed design is a convenience sample in which subjects choose to participate. Thus, any sample findings cannot be theoretically generalized to a broad population. This is a legitimate concern since online experiments tend to attract participants who are younger and less professional. The nonrepresentativeness of respondents may result in a "college sophomore problem" in which results may not safely relate to a broader population (Sears 1986). To my defense, college students from the ages of eighteen to twenty-four display the same qualities as news grazers generally. In fact, it is this age group and education level that news grazes with the most frequency. A final limit—and probably the most restrictive—of the design is that I do not have the degree of control over the news media treatment as would occur in a true experimental design. Subjects are not randomly assigned to watch a particular program; in fact, participants do not even receive a similar treatment depending on their clicking behavior.

The proposed design, though, has benefits. It at least approximates the effects of media choice as an intervening variable in assessing how opinion news affects viewers' political perceptions. In this regard, it complements experimental results that provide greater control over media treatments. The design also extends findings about political polarization to examining institutional and elite trust. Particularly, we want to test whether expanding media choice and corresponding growth in alternative news formats like opinion news programs have a measurable effect on individuals' perceptions of Congress and opposing party elites.

The principal alternative explanation is that media choice (and opinion news) merely promotes ideological sorting—conservatives view a conservative opinion news format while liberals choose liberal opinion news. According to this view, opinion news alone does not affect political perceptions independent of the viewers' ideological predispositions that are driving their media choices. Viewers merely sort themselves by their grazing decisions, and this self-selection is the real reason for any apparent behavioral differences across different news audiences.

In this case, opinion news does not promote public distrust but merely reflects it. Cynical, ideologically extreme viewers choose to watch opinion news because it offers confirming evidence of their current political views. If this alternative view holds, we would not find evidence that opinion news exposure affects political perceptions once controlling for their self-identified partisan and ideological beliefs. Before participants begin watching the different news and entertainment choices, I ask them questions about their partisanship, ideology, and news interest. Thus, the empirical test tries to statistically control for subjects' party and ideological views to assess the independent effect of opinion news exposure.

The results of this and other studies confirm that opinion news formats clearly do promote ideological sorting. Most individuals have political biases—a partisan identification and ideological predisposition that shape their political views, affect their media choices, and motivate how they process news information. Research has demonstrated how these predispositions affect how we gather, perceive, and remember news. This personal bias fits well into political psychologists' *online processing* and *memory-based models* of attitude formation. Television viewers most likely have developed preconceived notions about the political candidates, and they continuously update these perceptions cognitively, as they see and read new campaign information (Lodge, McGraw, and Stroh 1989; Lodge, Steenbergen, and Brau 1995; Rahn, Aldrich, and Borgida 1994). In the online processing model, individuals typically do not evaluate political candidates based on specifically recalled pieces of information but instead rely on a more general impression that reflects a summation of their media exposure. An individual may forget the exact nature of the material fairly quickly but nevertheless integrate this information into a summary evaluation of the candidate (also known as a "running tally"). In the memory-based model, there is no online tally, just a memory dump at the individual's decision point.

If we accept the online processing model, we might certainly expect that exposure to trusted—but possibly slanted—coverage may provide enough new information to a viewer's "running tally" to influence attitudinal change. This especially may be the case when combined with repetitiveness. Likewise, repetitiveness would seem to make a significant impression within a memory-based model because it would improve message recall.

As the cable news audiences have sorted, there is some evidence to suggest that the audiences react differently to televised political coverage. Scholars have investigated media effects of singular political events like entry into the Iraq War and government response to natural disasters. For example, following Hurricane Katrina in New Orleans, Republican viewers were much more responsive to news media framing that blamed the slow disaster response on state government rather than the Bush administration (Maestas et al. 2008). Also, the Fox News audience was more likely to believe that New Orleans citizens who took items from abandoned homes and businesses were "criminals," as opposed to "ordinary people who were desperate" (Pew Research Center 2005). It is difficult to estimate, however, what influenced the audiences' differing perspectives. Certainly, the responses were due, in part, to partisan predisposition and the consequent self-selection of like-minded news. Applied to the news-grazing phenomenon, political biases have a similar effect on who watches particular opinion news programs. We are more likely to watch opinion news programs that we think confirm—or at least do not conflict with—our political predispositions. In fact, this ideological sorting in news choices is more prevalent with expanding media choice.

As shown earlier, the Pew Research Center's survey studies confirm this general tendency for Americans to increasingly sort themselves ideologically when making news media choices, particularly when viewing opinion news programs. These political viewing biases affect individuals' news-gathering habits and news retention. This survey approach and results present some benefits to experimental approaches. Notably, surveys allow a representative sample of Americans to express their attitudes toward media choice. This random national sample allows us to more safely generalize results to all Americans. On the other hand, though, survey responses may be partly due to viewers' limited recall of news information. They also may not allow researchers to closely isolate the causal role of news-grazing media choice on viewer attitudes. Are survey results of respondents' attitudes caused by their media choices or caused by some other predisposed attitude or environmental condition, such as a pending election or emerging news story? Compared with a survey design, the opinion news quasiexperiment allows us to more closely test for a causal relationship between viewers' grazing practices and their political attitudes. By tracking specific viewers' media choices, we may be better able to isolate whether opinion news promotes not only ideological sorting but also other attitudinal changes. I discuss these attitudinal effects next.

Negative Stereotyping, Congressional Party Affect, and Bipartisan Trust

Opinion news promotes an ideologically sorted audience, and the format's news content displays clear agenda-setting and framing effects that may deliver emotional responses among like-minded partisan viewers. Given these conditions, I evaluate whether opinion news leaves its audience with negative stereotypes of opposing parties and leaders. There is substantial support from survey and election analyses of this negative stereotyping. Jacobson (2007), among others, has reported evidence indicating that Americans have had increasingly negative evaluations of a president opposite to one's party or ideology over time. Abramowitz (2010, 2014) also presents strong evidence that negative "affective" partisanship has strengthened over time among politically attentive partisan voters. That is, the partisan voters are experiencing increasingly negative feelings and associations toward opposing party leaders. Overall, the public is increasingly polarized by negative evaluations of opposing ideas and parties. This negative polarization is sharper among Americans when compared with other industrialized democracies (Mutz 2006).

These trends in polarization may be partly tied to my analysis of opinion news. An individual's partisan attitudes can be polarized by either (or both) an "in-group" or "out-group" assessment. In-group (or positive) polarization occurs when individuals move closer to elites, groups, or institutions that they already are predisposed to favor. If you consider yourself to be a conservative, for instance, and receive positive information for a conservative elite or party, this confirmatory evidence may strengthen your bond toward your conservative position. In contrast, out-group (or negative) polarization suggests that individuals further distance themselves from opposing partisan attitudes after receiving news critical of opposing partisans. How might opinion news affect either positive or negative polarization?

Conceivably, opinion news may result in positive polarization. Viewers may develop stronger positive stereotypes of groups, institutions, and elites that they typically agree with already. For instance, conservative opinion news may strengthen a viewer's predisposed attitudes toward some ideological issue—abortion, government spending, or military policy. Given the clear tendency for ideologically conforming audiences of opinion news programs—conservatives watching conservative news—the prospects for positive polarization are limited in practice. Ideological sorting by opinion news formats overwhelmingly reduces the potential effects of positive polarization. Partisans receiving confirmatory opinion news are already largely polarized toward this ideological position. Thus, the positive influences of opinion news are constrained.

Negative polarization, though, suggests that opinion news may primarily affect out-group assessments. In other words, opinion news results in viewers further distancing themselves from opposing attitudes. Viewers may adopt more negative stereotypes of opposing partisans or ideologues. For instance, a steady diet of liberal opinion news by liberal viewers may increase the likelihood that these liberals assume the worst stereotypical labels and beliefs of conservatives. Since opinion news tends to draw audiences disproportionately from individuals who are already prone to agree with the opinion's host, the prospects for out-group or negative polarization seem very possible.

The growing number and popularity of opinion news programming could have a negative polarizing effect on viewers. The growing prevalence of online opinion magazines and blogging are growing areas for this negative stereotyping phenomenon. Cass Sunstein has argued that media fragmentation promotes political polarization. With a focus on the Internet, Sunstein (2001, 2009) asserts that more viewing of online media would allow individuals to avoid news that conflicts with their preconceived political viewpoints. Exposure to like-minded opinion coverage, be it cable or online sources, may contribute toward stereotyping the opposition.

Opinion news journalists and broadcasters often rely heavily on negatives stereotypes of the opposition to make their arguments. Rush Limbaugh, for instance, is quick to place all liberals under labels such as "environmentalist wacko" or "feminazi" (1993, 1994), and Fox News' Sean Hannity and Bill O'Reilly regularly chastise liberals as weak and anti-American (Hannity 2002). On the left, Rachel Maddow and other commentators from MSNBC have found notoriety by harshly criticizing conservatives and defending liberals. Liberal comic Al Franken had considerable media success making the case for why "Rush Limbaugh is a big fat idiot" while revealing the "lies and the lying liars that tell them" of the political right. He was able to parlay this notoriety into a successful bid for the U.S. Senate in 2008 and served as a senator from Minnesota for eight years, until he announced his resignation in December 2017.

Partisan opinion news affects viewers' out-group perceptions, attitudes of opinions divergent from the host's views. This negative stereotyping—distorted, reductive generalizations homogenously applied to out-group members—is intended (like all stereotyping) to heighten perceived group differences to further bond like-minded members. This stereotyping effect may also discourage democratic values of institutional trust, tolerance, and political compromise by promoting negative stereotypes of out-group members.

Does opinion news promote, discourage, or have little significant effect on how individuals view opposing interests? News grazing, along with expanding media choice, is an important and intervening effect in the relationship between news and viewer perceptions. As discussed in the earlier chapter, a use and gratification theory of grazing suggests that most consumers of ideologically opinionated news seek out that programming because it is enjoyable and fits with their preconceived notions. From this perspective, people ignore news that has little relevance and appeal. Unsettling and unattractive news offers little in terms of gratification, so it will be avoided or disregarded (Graber 2006). With this in mind, the overall effect of conservative talk shows, for instance, may just be to reinforce the preexisting attitudes of their conservative regular viewing audience.

The construction of my experiment allows me to test for whether opinion news promotes either positive or negative polarization. To measure stereotyping tendencies, I included several ideological stereotyping statements in my post-test—the questions posed after participants grazed and watched different news formats. The participants could either agree or disagree with these statements on a five-point scale (1 = strongly disagree; 2 = somewhat disagree; 3 = neither agree nor disagree; 4 = somewhat agree; 5 = strongly agree) to a range of statements that asserted different stereotypical claims of conservatives and liberals. For examples, respondents were asked whether they agreed that "liberals don't care about traditional values" or that "conservatives only care about the rich."[5] Appendix II provides a list of all of these stereotyping statements. I created an additive index of all negative conservative and negative liberal stereotypes. Thus, higher scores indicate higher levels of negative stereotyping. The test is whether watching opinion news results in higher out-party negative stereotypes.

Table 4.3 shows the findings from two regression analyses in which my ideological stereotyping dependent variables were regressed against exposure to the two different types of opinion news exposure: Olbermann and O'Reilly. I control for subjects' self-expressed ideological and partisan beliefs reported before the experiment. As the results show, there are significant, though small, effects from opinion news exposure. Independent of their own conservative and Republican beliefs, viewers of the *O'Reilly*

Table 4.3 The Effects of Opinion News Exposure on Negative Ideological Stereotyping

	Liberal Stereotyping Index	Conservative Stereotyping Index
Time Watching Olbermann		.007 (.002)***
Time Watching O'Reilly	.006 (.002)***	
Ideology (7-point scale)	.971 (.108)***	−.521 (.103)***
Party Identification (7-point scale)	.663 (.102)***	−.518 (.099)***
Constant	5.18 (.251)***	
Adjusted *R*-Squared	.50	.31
N	442	442

Source: Created by the author using original data.
Note: Cell entries are regression coefficients with standard errors in parentheses.
*p < .10, **p < .05, ***p < .01 (one-tailed test).

Factor were significantly more likely to assert negative stereotypes of liberals. Again, this relationship holds even when controlling for ideology and partisan affiliation. Likewise, independent of liberal and Democratic leanings, viewers of *Countdown With Keith Olbermann* reported significantly stronger negative associations of conservatives.

In a similar analysis, I examined whether opinion news affects congressional party affect, the extent to which the respondent likes or dislikes the opposing congressional party. For instance, individuals were asked to place "Republicans in Congress" on a ten-point favorability scale, with higher numbers meaning a more favorable feeling toward congressional Republicans. Table 4.4 reports the effects of opinion news exposure on opposing congressional party affect. The results are mixed. Controlling for partisanship and ideology, viewers who chose to watch more of the *O'Reilly Factor* program were significantly less favorable of congressional Democrats. This result does not hold, though, for viewers of the liberal Keith Olbermann program.

Furthermore, both of these negative stereotyping and congressional party affect results are all small compared with the more apparent effects of ideological sorting. Generally, party and ideology strongly affect negative

Table 4.4 The Effects of Opinion News Exposure on Congressional Party Affect

	Favorable Feelings for Congressional Republicans	Favorable Feelings for Congressional Democrats
Time Watching Olbermann	−.001 (.002)	
Time Watching O'Reilly		−.005 (.001)***
Ideology (7-point scale)	.158 (.065)**	−.288 (.071)***
Party Identification (7-point scale)	.490 (.063)***	−.506 (.067)***
Constant	2.737 (.249)***	8.91 (.254)***
Adjusted *R*-Squared	.30	.38
N	442	442

Source: Created by the author using original data.
Note: Cell entries are regression coefficients with standard errors in parentheses.
*$p < .10$, **$p < .05$, ***$p < .01$ (one-tailed test).

out-party stereotyping and affect. Pew Research confirms that these negative assessments across party lines have grown over time. They compare public attitudes after the congressional party majority changed in 1995, 2007, 2011, and 2015. Generally, the results indicate that Americans have been more disapproving of the opposing party over time. They are more critical of the opposing party in keeping campaign promises and overall job approval. These growing negative associations are more pronounced among Republican respondents.

A final test of opinion news exposure on congressional perceptions relates to these out-party assessments. We would reasonably expect that negative ideological stereotyping and negative congressional affect would culminate in a decrease in the prospects for bipartisan trust. If you stereotype and do not like the opposition, you are not likely to trust a legislative process intended to promote civil deliberation, compromise, and bipartisan voting. I posed a series of post-test questions assessing respondents' bipartisan trust. Particularly, respondents were asked to place themselves on a five-point agreement scale with whether "I believe that the Liberals and Conservatives in Washington can put aside differences to do what is best for America." Additionally, respondents were asked whether "I trust the media to cover political events fairly and accurately" and whether "It is possible that I would vote for a Presidential candidate from a political party

Table 4.5   The Effects of Opinion News Exposure on Bipartisan Trust

	Bipartisan Trust	Bipartisan Trust
Time Watching Olbermann	−.001 (.001)	.002 (.001)*
Time Watching O'Reilly		−.002 (.001)**
Ideology (7-point scale)	.122 (.073)*	−.248 (.083)
Party Identification (7-point scale)	.527 (.083)***	−.449 (.080)
Constant	1.485 (.251)***	8.98 (.242)***
Adjusted R-Squared	.49	.34
N	442	442

Source: Created by the author using original data.
Note: Cell entries are regression coefficients with standard errors in parentheses.
*p < .10, **p < .05, ***p < .01 (one-tailed test).

different than my own." I created an additive index of these responses to assess respondents' feelings toward bipartisan trust. A higher score indicates a stronger bipartisan spirit.

Table 4.5 shows the results from opinion news exposure on bipartisan trust. Again, the results indicate that longer viewing times of partisan opinion formats are associated with lower bipartisan trust, even when controlling for viewers' ideological and partisan predispositions. The effects of opinion news exposure are small but significant, particularly for the *O'Reilly Factor*. The finding that politically right opinion news affects perceived bipartisan trust parallels other research findings. Perhaps it is a function of my particular research design and the news clips that were used; still, it supports the idea that negative stereotyping of out-groups affects perceived trust.

Conclusion

Senator Daniel Patrick Moynihan famously observed, "Everyone is entitled to his own opinion, but not his own facts." Opinion news formats have become a larger share of cable television, online, and radio news. Is this partisan opinion news reducing consumers' access to or interest in "the facts"? Are news consumers substituting facts with opinions? That is, are they less likely to see the complexity and ambiguity in public issues because news stories are increasingly presented to them in an opinion-based format?

This chapter begins to answer some of these hard questions. It provides some critical response by first placing the partisan news genre within the framework of news grazing. I argue that the growth of partisan news is one institutional response to our changing news-gathering habits. Opinion attracts and retains a distracted audience. I next answer these questions by assessing the evolution, audience makeup, and content of partisan opinion news. The growth, unique audience, and different story content of opinion news elevates the likelihood that regular partisan news consumers attach greater emotional connection with this news. I finally answer these questions by assessing the behavioral consequences of partisan news, particularly among news grazers. National Election Studies (NES) respondents who routinely listen to talk radio and watch opinion news programs are significantly more likely to perceive wider opinion divisions between presidential candidates. My analysis of experimental data supports this argument that news opinion marginally reinforces viewers' predisposed views and, more meaningfully, breeds distrust.

To clarify, media choice (not opinion news specifically) promotes sorting between news consumers. Partisan opinion news programs generally attract like-minded viewers, but they do not necessitate partisan polarization. Fox News or alt-right online blogs are not leading viewers to the right, for instance. Rather, right-leaning viewers simply prefer partisan opinion news formats. Opinion news intentionally includes affective appeal with the news, and predisposed partisan viewers respond by not clicking. The news-grazing argument is not that partisan news creates or significantly elevates partisanship among voters.

Still, the analysis also indicates marginal support for the idea that watching opinion news increases viewers' negative stereotypes toward opposing ideologues, negative affect toward congressional parties, and less agreement in bipartisan trust. Controlling for those viewers' ideological and partisan predispositions, greater exposure to opinion news marginally affects viewers. These reported experimental effects are not large, but they are significant. It is difficult to generalize from these experimental results given the lack of diversity and randomness in selection of our subjects. Additionally, our subjects' exposure to opinion news was brief and limited, much less than in a real-life setting. What might be the long-term effects over a broad audience of opinion news? More experimental and survey-based research should be done to further test these effects. The effects of opinion news are more complex than popular accounts suggest, but these effects are still not fully understood.

These effects from the media choice opinion news quasiexperiment coincide with earlier studies that examined the polarizing effects of partisan news. Levendusky (2013) notably reports experimental results showing the polarizing effects of partisan news in which subjects were randomly assigned to different news media treatments. Generally, media choice tends to decrease the size of negative affect and stereotyping effects. In a real-world setting, viewers always can click away or turn off news that they dislike. Still, the effects of expanding media choice extend beyond any experimental setting. In Part I, I argued that media choice has a more long-term consequence of altering how we collect news. This change toward news-grazing behavior correspondingly is affecting how news producers and makers present news to Americans, culminating in the growth of commentary news. Thus, while media choice empowers viewers to self-select news, it also promotes formats that inject commentary and engagement along with news.

The twin forces of media choice and news grazing will most likely continue the trend toward commentary news. The public is already voting with their remote-control clickers and computer mouses. The opinion news format has established a relatively small but loyal following in an increasingly fragmented news media market. A debate of broadcast media ethics, while informative, is unlikely to undo these market forces. Still, the changing reality also leads us to further evaluate the polarizing effects of these commentary formats. In the next chapter, I evaluate the effects of urgent and conflict-ridden news.

ENDNOTES

1. State of the News Media (2008) is at http://www.stateofthenewsmedia .com/2008.

2. Peter Laufer (1995) and Wayne Munson (1993) provide histories of talk radio.

3. State of the News Media (2008). http://www.stateofthenewsmedia .org/2008.

4. The 2010 Knight Report includes an impressive blue ribbon panel of journalists, as well as policy, business, and civic leaders. The commission report advocates for universal broadband, open networks, transparent government, a media and digitally literate populace, vibrant local journalism, and local public engagement. The report can be read at http://www.knightcomm.org/read-the-report-and-comment.

5. I confirmed that these different stereotyping responses are all strongly associated with each other using principal components factor analysis. The factor analysis gave principal components scores, and the results illustrate that the two sets of stereotypical statements (negative liberal and negative conservative) significantly load on the same dimension and are in the predictably opposite direction. With this confirmation, I created two different additive dependent variables (negative liberal stereotype and negative conservative stereotype, each on a two to ten scale).

Breaking News

M̲ost news consumers are very familiar with the breaking-news format. A news alert, bulletin, or special report is deemed "breaking" as emerging information is delivered in often an urgent tone or real-time graphics. The breaking-news genre is a more regular part of our news consumption diet with cable and Internet news. Cable and Internet news have elevated our expectations of immediacy and real-time coverage of news events. Looking back to the spring and summer of 2011, we see a case of how cable and Internet news has affected our tastes for breaking news. The case also illustrates how the breaking-news format may impact our perceptions of Congress and the media.

The preceding November 2010 midterm congressional elections provided much of the context for the congressional breaking-news events in the first year of the 112th Congress (2011–2012). The 2010 congressional elections resulted in House Republicans picking up a record-breaking sixty-three House seats to regain their U.S. House of Representatives majority. Tea Party Republicans, a strongly conservative faction within the House Republican Conference, won a large share of these new House seats, setting the context for an even greater ideological divide between House parties. On the other end of the Capitol, Senate Democrats retained their chamber's majority, despite losing six seats. However, since the U.S. Senate requires a supermajority to control the floor agenda, the resulting close party margin ensured that the Senate in the 112th Congress would also be extremely divisive.

Congressional deadlines, scandals, and partisan conflicts generally receive greater amounts of breaking-news coverage from media outlets than other congressional news stories. Emboldened by their new House majority, congressional Republicans in 2011 were poised to do battle with congressional Democrats and the Obama administration. Early in the 112th Congress, fiscal conservatives required deficit reduction legislation as a condition for their support of a short-term appropriations bill that kept the federal government open. This funding bill would extend the federal debt ceiling, the statutory maximum of money the U.S. Treasury Department is allowed to borrow. Absent this debt ceiling extension, the federal government would shut down, resulting in a furlough of some 800,000 government employees. About the same time, Moody's Investors Service also said it was considering placing a "negative outlook" on the AAA rating of U.S. debt as the country's budget deficit widened.

Given the widening partisan divide and impending debt ceiling crisis, the conditions were set for extensive congressional brinksmanship and prolonged breaking-news coverage. President Obama, Senate majority leader Harry Reid, and House Speaker John Boehner met regularly in the days preceding an April 15 shutdown deadline in an effort to avert the congressional crisis. Congressional Republicans pushed the president to negotiate over deficit reduction legislation in exchange for a short-term extension of the debt ceiling. Finally, on April 15, House members narrowly averted the crisis. At the eleventh hour, congressional and White House principals in the negotiation announced an agreement to stave off a government shutdown. The House agreement entailed $38 billion in deficit reduction but also left the likely scenario of a later congressional showdown over raising the debt ceiling later that summer.

All the while, cable and online news outlets reported continuously on the breaking news of the looming congressional deadline. Most of these news outlets included countdown clocks to the government closure embedded in a corner of the screen. The countdown clocks added visual drama, further heightening the urgency leading up to a April 15 midnight deadline. Internet news sources also provided immediate, ongoing coverage. The @GovtShutdown account on Twitter, started by the *National Journal*, posted a new message hourly about the impending deadline.

The breaking-news coverage of an impending shutdown extended for nearly two weeks in April 2011. According to the Pew News Media Index, cable news media filled 53 percent of their news hole with coverage of the deficit reduction vote event during the April 4–10 week before the shutdown deadline.[1] Both parties used congressional spokespersons during this extended breaking-news coverage to amplify their party's strategic talking points. Democratic spokespersons often portrayed Republicans as economic elitists indifferent to government employees' concerns of a shutdown; congressional Republicans frequently depicted Democrats as unconcerned about looming government debt. This extended coverage contributed to public perceptions of urgency but failure to act.

The April House deficit reduction agreement averted an immediate crisis but only bought a few months of time. The agreement portended another late summer congressional debt ceiling crisis. Before this late-summer showdown, though, other breaking news would continue to dominate cable and online outlets during the spring and early summer. In May 2011, cable and online news had a binge of breaking news with extended coverage of the killing of Osama bin Laden. Most of this coverage included White House, military, and international reactions to the event. However, congressional reactions to the event and its political implications were included in the breaking-news coverage.

In June 2011, a congressional scandal involving Rep. Anthony Weiner, D-N.Y., triggered yet another wave of breaking-news coverage. Representative Weiner attracted national attention after pictures surfaced on Twitter and the Internet showing Rep. Weiner in his underwear. Weiner initially denied so-called "sexting" allegations, claiming that online hackers had gained access to his Twitter account and posted manipulated photographs online to politically embarrass him. Weiner's denials resulted in a further frenzy of extended breaking-news coverage about his personal life, as well as other sexting photographs. At its peak during the week of June 6–12, 2011, the Weiner scandal filled 17 percent of the cable news hole, making it the top story of the week. Under intense media scrutiny, Weiner finally admitted sending the explicit photos. The extended congressional breaking-news coverage culminated with Weiner resigning his House seat on June 16.

Finally, the late summer of 2011 arrived, and, as predicted by April's news pundits, a July and early August summer debt ceiling showdown brought another round of extended breaking news from Congress. This time, House Republicans—again propelled by their Tea Party wing—were pushing the Obama Administration to agree to a deficit reduction bill before agreeing to raise the debt ceiling, a statutory increase in the maximum amount the Treasury is allowed to borrow. The breaking-news coverage during this induced budget crisis consumed most of two weeks leading up to an August 2 debt ceiling deadline.

The government shutdown countdown clock reappeared in this second round of 2011 congressional brinksmanship. According to Pew's News Media Index, cable news filled 75 percent of their news hole with debt ceiling coverage during the last week of July, the peak of the crisis. Typical coverage included Fox News' "America in Crisis" while CNN countered with a two-hour breaking-news event titled "Get It Done! Count-down to Debt Crisis." Cable news channels went into breaking-news overdrive. During and after the breaking-news binge, both congressional Republicans and President Obama experienced substantial decline in their public approval ratings. Between May and December 2011, according to Gallup, public approval of Congress declined from 24 to 11 percent.

The debt ceiling news drama ended once again with an eleventh-hour agreement. On August 1, the day before the debt ceiling deadline, the House passed the Budget Control Act of 2011 that raised the ceiling by about $900 billion, cut spending by some $900 billion over ten years, and established a congressional "supercommittee" that was charged with proposing the next round of substantial tax and spending changes by December 2011. Unfortunately, in late November, members of this super-committee declared the supercommittee process as unworkable. The failure of this supercommittee triggered another breaking-news binge, with both sides bemoaning the institutional failure.

The prevalence of breaking-news coverage throughout the spring and summer of 2011 underscores the current practice of news outlets covering Congress by emphasizing urgency, conflict, and drama. Morris (2006) characterizes this sustained breaking-news coverage as seeking to combine the shock of a car crash with the dramatic narrative of a soap opera. An initial news event is "broken" on screen, typifying the immediate shock of the car crash and compelling all news spectators to take heed. The second act of the breaking-news drama, though, is the soap opera. This soap opera drama involves a repeating narrative with a slowly developing story line, lengthy cast of characters, and extended speculation and analysis.

Cable news specializes particularly in the breaking-news format, often conforming to this crash and soap opera narrative. Internet news also has fueled the immediacy and speculation of breaking-news coverage. In reality, not many political stories include truly compelling "crash" and "drama" elements on their own. For this reason, scholars argue that it has become increasingly commonplace to infuse drama into the news to increase the number of stories that can be reported as breaking news (Aday 2010; Bennett, Lawrence, and Livingston 2008). Cable news audiences, particularly, tend to surge during periods of extended breaking news. For example, according to the Nielsen Ratings, CNN's breaking-news coverage of Osama bin Laden's death on Sunday, May 1, 2011, had a 981 percent increase in audience share compared with the preceding Sunday's audience size.

No doubt, cable and Internet news outlets are not wholly responsible for elevating news urgency. Public expectations for more immediate news also elevate the demand for urgent breaking news. News consumers' social media practices also drive news urgency. Individuals' Twitter feeds and Facebook postings raise this public expectation for immediacy. In many cases, certainly, the importance and global implications of news stories require no embellishment on the part of the news provider to communicate urgency. Perhaps the rise of global terrorism has truly increased the need for breaking-news coverage. News urgency is inherent to terrorism news events. Nevertheless, from a perspective of ratings, hits, and subscriptions, news providers are drawn to cover news that inherently contains urgency or can be at least communicated in urgent tones. Likewise, congressional partisans expect that breaking-news and conflict news formats may be means for potentially swaying public attitudes toward their issue positions. Legislative brinksmanship and partisans' coordinated media campaigns contribute to the news drama. Breaking news is a growing part of our news consumption habit partly because it holds news grazers' attention. We next analyze the evolution, audience makeup, and news content of the breaking-news format.

Understanding News Urgency

Breaking news is a style of delivery that has the effect of strengthening viewers' perceptions of news urgency. By news urgency, we mean news that signals immediacy, importance, and drama to viewers. This dramatized political news environment also garners increased audience size (Bennett 2016). Stories delivered in a breaking-news format may heighten viewers' recall of these news items by elevating audience attentiveness and interest. Cable and online news today serve as principal mediums for urgent news; these outlets have grown over time partly due to their capacity to deliver urgent news on demand.

Breaking news is often stories in which events are still unfolding while the news is being reported. Emerging news stories are covered live, often with dramatic tones. Typically, a rolling ticker at the bottom of the television screen may read "breaking news," "news alert," or some other attention-grabbing text. The immediacy of breaking news sometimes leads reporters to expedite or even forego confirming news accuracy. In some cases discussed later, this tendency has resulted in incorrect information being presented to the news audience. The coverage of a breaking news story is often repeated and expanded to fill a time block that may extend for hours, days, or even weeks. To fill this time "hole" and to continue the breaking-news coverage, news producers may ask experts or commentators to speculate or interpret meaning to the still-emerging event. This live, speculative commentary also may risk spurious or unconfirmed conclusions being presented to viewers.

News urgency is communicated in other ways besides the breaking-news format, though. News urgency is also increased by production elements like speakers' tone, their volume, the camera framing, and producers' editing techniques. First, the commentators' tone and volume may affect perceptions of news urgency. These sound elements include faster-paced discussion, heightened voices, frequent interruptions by the commentator, or *crosstalk*, in which multiple speakers talk over one another. Video production techniques also may raise perceptions of news urgency. Close-up frames around speakers, frequent cuts between speakers, rolling or flashing text overlaying the video, and colorful graphics, as well as live and unscripted reporting, may all serve as production styles that elevate perceived news urgency.

Primetime cable news programs are not alone in using these breaking-news techniques. Many of these sound and video production elements are common to the opinion news format discussed in the last chapter. For cable opinion news, a debate or roundtable news show format, one that has diverse commentators engaging with each other to interpret and evaluate a news story, combines opinion with urgency to retain audience. This debate format has the added feature of conflict between speakers to elevate urgency. This political conflict between "guests" and news hosts fits the breaking-news genre since it engages viewers with conflict-ridden drama.

Internet news sources also use production techniques to elevate news urgency. Notably, the tone and graphics used by Internet news sites often are intentional design elements to draw you to a news story. Sensational headlines and eye-catching thumbnail pictures may serve as "clickbait" to increase the click-through rate from a news aggregator site to the news online site. Tone and graphics on Internet news also affects how social media sites spread online news. The 2016 presidential election illustrated the use of social media as a tool for spreading breaking-news content. Thomas Patterson (2016) reveals the general tendency of the campaign news coverage during the 2016 election to have a critical, negative tone about the candidates. The Harvard Shorenstein Center study finds that Clinton received negative coverage in 64 percent of campaign stories while Trump coverage had a negative tone in 77 percent of the stories (Patterson 2016). Certainly, candidate Trump used tone and Twitter to advance salacious news with social media catchphrases like "Make America Great Again," "Build the Wall," and "Lock Her Up." Diana Owen (2017) presents a compelling overview of the campaigns' Twitter rants and press bashing during the 2016 presidential campaign. She also emphasizes the role of social media and Internet news in enflaming partisan voters.

Mutz (2015) analyzes the effects of "in-your-face" politics, particularly how uncivil tones and visual close-ups of cable news result in negative emotional responses with viewers. She makes a persuasive case that the growth of cable news, along with bigger computer and television screens over time, has led to more use of televised close-ups and uncivil political exchanges. Viewers of these uncivil exchanges, according to the experimental findings, have stronger negative perceptions of opposing partisans. Not all the findings are bad, though. Mutz also finds that this emotional arousal resulting from uncivil political exchanges stimulates higher rates of viewers' news attention and recall. In-your-face news formats may catch and hold our attention; however, it comes at a collective cost for our political system.

Evidently, the breaking-news format has a long history in network television and print news. Understanding the evolution, audience makeup, and news content of the breaking-news format clarifies how the breaking-news format is distinct from traditional news coverage. It also implies that the growth of breaking-news coverage is partly due to news providers' and makers' efforts to hold the attention of an increasingly distracted news consumer.

Evolution of Breaking News

Reporting on urgent, emerging stories remains a central purpose of journalism. Thinking broadly, newspapers in the nineteenth and early twentieth century regularly produced *extras*, special editions of the paper announcing important news. The origins of the breaking-news format, though, stems from the advent of radio and television. The term *breaking news* implies that the reporter interrupts, or "breaks from," the regular broadcasting schedule to report some shocking, significant news story. Breaking news may also imply news stories that are still happening as they are reported. In this regard, breaking or emerging news may evoke a metaphor of a breaking wave with the news reporter telling the story as it occurs. Regardless of how we conceive of breaking news, its frequency and influence on public attitudes has grown over time with the growing audiences of twentieth-century radio and television network news broadcasting.

The 1938 radio drama *The War of the Worlds*, for instance, was a fictional account of breaking-news coverage. In the radio drama, mock radio reporters interrupt regular programming to update listeners with special bulletins of a Martian invasion occurring in Grover's Mill, New Jersey. Despite disclaimers from producer Orson Welles that the drama was fictional, a handful of panicked listeners were fooled by the breaking-news coverage, believing that an actual Martian attack was occurring. The tension and anxiety prior to World War II, as well as the realism of the breaking-news format, contributed to the unintended prank.

The breaking-news format during the era of network television used terms like *special report, news bulletin, news flash,* or *news alert* to announce these interruptions from regular broadcasting. These news bulletins announced the assassination of John F. Kennedy, the Apollo moon landings, and Watergate scandal and are remembered by a generation of late-twentieth-century viewers. In 1979, the episodic breaking-news format was developed into a news commentary program. The ABC News program *Nightline* began as a way of keeping Americans informed about the ongoing Iran Hostage Crisis. News anchor Ted Koppel reported each night during the prolonged hostage crisis about the day's events. Koppel's *Nightline* program, though, far outlived the actual crisis, as he continued as host until 2005.

The birth of the Cable News Network (CNN), though, probably did the most to define the prevalence and future of the breaking-news format. CNN, the first twenty-four-hour news channel, was founded in 1980 by American media entrepreneur Ted Turner. It was not until 1996 that both Fox News Network and MSNBC news network joined CNN as competing twenty-four-hour news services. By this point, the role of breaking news for the twenty-four-hour cable news channel was partly defined. CNN had already established the style of news coverage in which news was repeated on a fixed interval to inform and capture the intermittent news audience. Additionally, CNN also established that the audience share for a twenty-four-hour cable news network is not uniform either by time of day or over time. The early morning and primetime (6 to 8 p.m.) viewerships were the peak times for the news audience. Additionally, breaking-news events resulted in a spike of audience share. A singular event defining the role of the breaking-news format and surging audiences was the Iraq I or Persian Gulf War in 1991. The Persian Gulf War coverage in 1991 catapulted CNN audience ratings, largely because the cable channel was the only outlet to provide continuous coverage and to have communications from inside Iraq during the initial hours of the American bombing campaign. As discussed in Chapter 2, the so-called *CNN effect* was coined to assert the influence CNN had on government decision making during foreign policy crises.

Other singular events that have further defined the breaking-news genre would certainly include the contested 2000 presidential election, the September 11 World Trade Center attacks, and Hurricane Katrina. Each of these news events resulted in prolonged breaking-news coverage and a sustained cable news audience. The amount of live coverage of emerging news stories, though, has been further fueled by Internet news, online news blogs and magazines, and social media sites like Twitter. News consumers' demand for immediacy and their attentiveness to the urgent style of news coverage have also resulted in a growing audience for breaking news.

Audience Makeup of Breaking News

The breaking-news format has become an integral part of cable and online news coverage. Generally, cable news outlets have a significantly smaller regular audience than the network nightly news programs. In 2014, for instance, according to Nielsen Media Ratings, an average of 22.6 million viewers tuned into one of the three commercial network news programs on ABC, CBS, or NBC. This network news audience is over seven times larger than the 2014 average audience of about 3 million regular viewers for the Fox, CNN, and MSNBC cable news outlets.

The size of cable news audiences, though, varies depending on the immediacy and nature of news events. News audiences are drawn to twenty-four-hour news channels or websites during an emerging news event, resulting in temporary spikes during the news events. Cable news audience size balloons during and after a breaking-news event. According to the Nielsen Ratings, for instance, CNN's breaking-news coverage of Osama bin Laden's death on Sunday, May 1, 2011, had a 981 percent increase in audience share compared with the preceding Sunday's audience size. News stories with compelling human and visual elements, such as political events, natural disasters, and military crises, temporarily elevate cable news viewership. Related to Congress, cable news audiences surge leading up to November elections, high-profile key votes, or scandals.

Despite these spikes in audience size, the breaking news audience is not substantially different by demographic standards from the news audiences of other news sources. According to Pew's News Consumption Survey, cable news audiences tend to be a bit older, lower income, and less educated than print, radio, and broadcast news audiences.[2] A wide range of Americans watches cable news during crucial breaking-news events. The challenge for cable news producers is retaining these irregular viewers as the breaking-news event fades.

Self-identified "regular viewers" of cable news tend to have a slightly higher level of political knowledge than the average American. The Pew Media Consumption Survey poses four questions about political and economic news events to gauge respondents' political knowledge. For example, 51 percent of regular MSNBC cable news viewers answered three or four of these knowledge questions correctly compared with 37 percent among all respondents.[3] Cable news regulars are more inclined to have higher political interest and enjoy following news compared with regular consumers of other news sources.

Regular viewers of cable news, not surprisingly, also are more likely to express views for preferred news outlets compared with the average American. They are more likely than average to prefer news that "shares your political point of view" and more likely to "trust a few news sources more than others." For example, 37 percent of regular Fox News viewers prefer like-minded news sources, compared with the 26 percent national average. It is worth pointing out again, though, that at least a majority of every regular news audience—radio talk shows, cable news, network news, online news blogs, print, political satire shows, and magazines—states a preference for news that does not have a political point of view.

Despite this last point, one of the most pronounced characteristics of cable news audiences is the emerging partisan and ideological divide between cable news channels. Sixty percent of regular Fox News viewers identify themselves as conservatives compared with 35 percent of all news media consumers. Fifty-eight percent of MSNBC regular viewers identify themselves as Democrats, compared with 32 percent on average. Regular cable news viewers tend to be significantly more politically opinionated; however, this allegiance to a particular cable network may be a function mostly of the opinion news programs aligned to each network, not necessarily the breaking-news programming. That is, the *O'Reilly Factor* on Fox News and the *Rachel Maddow Show* on MSNBC may drive the ideological divide rather than day or primetime headline news formats.

The distinction between breaking-news and opinion news formats also suggests that cable news audiences are attracted and retained for varied reasons. We found in Chapter 4 that the opinion news format tends to incite emotions of its like-minded audience, reinforcing their negative stereotypes of opposing partisans. The breaking-news format, independent of opinion news, may not widen the partisan or ideological divide between cable news channel loyalists. Still, as assessed in the next section, news urgency may elevate viewers' anxiety toward breaking news and political actors. With regard to Congress, breaking-news viewers' anxiety may reinforce other negative associations about Congress and Congress members generally. I assess these associations later in the chapter.

A final trait of the breaking-news audience is its growing reliance on online and social media, particularly among younger and better-educated news gatherers. Americans' hunger for immediacy increasingly is pushing them to Twitter, blogs, and online news sites to get the latest updates on news stories. Starting in 2010, more Americans stated that they relied on digital media sources than those relying on newspapers and radio news outlets. In fact, the percentage of regular consumers of all traditional (print, cable, and television) news sources has declined over the past decade while only followers of digital news sources have steadily grown.

The Internet news audience has undergone some changes as well. Nearly one in five Americans (17 percent) say they got news yesterday on a mobile device, with the large majority of these (78 percent) getting news on their cell phone. Evidently, smartphones and tablets are emerging devices for accessing online news and competing with cable channels for a breaking-news audience share.[4] Paradoxically, the growing availability and diversity of breaking-news sources contrast with the growing percentage of Americans who do not access news. For example, while young Americans are most reliant on mobile devices for news, Pew also reported in 2013 that 29 percent of those under twenty-five years old say that they did not receive any news yesterday either from digital news or traditional news platforms.

In summary, the breaking-news audience divides into a transient group and a regular group. The transients are episodic viewers who tune in when there are salient, emerging news events. Cable news, along with online news increasingly, is the primary basis for citizens to obtain this breaking-news coverage. Regular cable news viewers tend to be more ideological and have higher political interest than regular consumers of other news sources. Otherwise, regular viewers look like and behave like others. A broad range of news consumers rely upon twenty-four-hour cable news during breaking-news events. The public demand for immediacy in news coverage drives twenty-four-hour cable news providers to advance the breaking-news format. Additionally, cable news providers work to brand their news channels in an effort to sustain an otherwise fickle news audience. Breaking news is another means for this branding among these news outlets. Looking to the future, the demand for immediacy and emergence of digital devices is increasingly driving the public to online and social media to access news updates. The demand for breaking news is unabated.

Breaking-News Content

One way of supporting the claim that cable and online news sources use news urgency and conflict to increase their audience is to examine the content of their news agenda. Is the type of news covered in the breaking-news format different than other news sources? Since cable news specializes in the breaking-news format (particularly during the 6 to 8 p.m. time period), significant differences between news sources—print, network, cable, radio, and online—in the types of stories covered would support the view that the breaking-news format is distinct from traditional news.

As discussed earlier, the Pew News Coverage Index (NCI) presents an extensive account of news stories across cable, network, print, online, and radio news sources from 2007 to 2012. Particularly, the NCI presents a weekly summary of how different news outlets fill their respective "news hole," a prescribed time block for attracting a news audience. Each week, the NCI measured the percentage of the news hole filled by different stories across the news media sectors. Thus, we can contrast how the news agenda for network TV news, for instance, differs from cable news. For cable news, the news hole is defined as all news covered during a thirty-minute segment of daytime programming and two thirty-minute segments from primetime (6 to 8 p.m.) programming.

One basis for assessing the breaking-news agenda across news sectors is compare the percentage of the news hole consumed by the top story of the week. We can compare news agendas across outlets by examining how much time is devoted to extended coverage of a single story. Figure 3.2 summarizes the percentage of the news hole, averaged by year, filled by the top story for cable news channels, television network news, and print news. The graph indicates that cable news outlets—the predominant source of breaking news—tend to allocate more sustained attention to the top news story of the week relative to the other news media sources.

The widest departure between news sectors occurred in the presidential election years of 2008 and 2012. Cable news channels filled a much larger percentage of their news holes in these years with the top story of the week compared with print, online, and network news. Consider the week of April 23–29, 2012. During that week, cable news primetime coverage devoted 42 percent of its news hole to the presidential election, according the NCI data. Comparatively, network news filled 11 percent, online news filled 15 percent, and print sources filled 13 percent of their respective news holes to the election during this week. The news in late April 2012 included presidential primary elections in Connecticut, Delaware, New York, Pennsylvania, and Rhode Island, as Governor Mitt Romney approached the delegate count to capture the Republican nomination. This top-story bias of primetime cable news extends beyond presidential elections to include other breaking-news events.

One of the main topics of breaking-news reporting and commentary is political events, particularly coverage of campaigns and elections. Political coverage also includes reporting on Congress and the president. Clearly, though, politics and elections are not the only source of breaking news. Other singular events, such as disasters, extreme weather, violent or terrorist acts, other crimes, high-profile trials, military actions, and scandals, may offer a story line for extended breaking-news coverage. The general point, though, is that cable news content diverges from the news agenda of other media sectors partly due to its heavier reliance on breaking news. Given its 24/7 news mission, cable news aims to be the first place intermittent viewers go to for breaking news. As noted earlier, cable news receives an audience surge during breaking-news events. The breaking-news format evidently gives a heavier dose of political stories to news consumers. For political junkies, cable news can provide a steady dose of extended political coverage, analysis, and commentary. The breaking-news format, thus, affords a likely greater possible impact on our perceptions of Congress and politics broadly. I assess these effects of breaking news next.

The Effects of News Urgency on Attitudes toward Congress

Even if breaking news is distinct in its evolution, audience makeup, and content from traditional news, it does not necessarily mean that these differences matter in affecting public perceptions. We may still question whether these differences affect news consumers' perceptions of the political world. I next turn to an analysis of how news urgency—the expected impact of breaking news—may alter consumers' perception of Congress.

My expectations are grounded in my news-grazing theory that media choice is changing the public's news-gathering habits. More fundamentally, though, news grazing has correspondingly changed the style and content of the news that we receive. As with our earlier analysis of opinion news, I argue that news makers and producers use breaking news to hold the attention of an increasingly distracted audience. Urgent and drama-laden news formats have increasingly supplanted traditional, objective television news.

My analysis of breaking-news effects on perceptions of Congress specifically also builds on my earlier analysis of opinion news. In Chapter 4, my experiment results indicated that opinion news formats affected viewers' perceptions of Congress. Notably, opinion news formats generally leave negative affect toward opposing partisans, reinforcing opposing partisan stereotypes. Opinion news also strengthens viewers' perceptions of the degree of partisanship in Congress by targeting the opposing party leaders. The opinion news format leaves viewers with greater distrust and lower approval toward political institutions in general.

One of the purposes of delivering news in a "breaking" fashion is to create an audience perception of urgency and importance to the story. The tone and production features of the format may grab the attention of otherwise distracted viewers. Of course, the format's tone and production are not the only basis for holding the audience's attention. Clearly, many breaking-news instances are already urgent independent of the tone and production. Some breaking-news stories need no embellishment on the part of the news provider to communicate urgency. The obvious salience of the story itself is enough to attract an audience. Still, less salient breaking-news stories may retain an audience with coverage delivered in urgent tones, intense visuals, and engaging production elements. This breaking-news format may elevate the perceived urgency and perhaps audience anxiety associated with the story.

Two questions are central to assessing the effects of news urgency on viewers. First, are viewers less likely to change channels (click) from breaking news relative to news delivered with a less urgent tone? Second, what residual political attitudes or perceptions about Congress result from viewers who watch or read urgent news? Particularly, do viewers receiving greater amounts of urgent news feel more anxious or threatened by political events? Does news urgency leave viewers with negative assessments of Congress collectively?

Earlier studies address the first question—that greater exposure to news urgency does attract and hold viewers' attention. One study concludes that viewers are strongly attentive to television only about one-third of the time that they are in its presence (Anderson and Burns 1991). Communications and media psychology research has shown that viewers' attention and information processing are affected by news delivered in a breaking or live news format (Farhi 2002; Lang et al. 2002; Miller and Leshner 2007). When news is delivered in an urgent or live format, viewers' attentiveness and recall to the news story increase. Compelling negative visuals that often accompany breaking news enhance memory (Bolls, Lang, and Potter 2001; Lang, Dhillon, and Dong 1995).

As for the second question, news urgency may also alter public perceptions toward political institutions. Durr, Gilmour, and Wolbrecht (1997) find that periods of congressional action (including intra-Congress conflict) correlate with aggregate declines in congressional approval, perhaps even more than congressional inactivity. In fact, public attention to marginally productive congressional activities such as passage of legislation, veto overrides, or procedural actions may trigger lower public assessments of Congress as an institution. Ramirez (2009) extends this finding by showing that changes in congressional partisan conflict also correlates with lower public evaluations of Congress. He examines quarterly congressional approval data from 1974 to 2000 to show that higher party voting within Congress affects how citizens perceive Congress. The more congressional partisans divide on party lines, the less popular Congress becomes.

These studies offer aggregate-level evidence relating congressional activity to institutional approval. I extend this research by offering an individual or micro-level explanation of the relationship between congressional action and institutional disapproval. I test whether exposure to breaking news about Congress affects viewers' political attitudes or institutional approval. Does news urgency, in this case about the congressional brinksmanship related to the federal debt ceiling, leave viewers with negative assessments of Congress collectively?

Like the opinion news experiment discussed earlier, I designed an online, media choice experiment in which subjects' news-gathering habits and attitudes were assessed. The online experiment had participants watching cable breaking news, traditional news, and entertainment programs with a virtual on-screen television and remote control at the ready.[5] The online experiment recorded participants' viewing data throughout the experiment. This click data provides a record of what channel each subject was watching at a given second over the five-minute experiment.

Participants first responded to a series of behavioral "pretest" questions asking their political ideology, television news habits, news program preferences, political knowledge, and partisanship. The research appendix (Appendix I) includes these pretest questions. The battery of questions allows us to control for participants' political and media predispositions that may correlate with news-viewing habits. The principal alternative explanation is that media choice promotes only partisan or ideological sorting. According to this view, commentary news formats, including urgent breaking news, do not affect viewers' perceptions independent of viewers' ideological and partisan predispositions. Viewers merely sort themselves by their grazing decisions. In this case, commentary news formats do not promote institutional distrust but merely reflect it among an already distrustful audience.

The experiment followed the earlier media choice design. That is, subjects selected or chose their level of exposure to any news or entertainment channel. Just like a normal media viewing, subjects had access to a simulated remote control activated with a click of the participant's computer mouse; participants had the opportunity to view programming that included four different news formats and two entertainment programs. Particularly, subjects could choose to watch CNN, Fox News, *NBC Evening News*, the *PBS News Hour*, an ESPN sports clip, or the NBC reality show *The Amazing Race*, all taken from the same mid-December 2011 time period. The CNN and Fox News breaking-news frames included more visual cues related to the breaking-news format compared with the NBC and *PBS News Hour* frames.

The experiment, in this case, assesses whether the choice and length of exposure to breaking-news frames affected respondents' political attitudes. All of these urgent news frames relate to the congressional "supercommittee" and budgetary actions to extend a payroll tax reduction before the end-of-year legislative holiday. The "supercommittee" was a select, bipartisan committee of congressional leaders who attempted to forge a deficit reduction deal in Congress. The committee leaders announced their failure in the urgent news clip. The CNN and Fox News frames include a banner labeling the story as "breaking news" or "news alert," respectively. All four news frames include live coverage and critical (and, at times, emotional) commentary from opposing partisans to elevate news urgency.

The experimental stimulus for subjects, in this case, is the interaction of both media choice and the breaking-news format. Subjects in the experiment were free to view any of the six channels and to decide on the length of their viewing. Subjects that chose to be exposed to longer periods of the breaking-news format received a high "dose" of the experimental condition. In this case, the tones and rhetoric of opposing partisans, along with the production elements of the breaking-news format, may have triggered a stronger emotional response with these viewers about the news story.

There was some variation in the amount of time viewed across channels, but there is not much evidence to suggest the breaking-news formats attracted significantly more viewing than other forms of news that covered the same material. Both CNN's breaking news and Fox News' news alert were successful in attracting more attention than the non-news programming. Perhaps subjects watched more news because they believed that this was purpose of the experiment or that it was the socially acceptable choice. Regardless, I did not find support in my breaking-news experiment that the format attracted or retained an audience.

Particularly, my expectations are that news urgency may have a measurable effect on individuals' perceptions of anxiety toward Congress. I posit that news urgency triggers emotional responses from viewers that often result in higher levels of anxiety and lower levels of institutional approval. After subjects finished the five-minute viewing period, they completed "post-test" behavioral questions about their level of anxiety toward news and their assessment of congressional performance. Again, Appendix I lists the post-test questions.

This series of questions ask subjects a series to gauge whether they felt "nervous," "angry," or "optimistic" about current affairs. The participant's responses are combined to create a measure of news anxiety. The "news anxiety" score increases as respondents express that programming made them feel more angry, more nervous, or less optimistic toward our political system.

Likewise, I assessed my second hypothesis—that breaking news affects viewers' assessments of congressional performance. Participants were asked how Congress was handling its job, whether it could resolve the key issues facing the country, and whether Congress acts in the public interest. A participant's responses to these questions were combined to construct a measure of institutional distrust. Higher values indicate greater distrust of Congress.

Table 5.1 illustrates whether or not an individual's emotional or institutional responses were related to the degree of breaking news they watched in the experiment. The primary independent variable of interest is the number of seconds spent watching breaking news versus nonbreaking news and entertainment-based programming. Nonbreaking news is the excluded variable. We also control for race (white = 1; nonwhite = 0), gender (male = 1; female = 0), age, party identification (seven-point scale, 1 = strong Republican . . . 4 = middle of the road/don't know . . . 7 = strong Democrat), political ideology (1 = very conservative . . . 4 = moderate . . . 7 = very liberal), and political knowledge (0 to 4 index based on the number of correct answers to four fact-based questions reported in Appendix I).

The results reported in Table 5.1 are mixed but provide some evidence that breaking news affects congressional perceptions. Compared with traditional news and entertainment, breaking-news exposure marginally but significantly influences perceived news anxiety and institutional evaluations of Congress. Also, those who spent more time following non-news programming on ESPN and *The Amazing Race* were less anxious about the news, though were no less supportive of the Congress (institutional index). These results indicate that exposure to news coverage of congressional legislative infighting leads to more anxiety, more distrust toward legislative process, and a lower level of institutional support. And when we look at the conventional

Table 5.1 The Effects of Breaking-News Exposure on News Anxiety and Institutional Disapproval of Congress

Variable	News Anxiety	Institutional Disapproval
Seconds of Breaking-News Exposure	.003 (.001)*	.002 (.001)*
Seconds of Entertainment TV Exposure	−.007 (.001)*	.004 (.001)*
Race	.634 (.178)*	−1.413 (.197)*
Gender	−.059 (.169)	−.315 (.187)
Age	.071 (.074)	−.163 (.082)*
Party Identification	.006 (.069)	−.005 (.077)
Political Ideology	.065 (.070)	.010 (.077)
Political Knowledge	.036 (.062)	−.254 (.068)*
Constant	6.150 (.388)*	6.489 (.428)*
R-Squared	.155	.220
N	466	466

Source: Created by the author using original data.
Note: Cell entries are regression coefficients with standard errors in parentheses.
*$p \leq .05$ (two-tailed).

news coverage of Congress versus the breaking-news format, the significant difference is in the level of anxiety. That is, breaking news generates significantly more anxiety among viewers than nonbreaking news.

The reported effects of breaking-news exposure are not large, and it is hard to generalize whether a brief exposure to urgent news has lasting consequences. In reality, most breaking-news stories do not relate to Congress directly. Additionally, the experiment cannot capture the "car crash to soap opera" narrative discussed at the start of the chapter that is common to prolonged breaking-news coverage. Breaking news can be inherently stressful for viewers; thus, it is not surprising that exposure is related to heightened anxiety. Still, the premise is that the breaking-news format is a more common form of news coverage with media choice and news grazing. Thus, Americans generally receive greater exposure to this format and, consequently, are more likely to be affected by it.

Conclusion

This chapter extends the news-grazing phenomenon to another commentary news format: breaking news. First, I tried to substantiate that the breaking-news format has a distinct history, audience, and news content that differentiates it from traditional news delivery. Like opinion news, a breaking-news format engages the audience while also informing them. This engagement occurs through protracted coverage of a single, emerging story line. This coverage of the emerging story often integrates extended live reporting, expert commentary, drama-laden visuals, and a repetition of information.

I also discussed how the tone and production elements of the breaking-news format also differentiates this style of news coverage from traditional formats. Commentators' tone may communicate the urgency and immediacy of the news story. The production elements, with multiple commentators, close-ups, and sometimes uncivil crosstalk, are also identifying qualities of this format. Social media and Internet news sources also make use of tone and other production elements to attract and retain a breaking-news audience.

Today's breaking news is an understandable extension of new media technologies, growing media choice, and our changing news-gathering habits. I discussed the evolution of the breaking-news genre, emphasizing particularly the role that cable news channels have had in elevating public expectations for news immediacy. The breaking-news audience is unique from other news sources in that it expands and contracts greatly with particular news events. This variable audience size to cable news, I argue, incentivizes news producers to prolong breaking-news coverage in order to retain intermittent viewers. Finally, the news content of breaking news is also distinct from other news outlets. Breaking-news coverage provides a much heavier dose of a single, emerging story, in contrast to the news agenda that includes a more diverse presentation of news. National elections are the biggest source of news content for sustained breaking-news coverage. The 2016 election was the most recent and prevalent case. Cable and Internet news sources used elements of the breaking-news format to saturate news consumers with continuous 2016 presidential election commentary.

Finally, I conducted a media choice experiment to test for possible attitudinal effects of breaking-news exposure, allowing participants to watch conventional news coverage and nonpolitical entertainment. Overall, I found some evidence that longer exposure to the breaking-news format may elevate perceptions of news anxiety and congressional disapproval, all else being equal. I am quick to note the limits of this analysis. It is possible that breaking-news effects are ephemeral and short-lived. Additionally, effects may take form with only some viewers or may require a much longer exposure than occurred in the experiment. More research within a media choice framework would be helpful in addressing these limits of the current results.

Despite these limits, I argue that media choice and news grazing promote greater use of commentary news formats and that these formats trigger emotions, along with informing their audience. I also argue that these emotional responses, when applied to Congress, do not present the institution in a positive light. News grazers are more apt to receive negative messages about Congress from commentary news. Breaking news, particularly, delivers a dose of anxiety in which viewers are more likely to perceive that they are nervous, angry, or pessimistic about our political system.

For Congress and the media, breaking news tends to remind viewers of the things they do not like about politics: excessive partisanship, uncivil discourse, or stalemate. The government shutdown case at the start of the chapter illustrates how these negative messages might be filtered through a breaking-news story frame. Ultimately, Congress may be guilty, to some degree, of all these perceived stereotypes. It is undeniable that Congress is slow to act and rife with political conflict. That is, in fact, the nature of representative government. It is important, though, to see that the lens through which we view the institution may accentuate and thus reinforce our stereotypes.

ENDNOTES

1. In this and later chapters, I report evidence from Pew Research Center's News Coverage Index (NCI). Pew systematically sampled and coded news stories by news outlet and week between 2007 and 2012. This content analysis of news coverage followed a multistage sampling process that covered five main sectors: network TV news, newspapers, online news sites, cable news, and radio news. The industry term, "news hole," refers to the space (or time) given to news content during the prescribed time periods. The NCI Project measures a "news hole" for cable news as all news covered during a thirty-minute segment of daytime programming and two thirty-minute segments from primetime (6 to 8 p.m.) programming. The NCI methodology is explained in detail at http://www.journalism.org/news_index_methodology/99.

2. The Pew Research Center reports trends in news consumption from 1991 to 2012. The 2012 Pew report, *In Changing News Landscape, Even Television Is Vulnerable*, analyzes these trends. See http://www.people-press.org/2012/09/27/in-changing-news-landscape-even-television-is-vulnerable.

3. These audience profiles of different news sources make use of Pew's 2012 Media Consumption Survey. The survey results are available at http://www.people-press.org/2012/09/27/in-changing-news-landscape-even-television-is-vulnerable.

4. The Media Insight Project's 2013 report, *The Personal News Cycle*, presents interesting evidence of how media devices are altering how Americans get their news.

5. The breaking-news experiment follows a similar protocol as the earlier ones. Appendix I presents the survey script and gives more detail about the analysis.

CHAPTER 6

Fake News

The term *fake news* broadly refers to news content that consists of deliberate misinformation. The purpose of this fake news presumably is either to intentionally mislead the audience, to entertain the audience (often when they understand the hoax), or to make money for the fake-news producer. Certainly, more than one of these goals may possibly motivate fake-news producers. Fake-news stories that go viral on social media, for instance, can generate significant advertising revenues (as consumers click through to the originating site) while also achieving the producers' political or entertainment ends.

Allcott and Gentzkow (2017) discuss the economics of fake news, offering a market-driven explanation for this emerging news format. They argue that fake news arises rationally from news media providers who generally gather and sell information about the true state of the world. They argue that news consumers cannot costlessly infer the accuracy of news information, particularly in an age of expanding media choice. As presented in earlier chapters, news audiences also are increasingly attracted to news that engages them with emotional appeals. Thus, divisive partisan news and sensationalist breaking-news formats compose a growing share of our news diet. Allcott and Gentzkow argue that fake news generates value for consumers seeking engagement without requiring producers to pay for reporting and fact-checking costs (since the news is fabricated). The social costs imposed on us all, though, due to fake news could be substantial. Generally, they argue fake news makes it more difficult for news consumers to monitor and assess news accuracy and results in skewed public beliefs. These skewed public beliefs potentially reduce public trust in political actors and the news media.

Broadly, this still-emerging fake-news format includes patently false, exaggerated, and satirical stories that appear as regular news to attract an audience. The fake-news concept took a more specific meaning, particularly the patently false brand of fake news, during and after the 2016 election. False campaign stories during the 2016 election inaccurately and negatively portrayed both Democratic nominee Hillary Clinton and Republican nominee Donald Trump, with Clinton featured in a disproportionate share. These fake-news stories were spread to significant numbers of voters largely through social media and political Internet blog sites. This viral spread of fake news via social media platforms and blogs resulted in little independent fact checking or filtering from news consumers. Allcott and Gentzkow (2017) estimate that there were 760 million instances of an Internet user clicking through to read an online fake-news story during the 2016 campaign, about three fake news stories per American adult.[1]

I discuss the different types and broader political significance of fake news in this chapter. However, the focus is largely on one relatively ubiquitous source of fake news, political satire. Satire is a type of fake news, and it is a commentary news format that clearly combines engagement with news content. Current practitioners of political satire cable news programs include Samantha Bee, Trevor Noah, and John Oliver. In the recent past, though, comedians Stephen Colbert and Jon Stewart greatly expanded the fake-news audience, reaching new popular heights with the political satire genre. Appearing on NBC's *Meet the Press*, Stephen Colbert reflected on how his comedic style is a commentary news format expressing political points of view. "I'm a satirist," Colbert remarked. "All satirists make points. Satire is parody with a point. So if I was doing satire and didn't have a point of view, then that would be schizophrenic."[2]

From 2005 to 2014, Colbert's "parody with a point" involved playing the character of a mock political conservative, a bloviating, right-wing parody of the former Fox News commentator Bill O'Reilly. Playing the role of his right-wing character on Comedy Central's *Colbert Report*, Colbert used irony and sarcasm to poke fun at the supposed false reasoning, ideological dogma, or presumed pomposity of politicians. In the National Public Radio interview, Colbert explained what he told his *Colbert Report* program guests before they were interviewed before the live audience: "I say thank you for coming, have you ever seen the show? I do the show in character. He's an idiot. He is willfully ignorant of what you know and care about. Please honestly disabuse me of my ignorance, and we'll have a great time . . . but sometimes they forget" (National Public Radio 2012). In the case of Colbert and other humorists, satire serves as a rich source for humor and real political commentary.

Congress has always been a natural target of humorists' satire. Recent practitioners of the satirical news format have only refined the art. *The Colbert Report*, for instance, had a recurring segment, "Better Know a District," in which Colbert gave a humorous account of a congressional district and an interview with the House member. As part of a "435-part series," the Colbert segment was repeated eighty-four times from 2005 to 2014. The segment followed a common structure, beginning with the district being introduced as "fightin'" (the "Fightin' 15th") and culminating in a mock interview with the House member. Over time, House members became more aware that the segment was not merely free media attention but also a sardonic look at their district and legislative work. Less savvy members unwittingly became drawn into answering Colbert's strange interview questions and made often embarrassing comments. For instance, Rep. Lynn Westmoreland, R-Ga., the cosponsor of legislation to have the Ten Commandments placed in the Capitol Building, was quizzed by Colbert in one episode to name all of the Ten Commandments. The socially conservative Westmoreland, unfortunately, could only name three, and the repeated media coverage of his struggling response did not present him favorably. Several years later, his press aide stated, "I deeply regret letting him go on 'The Colbert Report.'"[3] Eventually, both House Republican and Democratic congressional leaders advised their party caucus members to not appear in the satirical segment.

In 2010, Colbert presented another, more policy-centered take on Congress. He did a series of satirical news stories on safety and legal issues faced by migrant farm workers. United Farm Workers (UFW) president Arturo Rodriguez appeared with Colbert to discuss the UFW initiative "Take Our Jobs," a campaign that challenged U.S. citizens to replace immigrants in farm work. The point of the campaign was to show that few Americans are willing to take on difficult farm labor, and thus, immigrant laborers are not really "taking our jobs." Following the satire, Colbert accepted the UFW challenge, agreeing to take a farm worker's job for a day. Colbert gave a satirical account of hardships faced by migrant farm workers while picking beans and packing corn as his suit-wearing, straight-laced conservative character.[4]

Colbert's satirical UFW story led Representative Zoe Lofgren, D-Calif., then chairwoman of the House Judiciary Committee's Subcommittee on Immigration, to invite Colbert to testify before her congressional subcommittee. And in a surreal moment, Colbert presented yet another layer of satirical irony by testifying before actual House members as his mock conservative persona. "As we've heard this morning, America's farms are presently far too dependent on immigrant labor to pick our fruits and vegetables," Colbert stated in prepared congressional remarks. "Now the obvious answer is for all of us to stop eating fruits and vegetables. And if you look at the recent obesity statistics, you'll see that many Americans have already started."[5] Colbert then continued with a brilliant satire of migrant worker restrictions and congressional dysfunction. He ends with a biting comment of congressional partisan polarization: "I trust that following my testimony, both sides will work together on this issue in the best interest of America, as you *always do* [audible laughter]."

Colbert's satirical treatment of Congress extended to campaigns and elections as well. Most famous was his satire of federal campaign finance, particularly the issue of super PACs. Super PACs are "independent expenditure campaigns" and thus are not allowed to coordinate their spending directly with campaigns by candidates or political parties. Colbert's news segment on the subject followed the landmark U.S. Supreme Court ruling known as *Citizens United v. FEC* (2010), which allows unlimited super PAC campaign contributions and spending by corporations, labor unions, and individuals, again, so long as the spending is "uncoordinated" with candidate's campaign committees. This tenuous distinction between these supposedly uncoordinated, outsider campaigns and candidate campaigns became the butt of the satirical news joke.

Playing his satirical right-wing character, Colbert created his own super PAC—called Americans for a Better Tomorrow, Tomorrow—in 2011 with the professional advice of his guest, Trevor Potter, the former commissioner and chairman of the U.S. Federal Election Commission. After declaring his candidacy for the 2012 presidential election, Colbert signed over control of his super PAC to fellow satirist, Jon Stewart, announcing that the organization would now be referred to as The Definitely Not Coordinating With Stephen Colbert Super PAC. Raising over $1 million, Colbert's super PAC spoofed the unregulated practice of independent expenditure campaigns while labeling campaign finance as the "politico-industrial complex." Speaking as his mock-conservative character, Colbert said his super PAC money would fund not only political ads but also "normal administrative expenses, including but not limited to, luxury hotel stays, private jet travel, and PAC mementos from Saks Fifth Avenue and Neiman Marcus" (Kahn 2010).

Colbert's super PAC satire ultimately won him a Peabody Award as an "innovative means of teaching American viewers about the landmark court decision" (Subramanian 2012). The comedic spoof ultimately drew attention both to the lax state of campaign finance regulation and the inability of Congress to resolve these issues. More broadly, the Colbert case exemplifies how political satire today acts as a powerful and engaging form of news commentary.

Fake News and Political Trust

The broad types and audiences of fake-news stories underscore this format's potential for affecting public trust of Congress and the media. Congress's procedural inefficiencies and partisan nature, in particular, make it a rich target for satirists' humor. Additionally, perhaps there is a reinforcing effect of fake news and media distrust as news audiences further doubt the accuracy of mainstream news sources. Two in three Americans today express a view that fake-news stories cause a great deal of confusion about the basic facts of current events (Pew Research Center 2016).

This fake-news genre took on a nefarious and disturbing turn in the 2016 election as made-up news campaign stories appearing first on ideological Internet sites were spread more broadly through Facebook and Twitter. According to Pew Research, 23 percent of Americans reported soon after the 2016 election that they had shared a made-up news story either knowingly or not. In addition to sharing fake news, 71 percent of Americans after the 2016 election said that they often or sometimes see made-up political news online. The perceived prevalence of fake news is on the rise. These fake-news stories included accounts intended to at least manipulate the public's belief in the integrity of the electoral process, if not their actual vote.

Delivering "fake," "pretend," or faux" news, political satirists often marginalize their influence, dismissing themselves as merely comedic entertainment. However, as the Colbert case shows, the line between political comedy and journalism has blurred (Baum 2003; Reinemann et al. 2012). Geoffrey Baym and Jeffrey Jones (2013) argue that Colbert's (and other satirists) insistence that he is only a host of a fake-news show should not prevent us from recognizing the political impact of satire in a fake-news format. In fact, Baym and Jones (2013) investigate the global significance of satire as this news commentary format extends across many political cultures.

The satire format, while clearly diverging from the standards of traditional news, fits well with other commentary news programs. News audiences increasingly look to these commentary formats just as newspaper readers may have looked to the op-ed page. Political satire affords viewers a mix of news, humor, and commentary (Peterson 2008). The satirical news format certainly does not aspire to or obtain the journalistic values of objective and accurate news. Thus, some may question the claim that satire is a "news format" rather than merely entertainment with some news by-product. Nonetheless, survey research indicates that political satire has growing importance as a news source among American viewers (Pew Research Center 2012b). Further defying this supposed separation between comedic entertainment and news, respondents to a Pew Research Center poll recently named satirist Jon Stewart as the fourth-most-respected journalist (Kakutani 2008). While audience share and reach are limited, political satire represents a fairly unexplored and emerging area of media effects on political attitudes.

As in the previous two chapters, I first give an accounting of the emerging satire news format—its evolution, audience, and news content. Political satire has growing relevance to American politics given the multiplicity of platforms, popularity of contemporary practitioners, and growing audience share. Also, like in the previous chapters, I then turn to explaining why and how political satire matters in shaping public perceptions of trust in Congress. The explanation for why political satire matters is that humor can act as a powerful means for understanding and remembering news. I discuss the role of selective exposure in shaping what citizens understand and remember from consuming political satire. As for understanding politics, satire matters as political humor can serve a very positive democratic role; a growing body of academic research shows that it may sometimes act as a gateway for less informed voters to not only gain political information but also possibly heighten their political interest and later participation. I also relate, though, a more pessimistic account of how satire matters. Particularly, I discuss how satire may elevate viewers' cynicism toward Congress and opposing (or out-)partisan groups. Satire, generally, is an antiestablishment genre poking fun at authority and elite hypocrisy (Peterson 2008). Applied to politics, though, I question whether political satirists have a greater effect on Congress as an institution, beyond just those who are the immediate brunt of the jokes.

This chapter then turns to an empirical assessment of the political relevance of satire aimed at Congress. I report results from two experiments that assess how satirical news affects our political attitudes toward Congress. Political satire has an immediate target and narrative that become the basis for both humor and commentary about Congress (Gray, Jones, and Thompson 2009; Lichter, Baumgartner, and Morris 2014; Yarwood 2004). This research adds to earlier work examining the effects of media choice on news viewers' attitudes toward Congress. Grounded in the larger theory of news grazing, I explore whether viewers' media choices and screening allow viewers to avoid news that they find is less engaging and intentionally choose news that engages and tends to reinforce attitudinal predispositions (Prior 2007). I conclude with some thoughts about becoming more self-aware of our news consumption and its implications for how we see Congress.

Fake Satirical News:
Evolution, Audience, and Content

Earlier forms of televised political humor were generalized in nature, making vague references to corruption of politicians in general. Starting with Johnny Carson's lampoons of politics and politicians on *The Tonight Show* and moving to *Saturday Night Live*'s mockery of President Ford, late-night political humor has become increasingly politicized (Voth 2008). Throughout the 1980s and 1990s, comedic portrayals of presidents Reagan, H. W. Bush, and Clinton became commonplace in sketch comedy programs, as well as in late-night talk show monologues (Compton 2008). During the 2000s, televised humor's focus on the political world became a mainstay in political discourse with the growing popularity of Jon Stewart and Stephen Colbert's mock-news programs (Baumgartner and Morris 2006). The intersection of televised satire and popular culture may have hit its zenith in 2008, with Tina Fey's iconic portrayal of Republican vice presidential candidate Sarah Palin.

The nature of late-night televised political humor, however, varies from source to source. *Saturday Night Live*, for example, is unique with its sketch comedy approach, often parodying the behavior of political candidates during debates but also paying close attention to presidents—particularly during times of high-profile events. The sophistication of this sketch comedy satire on *Saturday Night Live* varies, with some sketches illustrating nuanced satire while others are basic slapstick comedy (Peterson 2008). The programs that are nightly talk shows on the broadcast networks, such as the former *Tonight Show With Jay Leno* and *Late Show With David Letterman*, are blunter instruments that almost exclusively focus on physical traits, scandal, and political blunders (Niven, Lichter, and Amundson 2003; Young 2004, 2006).

Some observers have argued that the talk show forum on late-night talk shows allows the candidates and government officials an opportunity to bypass the "journalist filter" and speak directly to voters, thus facilitating greater communication between political elites and voters (Davis and Owen 1998). Thus, late-night talk shows are part of the larger "soft-news" genre that has the potential to spark political interest and knowledge among Americans who were previously disengaged from the political process (Baum 2003).

Others have argued that the impact of late-night humor on the political process has been less positive, although still significant. As the comics unleash their barrage of jokes that mostly highlight the personal shortcomings of politicians (Niven, Lichter, and Amundson 2003), these characterizations become more prevalent in the mind of the public (Young 2004, 2006)—Bill Clinton as the philanderer, Bob Dole as the old grump, Al Gore as the robotic exaggerator, George W. Bush as the dimwit, and Donald Trump as the angry demagogue. Certainly, late-night comics were not exclusively responsible for establishing these characterizations, but several scholars note their important role in the proliferation. West and Orman (2003) explain,

> Through these jokes, satires, and monologues, it becomes apparent that not only have stand-up comedians become political activists via the impact of their political jokes, but also they help shape the manner in which prominent politicians are seen. (97)

Several scholars contend that the power of comedians to frame the public portrayal of politicians negatively influences democracy. Russell Peterson (2008) argues that simplistic jokes of network comics are antipolitical in nature. Specifically, he classifies the Leno/Letterman/Fallon brand of network late-night comedy as pseudosatire. Instead of genuine satire, which uses humor to "speak truth to power," pseudosatire capitalizes on antipolitical sentiment to "poke fun at" or "kid" those in power. Pseudosatire is typically rooted in the cynical perspective that politicians are self-interested and corrupt, the American public is getting sold a bill of goods, and the system is broken beyond repair (i.e., antipolitics). Peterson (2008) puts forth the perspective that

> late-night's anti-political jokes are implicitly anti-democratic. They don't criticize policies for their substance or leaders for their official actions (as opposed to their personal quirks, which have little to do with politics per se); taken as a whole, they declare the entire system—from voting to legislating to governing—an irredeemable sham. (14)

Similarly, West and Orman (2003) observe that "rather than using humor to engage the public in serious substantive issues, humor deflects from substance and draws our attention to personal or trivial aspects of the political process. When voters form impressions based on a comedian's monologues, they risk debasing civil discourse" (98).

While the traditional network comics continue to rely on simple punch lines that exploit negative stereotypes to generate laughs from a broad audience, sharper political satire has emerged on late-night cable television.

On HBO, Dennis Miller's comedy-based talk show, *Dennis Miller Live*, which emerged in the early 1990s, was heavily political in nature. More recently, *Real Time With Bill Maher* aired on the same channel. These programs have been classified as genuine satire (Jones 2005; Peterson 2008). Instead of simply exploiting antipolitical sentiment to dismissively chaff ancillary shortcomings of politics and politicians (pseudosatire), genuine satire expresses "meaningful indignation" about political issues, ideology, and public policy (Peterson 2008, 25).

Of course, HBO does not have the cable television market cornered when it comes to late-night political satire. Comedy Central began featuring political satire with *Politically Incorrect* in 1993, followed by *The Daily Show* in 1996. Both were presented as "mock" news programs that were integrated with a talk show element. The driving force behind both programs was to create a humor-based talk show environment that dealt more exclusively with politics and current events than their network competitors. Initially, *Politically Incorrect* took this charge more seriously than *The Daily Show*, which was hosted by Craig Kilborn (Jones 2010). However, *The Daily Show* took a much sharper turn toward the political in 1999 when Kilborn left the show and was replaced by Jon Stewart. Stewart took over at an opportune time—right before the controversial 2000 presidential election. During the time of *The Daily Show's* "Indecision 2000" coverage of the election and its aftermath, the program began drawing praise as the best political satire on television. And in the time following the 9/11/2001 terrorist attacks and the subsequent invasion of Iraq in 2003, Stewart began to gain wide recognition not only as a comedian but also as a political commentator (Jones 2010; Peterson 2008).

In recent years, the one satirist who has gained as much notoriety as Jon Stewart is Stephen Colbert, as discussed at the start of this chapter. Initially a correspondent on *The Daily Show*, Colbert began hosting a spin-off titled *The Colbert Report* in 2005. *The Colbert Report* aired Monday through Thursday at 11:30 p.m., immediately following *The Daily Show*. Together, the two programs constituted the core of Comedy Central's political coverage and were widely recognized as the smartest political satire on late-night television, with their credibility rising far above that of "comic" and into the realm of legitimate political commentators (Baym 2005, 2010; Peterson 2008).

Because they were both Comedy Central programs (with the same producer for a time), appeared back to back, and were both "mock" news programs, Stewart and Colbert are often mentioned in the same breath as the "new" brand of political satire in America. However, the two programs took different approaches to lampooning the political world. Jon Stewart satirized by playing the part of the rational outside observer looking inside the often-absurd political world. Colbert, on the other hand, satirized politics by placing himself inside the absurd political world and allowing others to look from the outside. Colbert's format was modeled after conservative talk shows broadly and, in particular, *The O'Reilly Factor* on the Fox News network. Taking on the blustery, hyperpartisan conservative-host role, Colbert would reject "mere" facts in his discussion and debate about politics. The show even included a segment titled "The Word," modeled after O'Reilly's "Talking Points," in which Colbert editorialized with on-screen text to accompany his discussion.

Regardless of their differences in style, the satire of Stewart and Colbert was successful in gaining ratings, and it continues now with new hosts. According to the Pew Research Center's 2012 Biennial Media Consumption Study, the portion of the public that reported watching *The Daily Show With Jon Stewart* at least sometimes rose from 12 percent in 2002 to 26 percent in 2012. *The Colbert Report*, which began in 2005, saw its ratings portion increase from 19 percent in 2008 to 23 percent in 2012. These numbers compare favorably with featured primetime cable television news programs such as *Hannity* (15 percent), *Hardball With Chris Matthews* (18 percent), *The O'Reilly Factor* (26 percent), and *The Rachel Maddow Show* (11 percent).

Stephen Colbert has moved on to CBS's *The Late Show*, but a new generation of comedians is extending the satirical news format. Satirists like Trevor Noah, John Oliver, Larry Wilmore, and Samantha Bee are developing new audiences. The satirical news format, late-night talk format, animated situation comedy shows, and online satire all continue to skewer politicians for their ideological inconsistencies, moral failings, or occasional faulty reasoning. While Congress presents an easy target, in truth, political satire of Congress is relatively rare compared with presidency-centered satire. Lichter, Baumgartner, and Morris (2014) report that only about 5 percent of all jokes on political satire shows actually relate to Congress.

Relative to Congress, the presidency presents a more reliable comedic target for satirists. There are several reasons for this humor bias favoring the executive. Foremost, the audience is likely to have more media access and news information about the president compared with Congress. Thus, this audience has a greater shared context for understanding the humor directed to the executive. Additionally, the president as a singular individual, in contrast to the 535 members of Congress, is more likely to draw satirical humor based on individual attributes or verbal statements. The rhetoric of presidents and presidential candidates is more closely watched and assessed by the news media.

The general effect of presidency-dominated political humor, though, is that it further contributes to public perceptions of an executive-led and -dominated federal system. Defying Article One, Congress is typically presented as a reactionary and obstructionist institution to executive action. Washington-based news coverage generally may be guilty for presenting this media-driven perception, not just political satire. Regardless, political satire adds to public sentiment of a strong executive that transcends constitutional authority.

Political Satire and Public Attitudes toward Congress: Why and How Does Political Satire Matter?

Satire may not affect all news consumers in the same way. In this section, I explain why and how political satire may matter. I present some theoretical motivations for studying satirical news and suggest some expectations for behavioral consequences of political satire. To begin, though, why might political satire affect our perceptions of Congress? I argue that political satire matters by triggering preexisting political beliefs among some recipients. Particularly, I argue that prior political knowledge, selective exposure, and partisan strength frame how this satire triggers preexisting political beliefs. Finally, I argue that humor broadly—and satire specifically—is a potent mechanism for political persuasion. I briefly review cognitive psychology findings that explain this relationship between humor and persuasion.

Political knowledge refers to the capacity to identify, recall, and apply information relevant to understanding political events or institutions. Selective exposure relates to the tendency to increase the length or amount of contact to information that supports an individual's preexisting beliefs. Partisan strength refers to the intensity of one's partisan identity. I argue that satire triggers stronger effects for those recipients with prior political knowledge, longer exposure, or partisan beliefs since they receive a greater sense of the humor. Generally, the ability of satirical news to inform and be retained, as well as entertain, determines whether it has behavioral effects.

This theoretical framework for behavioral effects of satire is grounded in Zaller's receive-accept-sample (R-A-S) model. The R-A-S model proposes that viewers' level of engagement is determinative of whether or not they will "receive," or be able to understand and retain, a given message. If that message is able to fit in with viewers' previously held opinions or outlooks, they are then likely to "accept" the message. Consequently, when asked their opinion about an issue, satirical news audiences will then "select" the opinions that have most recently been "received" and "accepted." By tuning in to a program that seems relevant to their interests, a satire audience is not only receptive to what is being broadcast but likely to accept and store the messages that they are receiving (Zaller 1992).

Satire's effects on knowledge may vary by the satire format and audience makeup. I noted earlier that political satire varies in format and audience from stand-up comedy to the fake-news format. The fake-news program audience, particularly, may have greater political knowledge compared with a general comedy audience. First, the fake-news format is almost exclusively political in its coverage, thus elevating viewers' political knowledge. Second, this political format attracts and requires viewers that have at least minimal background knowledge of politics sufficient to "get" the jokes.

The political sophistication of fake-news audiences (for instance, audiences for the *Colbert Report* and *Daily Show*) have been demonstrated in earlier studies (Baumgartner and Morris 2006; Baym 2005, 2010; Peterson 2008). Additionally, some past survey research has shown positive correlations between exposure to *The Daily Show* and other measures of political knowledge (Young 2004). Baum (2003) and others have argued that soft-news programs, including political comedy, have the potential to inform some segments of the viewership (Baum 2003; Brewer and Cao 2006; Moy, Xenos, and Hess 2006; Parkin 2010).

Selective exposure—the nature and length of a viewer's media choices to news and entertainment media—is a second response to why satire matters. As I have discussed throughout my discussion of news grazing, growing media choice begets audience fragmentation. Particularly, news media choice and the emergence of different news formats have resulted in greater variability among Americans in the amount and nature of news consumption. Some consumers opt for entertainment over news or vice versa.

Prior (2005) argues persuasively that media choice correspondingly increases variability in political knowledge and news informedness. Citizens' media choices between entertainment and news are largely directed by their predisposed levels of political interest. Stroud (2008, 2011) finds evidence of a broad relationship between citizens' partisanship and their news choices. She finds that partisan selective exposure may encourage citizens' participation and help them understand complex issues. However, partisan sorting by niche news sources may also contribute to an already fragmented, polarized electorate. Arceneaux and Johnson (2013) contextualize this finding. They argue that media choice decreases the like-lihood that partisan news polarizes, since like-minded viewers are much more likely to tune in, and opposing-minded viewers are more likely to tune out.

Selective exposure to political satire, though, may affect viewers differently from partisan news. There are several reasons for this differ-ence. First, as noted before, satirical news is watched more regularly by a younger audience with variable political sophistication. Recent works have demonstrated that younger Americans particularly seem to learn substan-tive political issues better through comedic programming than through "straight-news" programming (Parkin 2010). The Pew Research Center found that young (eighteen- to twenty-nine-year-old) males, particularly, use and trust satirical news as a source of news about government and poli-tics (Gottfried and Anderson 2014). Second, selective exposure elevates the framing effects of satire (humor) on a political message. Humor may pro-vide a psychological trigger for receiving and retaining political informa-tion, particularly among younger, less sophisticated viewers. Third, greater selective exposure to satirical news elevates the impact of partisan congru-ence. Satirical news emphasizes emerging, national stories with a clear ten-dency toward election-oriented commentary. Arceneaux (2012) finds that individuals' anxiety toward stories and events may trigger cognitive biases, particularly for loss aversion. Humans' innate distaste for loss triggers an emotive response to information that threatens or counters their partisan predispositions. Greater selective exposure to satirical news thus increases the amount of content parodying political antagonists that implicitly pres-ent a potential threat or loss to most viewers. In these ways, selective expo-sure increases the likelihood of attitudinal effects.

Finally, satirical news may have a differential effect on those who have strong, predisposed partisan identities that are consistent with the humor. The *Colbert Report* and *Daily Show* programs "report" on news that disproportionately pokes fun at conservatives or implicitly supports progressive political agendas. Recent academic and survey studies report that the audience tends to be younger, better educated, left leaning, and more likely to live in an urban area than the typical television viewer (Baumgartner and Morris 2006; Cao 2008; Lichter, Baumgartner, and Morris 2014; Young and Esralew 2011). A 2012 Pew Research Biennial News Consumption Survey found that 12 percent of *The Colbert Report* viewers were Republicans while 38 percent were independents and 45 percent identified themselves as Democrats. In their 2014 report, Pew reported that roughly a quarter of consistent liberals report, use, and trust satirical news (*The Colbert Report*) as a source of information about government and politics compared to a mere 1 percent of consistent conservatives (Mitchell, Gottfried, Kiley, and Matsa 2014).

Academic studies that discuss older satirical programming discuss how the target audience for the antiestablishment form of entertainment fits this same relatively young, left-leaning mold. Cantor (1999) discusses how *The Simpsons* influences the way Americans think, "particularly the younger generation" (Cantor 1999, 734). Carr (1992) discusses the clashes between CBS and the comedic duo the Smothers Brothers regarding the political content of the program *The Smothers Brothers Comedy Hour*, culminating in the network's decision to cancel the program in 1969. Carr (1992) describes how the satirical program's appeal with younger, more urban viewers "created a kind of us versus them rhetoric" (Carr 1992, 13).

A final reason why political satire matters relates to its power to persuade. Contrary to a view that humor is simple or light-hearted, psychology research indicates that humorous messages require more effort to process than nonhumorous messages. A dominant explanation of humor is the incongruity-resolution theory, stating simply that humor occurs when there is an incongruity between what we expect and what actually happens (see Alden, Mukherjee, and Hoyer 2000; LaFave, Haddad, and Maesen 1996). Processing this incongruity involves two phases: a cognitive phase and an affective phase.

The cognitive stage requires us to first compare the message with what the brain knows to be true—based on assumptions and expectations of appropriate behavior—and find that it doesn't line up. This schema inconsistency must be resolved in order to "get the joke." It involves suppressing information recently stored in working memory and replacing it with an alternative narrative that must be retrieved from long-term memory. Then, the affective phase involves determining whether the joke was funny. If it was too absurd or complex for the recipient to comprehend, he or she will not get it—and may not even realize that a joke was intended (Wanzer, Frymier, and Irwin 2010). Neuroscience has found that humor first activates the part of the brain that is associated with ambiguity resolution and then activates the brain's reward network (Goel and Dolan 2001; Mobbs et al. 2003). This complex process instigated by humor may cause the humorous message to leave a greater lasting impression, which will be remembered for longer periods of time than a nonhumorous message.

The satirical news format often combines rhetorical styles like irony and sarcasm to relate a joke with a political message. Irony and sarcasm are complex forms of communication requiring an audience to dissect subtleties in language. This complex language combines exaggeration, caricatures, sarcasm, and parody to clue the audience to a joke. The linguistics scholar John Haiman gives more than two dozen ways that a person can indicate sarcasm with either pitch, tone, volume, pauses, duration, and punctuation (Haiman 1998). The humor requires an engaged, attentive audience. If the audience "gets" it, then they may appreciate the comedy; if they don't, though, they can often feel lost or even mocked.

The persuasive power of political satire partly comes from this higher level of cognitive engagement required by its audience. The comedy audience is more fully engaged. As noted, the comedy audience must follow the satirist's rhetoric and also be sufficiently informed of the news content to appreciate the humor. The side effect of this audience engagement is that it may elevate retention and potentially shape attitude formation.

In summary, my explanation for why satirical news matters in affecting perceptions of Congress rests in how we process political information. As citizens, we do not recall and use all the political information that we may consume. Political information is more likely to matter when consumers have prior political knowledge, when viewers watch more regularly or for longer times, and when viewers share the partisan or ideological views of the information. Finally, humor acts as a powerful means for triggering and retaining information. I discussed the complex cognitive and affective processing required to get a joke. This heightened cognitive demand of humor elevates the likelihood that its audience will use satire to generalize about the political world.

How Satire Matters:
The Effects of Political Satire on Congress

The question of how political satire affects political perceptions has led to a limited amount of research offering tentative but provocative conclusions (Baumgartner and Morris 2012). These conclusions present both optimistic and pessimistic accounts of how humor impacts Congress. The fake-news experimental analysis discussed later in the chapter examines how satire may trigger negative affect (emotions) toward politics. This affective response may lead to heightened cynicism toward politicians and political systems. When Congress is their target, satirists tend to draw attention to individuals or events that confirm viewers' negative predispositions toward the institution. This more negative assessment of satirical effects, though, is not the only view.

There are broader and more optimistic effects of political satire on politics. There is some scholarly support that satire has the potential to elevate viewers' political interest. The affective responses of satirical news may increase viewers' general interest in politics, and political interest is a strong predictor of later participation. The social value of political comedy lies in generating a familiarity with the political world, heightening political interest, and promoting higher political engagement among an otherwise less engaged population of young adults. A second broader effect relates to the persuasive power of humor—and satire specifically. As partisan polarization and political gridlock often prevail in our system of divided powers, satire may serve as a means of changing minds and focusing attention across crosscutting groups.

Prior studies flesh out this argument by exploring the theoretical claim that political humor indirectly promotes participation. Jones (2010) contends that political satire, though often falling short of informing the electorate compared with traditional news, may be a gateway to political participation by strengthening citizens' affective or emotional engagement with politics. While it may fall short in the amount of news content delivered compared with traditional news, political satire may elicit stronger emotional responses, thus increasing viewers' motives for watching politics. Viewers' emotional responses of anger, joy, or playfulness from watching political satire may strengthen their personal identity of beliefs and their perceived connection with like-minded others. Following this argument, this strengthened personal identity affects one's internal political efficacy. Internal political efficacy refers to the belief that one can understand politics and thus meaningfully participate in politics. Political satire may indirectly lead to greater political participation by strengthening less politically engaged viewers' internal political efficacy.

Other studies have tried to test this participation argument with social experiments and survey data (Cao and Brewer 2008; Hoffman and Thomson 2009; Lee and Kwak 2014). These studies have found generally positive but weak results affirming the relationship. The weakly positive results underscore the difficulty in disentangling whether one's preexisting political interest leads to political satire consumption or whether satire leads to new political interest. The chicken-or-egg problem is common in media effects research, and even when disentangling it through experimental situations, latter views imply that regular viewers of political satire programs are solely motivated by their desire for entertainment. The political commentary and interest is a mere by-product of this entertainment. Research on Comedy Central's *The Daily Show* audience indicates that viewers have higher levels of political interest and knowledge than nonviewers (Young and Tisinger 2006). Still, most satirical news viewers claim to watch mostly to be entertained (Young 2013). About 20 percent of *The Daily Show* audience claim to be apolitical (Cao and Brewer 2008), and thus, political information may be an unintended by-product of the laugh.

An individual's level of political interest is stable over one's life compared with other attitudes (Prior 2010). Thus, the determinants of political interest early in one's life are formative to sustaining political interest (and active citizenship) at later stages. Political satire programs tend to attract a younger audience compared with traditional news; thus, there is reason to think that these formats could promote a lasting change in viewers' political engagement. Their relatively youthful audience, reason stands, would have less well-developed news-gathering, partisan, and voting habits. Political satire thus may trigger heightened political engagement over time. The social value of political comedy lies in generating a familiarity with the political world, heightening political interest, and promoting higher political participation among an otherwise less engaged population of young adults.

Beyond the claim that political humor promotes political engagement, there are other claims that it may affect political attitude formation. Political psychology and communications research has found that political humor might have persuasive effects, leading to attitude formation or even change. Advertising studies have long shown how humor can affect persuasion simply by increasing the attention paid to the ad for a particular product (Madden and Weinberger 1982; Zhang and Zinkhan 2006). Positive evaluations of one product over another can be influenced by associations with humor. Humor can elevate audience attention and result in positive associations to a related, substantive message. Political messaging is not entirely distinct from product advertising. A political message associated with humor can persuade an audience with either negative or positive associations. This persuasive capacity of humor is partly due to the higher degree of cognitive engagement required for processing humorous messages that I discussed earlier. Since both cognitive and affective processing is required for getting the joke, the likelihood of the joke having some persuasive influence may be greater than other information.

Besides the possible positive effects of political humor, there are also claims that satire may have detrimental consequences. How, then, does satirical news have negative effects on politics? I argue that satire heightens political cynicism toward political elites and institutions (and, in my study, Congress particularly). The intent of satire, generally, is both to tell a joke and to invoke constructive social criticism. The wit draws attention to the societal condition. Applied to politics, satire serves to reveal the inconsistencies and failings in politics broadly. Thus, as a regular source of information, satire may act to confirm and, in fact, elevate public cynicism toward Congress. Political satire, like uncivil debate and crosstalk discussed in Chapter 4, tends to lead viewers to generalize these negative behaviors toward Congress as a whole. Mutz and Reeves (2005) report experimental results showing the effects of incivility among political elites. Subjects were exposed to a mock political debate between two candidates that was professionally staged and produced using trained actors. The experimental manipulation was whether the candidates used civil or uncivil language, with the scripts being carefully modified to control for the effect of uncivil language. The results are subtle but generally show that uncivil political discourse suppresses viewers' trust in politicians and politics.

Other studies corroborate Mutz and Reeves's (2005) conclusions. Forgette and Morris (2006) extend this finding by showing similar effects of conflict (or debate-style) commentary news shows. They find, through experimental results, that subjects exposed to political talk programs in which dueling hosts interrupt, name-call, and talk over each other leave with a heightened cynicism toward politics. Baumgartner and Morris (2006) compare election coverage between political satire and traditional news formats. They show that viewers of *The Daily Show*, compared with viewers of traditional news, are more likely to receive an exaggerated, negative portrayal of candidates, and consequently, these satire viewers report less trust in the political system. Viewers of *The Daily Show* report not only higher levels of confidence in their own abilities to understand the political landscape, they also report stronger negative feelings toward political candidates, a wide spectrum of political institutions, and the news media generally (Baumgartner and Morris 2006).

Beyond political cynicism, another effect of satire may be alienation toward select political elites or groups, particularly those elites and groups that are the target of the satire and which the viewer is predisposed to oppose. I will refer to these opposed targets of satire as *out-groups*. They represent those organizations—opposing parties, partisans, or media—that a significant share of the audience already may distrust. Political satire serves to prime and reinforce those predispositions. I would expect that viewers' alienation or dislike would be stronger after exposure to political satire, particularly for out-groups.

In the next section, I present and report results from two political satire experiments evaluating my expected political effects of satire on congressional cynicism. The first design and experiment is a forced-choice experiment in which subjects are randomly assigned to one of three conditions or to a control group. The latter research design parallels the earlier selective-exposure experiments assessing how public attitudes toward Congress are affected by opinion (partisan) news and breaking-news formats. Like the earlier experiments, this second political satire experiment integrates media choice, allowing subjects to engage in news grazing, a behavior of casual or unintentional news gathering. I elaborate on these results next and present results from the two experiments.

Assessing the Effects of Political Satire on Congressional Cynicism

I have presented a case of why and how satire may matter to public perceptions of Congress. Notably, I have argued that political satire triggers and reinforces viewers' political predispositions via consumers' selective exposure. Media choice elevates selective-exposure effects, and political satire tends to reinforce a predisposed view of political institutions and actors. Applied to Congress, satirical news typically reinforces a negative view that legislators are less than wholly public minded, and congressional processes obstruct positive change. These reinforced perceptions contribute to greater public distrust toward Congress.

I hypothesize that this selective exposure results in greater distrust toward Congress, cynicism toward politicians, and out-group alienation. Following the discussion of why and how political satire matters, I hypothesize that satire will have a greater impact depending on subjects' prior political knowledge and stronger partisan identity, partly by increasing selective exposure. As noted, younger, left-leaning individuals with slightly higher political knowledge are more likely to regularly consume satirical news. Satirical news is more likely to matter when consumers have political knowledge, when viewers watch more regularly or for longer times, and when viewers share the partisan or ideological views of the humor.

I assess the conditional impacts of satire on political attitudes toward Congress. Particularly, I offer three explanations for why behavioral effects are elevated from satirical news. First, satirical news may attract viewers who have political knowledge sufficient to get the joke but not enough that their attitudes are resistant to change. This political sophistication, additionally, may elevate their attention to satirical news and thus may elevate their capacity to retain new information. Political satire combines news content with a powerful framing device: humor. The humor frame promotes subjects' capacity to recall that information. Second, I argue that a recipient's self-exposure to satirical news increases the likelihood of attitudinal effects. The length of satirical news exposure is conditioned partly on the congruence of political views between the humor and the audience. Political satire likely triggers viewers' cognitive biases for agreeing with congruent information. Sustained, self-exposure elevates the likelihood that these biases are triggered and information will be retained. Third, current satirical news programs attract a left-leaning audience that includes viewers who may be predisposed to agree with the political message of the jokes. These confirmatory cues elevate the likelihood that information is received and retained. Viewers are more likely affected when congressional targets of satirical news are to the political right.

I designed two experiments to test these hypotheses. Both of these experiments were conducted online and drew nonrandom samples using Mechanical Turk. They both followed the same pretest/post-test questionnaire design and used congressional budget news stories as conditions for assessing congressional attitudes. The main difference between the two experiments, though, was in the role of media choice and selective exposure. The first research design was a forced-choice experiment that restricted subjects from selectively choosing between entertainment and news options. Subjects in this forced-choice experiment were asked a series of pretest questions regarding their perceived feelings (warmth) toward political leaders and parties and their political knowledge, partisanship, and demographics. Subjects were then exposed to a different news stimulus and were then asked to complete a battery of post-test questions regarding their perceived trust in Congress, political cynicism toward politicians, out-group alienation, and media trust. The pre- and post-test questionnaire is included as Appendix II.

This first satirical news experiment randomly assigned subjects to one of four conditions: a "fake" satirical news condition, a satirical news condition, a straight-news condition, or a control group (that received no news story). The first two conditions were the primary test stimuli for assessing the satirical news hypotheses. They differed only by a prompt in which Condition 1 subjects were told explicitly that the forthcoming story was "fake" satirical news, thus allowing me to test whether satirical news consumers mistakenly believe that the satirical story is actually a real news story. The satirical news conditions then included a brief story from the online satirical news site, *The Onion*. The brief satirical news story was titled "Obama, Congress Must Reach Deal on Budget by March 1, and Then April 1, and Then April 20, and Then April 28, and Then May 1." The story parodied the procedurally complex and highly partisan congressional budget process. According to the parody, "[e]xperts say that without reaching a deal this Friday, the automatic $85 billion reduction in government spending will immediately slow the U.S. economy and impact thousands of middle-class citizens. Officials said the same exact thing will happen next month, the month after that, and the month after that if Obama and Congress fail to meet deadlines created by the preceding, incomplete deals."

This "fake" satirical news experiment permits an initial test of whether political satire affects attitudes toward Congress. Since it does not permit selective exposure, I expect results to be muted. I assess effects across three different dependent variables: congressional distrust, political cynicism toward politicians, and out-party alienation. Again, Appendix II includes the post-test questionnaire. The political cynicism measure is an additive index score including three questions asking agreement with whether "most politicians are competent," "politicians put their own interests ahead of the public's interest," and "politicians are not in touch with life in the real world." Similarly, I assess out-party alienation with subjects' agreement to whether "Democrats [Republicans] in Washington don't seem willing to work with Republicans [Democrats]." I hypothesize that exposure to satirical news would increase out-party alienation.

Table 6.1 presents the findings across the different dependent variables. I find no significant effects for my satirical news conditions. There is no difference in results between Conditions 1 and 2, and thus, I report results combining these two test conditions to simplify presentation. The political knowledge index and partisan identification variables are both strongly significant. Subjects with lower political knowledge (an index score of four different knowledge questions) who indicate stronger Democratic Party identification (a seven-point party identification scale) have significantly higher congressional distrust and cynicism. However, the main finding of this initial forced-exposure experiment is that I do not find the satirical news condition independently affects public attitudes toward Congress.

I also completed a second, media choice experiment. This media choice experiment allowed subjects to avoid news or to choose between different news formats, including satirical news. Arceneaux and Johnson (2013) employ innovative experimental methods—particularly selective-exposure and participant preference experiments—assessing how media choice alters the relationship between partisan news exposure and perceived party polarization. Their studies examine how media choice affects partisan polarization as opposed to attitudes toward Congress. Nonetheless, they argue convincingly that traditional, forced-exposure designs limit the external validity of many news media experiments.

Table 6.1 "Fake" Satirical News Experiment Results on Attitudes toward Congress

	Congress Distrust	Cynicism of Politicians	Democratic Alienation	Republican Alienation
Satire	.124 (.078)	−.045 (.209)	−.072 (.110)	.158* (.080)
Party ID	.071* (.016)	.016 (.046)	−.015 (.023)	.057* (.016)
Pol. Knowledge	.157* (.024)	.239* (.064)	.133* (.032)	.116* (.025)
Gender	−.087 (.059)	−.001 (.161)	.143 (.084)	.179 (.061)
Race	.004 (035)	.129 (.091)	.003 (.046)	.015 (.031)
Age	.029 (.048)	−.031 (.121)	−.089 (.066)	.011 (.044)
Constant R^2 N	2.91* (.188) .09 807	10.40* (.489) .03 807	3.02* (.264) .04 807	3.21* (.183) .05 807

Source: Created by the author using original data.
Note: Cell entries are regression coefficients and standard errors.
*$p \leq .05$ (two-tailed).

I contrast findings from a second online selective-exposure experiment with the earlier results. In this second experiment, participants watched a simulated television with a virtual remote control at the ready. This simulated television allowed subjects to watch and click between six different cable news and entertainment programs for about five minutes. Subjects may have viewed programs that include conventional news formats, political satire (fake) news, and entertainment programs. Specifically, subjects may have chosen to watch *CNN Headline News, NBC Evening News, The Daily Show With Jon Stewart, The Colbert Report,* an ESPN sports clip, or the CBS reality show *The Amazing Race.* All these video clips were taken from the same time period, and all of the conventional and satirical news programs focused on congressional budget negotiations. I thus controlled for temporal and news content effects.

The online satirical news experiment allowed me to record "click" data for each participant. That is, I recorded what program each subject was watching for each second of the five-minute experimental condition, allowing me to gauge grazers' news and entertainment decisions. Broadly, this click data gives information about when, where, and how often subjects clicked between programs. I sum the total seconds viewed per channel for measuring strength of program exposure. Particularly, I use each subject's seconds watched of satirical news as a measure of his or her selective exposure. The experimental stimulus thus is an interaction of satirical news and a subject's media choice. Within this selective-exposure experiment, subjects' viewing decisions allowed for them to avoid all news or to intentionally select a preferred news format, thus increasing the external validity of the study's findings.

Again, the media choice experiment assesses whether the length (seconds) of subjects' viewing of satirical news affects their perceptions of Congress, politicians, opposing parties, and the media. A control group of random participants did not have the remote control along with the virtual TV. They only could watch ESPN for the experiment before completing the post-test questions. This media choice design does come at a cost of internal control since I did not randomly assign subjects to specific treatments. Instead, subjects chose their level of treatment. Additionally, subjects could have the same number of seconds viewed of satirical news but have watched at different times during the five minutes. Thus, the selective-exposure experiment does not ensure an identical treatment among supposedly similar subjects. Despite these limits, media choice and selective exposure offer greater external validity in comparison to the forced-choice experiment. Forced-choice news media experiments artificially constrain viewing habits in an age of media choice.

The media choice experiment also offers a test of the self-selection thesis. I argue that media choice increases effects of distrust or cynicism toward Congress. Selective exposure results in viewers seeking and retaining information that conforms their political predispositions. The hosts and content of the two satirical news formats—the *Daily Show* and *Colbert Report*—are more overtly left leaning than the earlier *Onion* satirical news condition. Satirical news may also attract a younger, less informed audience compared with other news formats.

Table 6.2 reports the results from the selective-exposure satirical news experiment. After grazing between news and entertainment for about five minutes, participants were next asked the post-test questions presented in

Table 6.2 Selective-Exposure Satirical News Results on Public Attitudes toward Congress

	Congress Distrust	Cynicism toward Politicians	Democratic Alienation	Republican Alienation
Satire	.002*	.008*	−.004*	.003*
	(.001)	(.003)	(.001)	(.001)
Party ID	−.005*	−.142	−.431*	.257*
	(.030)	(.110)	(.037)	(.037)
Pol. Knowledge	.169*	−.443*	.020	.138*
	(.030)	(.114)	(.047)	(.040)
Gender	.244*	−.392	.185	.027
	(.082)	(.316)	(.118)	(.103)
Race	−.046	.431*	−.034	−.069
	(.052)	(.186)	(.058)	(.055)
Age	.002	−.136	.044	.023
	(.032)	(.121)	.046	(.038)
Constant	2.91*	12.02*	5.05*	2.28*
R^2	(.235)	(.948)	(.355)	(.333)
N	.12	.09	.28	.21
	394	394	394	394

Source: Created by the author using original data.
Note: Cell entries are regression coefficients and standard errors.
*$p \leq .05$ (two-tailed).

Appendix II. These post-test questions and measures are the same as in the forced-choice experiment. However, the "satire" independent variable is the selective exposure of viewing satirical news, in seconds.

The results indicate some support that selective exposure to satirical news may contribute to negative affect toward Congress. Longer viewing of the satirical news is significantly related to greater distrust toward Congress and cynicism toward politicians. Subjects who viewed *The Daily Show* and *Colbert Report* for longer periods reported slightly less alienation toward Democrats and greater alienation toward Republicans. Republican identifiers are more likely to distrust Congress and express cynicism toward politicians. Expectedly, Republican identifiers report stronger alienation toward Democrats, and Democratic identifiers report more alienation toward

Republicans. Overall, these results, compared with the forced-choice model, provide stronger evidence for the argument that selective exposure to satirical news marginally contributes to jaded views of Congress.

Conclusion

Fake news fits with the general thesis that commentary news formats are partly outgrowths of expanding media choice and our growing news-grazing tendencies. This news grazing implies that viewers increasingly engage in directed browsing and screening of their news. Expanding media choices are elevating the potential of selective exposure. The news-grazing habit draws us to emerging news formats like opinion, breaking, and satire news that engage us while also informing. That mixture of engagement and information, though, often leads to more critical, negative reports of Congress and the media.

This chapter places political satire within the broader class of commentary news formats and assesses how fake news broadly may alter our views of public trust in Congress. I began by introducing the broad idea of fake news, underscoring its impact in the 2016 election. The chapter then discusses the evolution of satirical fake news while reviewing why and how political satire may matter in our perceptions of political institutions. Finally, I assessed these explanations with two experiments testing how satirical news affects public attitudes toward Congress. These experimental research designs were grounded in a selective-exposure theory of news consumption, allowing participants to make their own media choices within the constraints of select programs. While reality permits even more media choice than viewing news options presented in the experiment, I can at least approximate the effects of media choice as an intervening variable in assessing how satirical news affects viewers' institutional distrust and out-group alienation.

An alternative explanation to these effects, as discussed earlier, is that media choice (and news grazing) merely promotes political sorting—conservatives view conservative partisan formats, liberals view liberal partisan news, and, in the case of satire, cynics watch satirical news programs. According to this alternative view, commentary news formats broadly do not independently contribute to viewers' negative assessments and distrust of political institutions. Viewers merely sort themselves by their grazing decisions. Satirical fake news does not promote negative attitudes toward Congress but merely channels or reflects an audience already cynical toward politicians. Cynical or partisan viewers choose to consume satirical content because it offers confirming evidence for their current political views.

The selective-exposure experiment offers some challenge to this alternative view. I find some evidence that satirical fake news promotes greater cynicism or out-group alienation once controlling for self-identified partisan and ideological beliefs expressed before the experiment. The findings may further indicate the importance of including choice into news media experiments. They also underscore that the satirist's joke is often on Congress and that these jokes are not benign toward viewers' institutional assessments.

As with the earlier assessments, my conclusions regarding satirical news are troubling for Congress as an institution. Satirists may claim that they are mere comedians who tell jokes, and no doubt, congressional polarization and obstruction promotes political cynicism independent of commentary news. Still, the lens through which this institution is viewed may alter citizens' perceptions. Satirical commentary may affect viewers' perceptions of congressional and opposing party distrust. Viewers of political satire may be slightly less trusting toward Congress, politicians, opposing partisans, and the media. I argue that commentary news tends to communicate a more salacious view of members' behavior, partisan polarization, and institutional dysfunction that heightens viewers' emotion and anger toward the institution. Satirical news viewers tend to be younger and left leaning; thus, this heightened political cynicism may have particular electoral and partisan implications.

Ultimately, congressional distrust matters in how citizens interpret congressional actions and how voters perceive partisan choices. Low levels of public trust may ultimately undermine popular legitimacy in the legislative process and legislative outcomes. When legislative institutions fail to promote compromise and crosscutting coalitions that promote responsive government, Americans lose faith in their democracy, and there is less credibility in policy outcomes. The final chapter builds on these concerns. I analyze the significance of an increasingly unpopular Congress, linking it back to news grazing and commentary news formats.

ENDNOTES

1. Despite the prevalence of fake news during the 2016 campaign, Allcott and Gentzkow also argue that it was unlikely that fake news was determinative in the Trump victory. News consumers rely on many news platforms and sources, and they find that social media was not the most important source of election news for most Americans. Consequently,

while there may be broader social effects of fake news, the authors conclude it did not change the election result.

2. Colbert appeared on *Meet the Press* on October 14, 2012. For a transcript of the interview, see http://www.nbcnews.com/id/49406385/ns/meet_the_press-transcripts/#.VsNXzuZGmYt.

3. Read "Congress Cools on Congress" at http://www.politico.com/story/2010/09/congress-cools-on-colbert-042929#ixzz43jko0NqN.

4. The Colbert Report episode occurred in two parts and can be found online at http://www.cc.com/video-clips/xr7q4y/the-colbert-report-fallback-position---migrant-worker-pt--1 and at http://www.cc.com/video-clips/puxqvp/the-colbert-report-fallback-position---migrant-worker-pt--2.

5. Colbert's testimony can be found online at https://www.youtube.com/watch? v=k1T75jBYeCs.

Overexposed

Americans' changing news consumption habits are affecting their political trust. News grazing affects what news we view and, correspondingly, how we view Congress and the media. The growth of media choice and grazing behavior is altering the relationships between news producers, news makers, and news consumers. In some ways, media choice lessens media effects on viewers by permitting us to merely avoid the news content we do not want to consume. For instance, I found that viewers most likely to have negative responses to conflict-ridden news or who are ideologically opposed to a specific, partisan news format can simply tune out.

In other ways, though, media choice and news grazing indirectly increases the potential for media effects. Particularly, news producers have increased the amount and variety of commentary news formats in order to hold the attention of the increasingly distracted news grazers. News makers have also directed more effort and resources toward communications strategies to advance their political goals. Congressional partisans, particularly, have used the expansion of online and cable news, as well as social media, as means to mobilize and extend their electoral base. As a result of these mediating changes from news producers and makers, viewers are more likely to be exposed to commentary news formats. Additionally, news consumers are increasingly sorting themselves politically through their news media choices. This heightened exposure to like-minded commentary news formats reinforces viewers' political predispositions and heightens their emotional response to news.

Broadly, our changing news-gathering habits are affecting our political attitudes. The lens from which we see the political world is more colored. In this concluding chapter, I start with a quick review of the news-grazer thesis, arguments, and evidence. The next part of the chapter evaluates the implications of the grazing phenomenon. Particularly, I return to my discussion in Chapter 1 about Americans' dislike of Congress and the media. What does it mean for Congress to have public approval rates persistently in the low teens or even single digits? What do these low approval rates say about not only Congress but also today's voters and the media?

I argue that Congress and the media suffer from *overexposure*, an over-reporting of commentary that activates the public's affective partisanship, presents more negative media frames of the legislative process, and increasingly distracts members from their legislative business. Overexposure denotes that Congress receives too much media attention in formats that are more likely to trigger emotional responses among news consumers. Congress is overexposed because it presents an accessible and willing target for negative and polarizing media coverage. I argue that congressional partisans increasingly seek out this polarizing media to mobilize their partisan base and advance partisan issues. Additionally, commentary news formats retain a distracted, news-grazing audience. However, overexposure comes at a collective cost.

This overexposure thesis implies negative consequences for voters, Congress as an institution, and the media. Overexposure contributes to voters' distrust of opposing congressional leaders and disenchantment with the legislative process. Low congressional approval contributes to higher congressional electoral volatility. An overexposed Congress has institutional implications as well. Congress's capacity to use its internal organization to form bipartisan agreement has eroded with excessive media attention. I note the decline of the congressional committee system and conference committees as mechanisms for forming legislative majorities as parties have captured greater agenda control in the House and Senate.

Finally, I extend the overexposure argument to the media itself. Salacious coverage of Congress reflects badly on both Congress and those who report the news. Media distrust contributes to less public learning from the news and promotes a growing partisan electoral divide. This partisan divide in media distrust has expanded as strong Republican identifiers' express disaffection from mainstream news. This Republican disaffection has been reflected and fueled by the 2016 election of Donald Trump. In short, an overexposed Congress promotes low institutional trust and has political significance for voters, Congress, and the media.

A Summary of the News-Grazing Theory

First, let me review the argument and evidence presented in earlier chapters. I began by introducing the news-grazing concept and evaluating its origins. I also presented a news-grazing theory in which media choice is transforming how we gather the news, how news is made and produced, and, ultimately, how we perceive the news. The news-grazing model, presented in

Figure 1.1, implies that our news-gathering habits are transforming the way news makers and producers present Congress and conflict. Greater exposure to news urgency contributes to a growing public agitation toward public affairs generally. Greater exposure to conflict-oriented coverage contributes to a growing public distrust toward opposing sides. Finally, greater exposure to fake news leads to public cynicism or disengagement toward the institution. This news-grazing theory has broad implications, but I focus on its effect on politics and political institutions, notably the U.S. Congress. While Americans have rarely expressed high approval of Congress, public approval more recently is reaching lows. The news-grazing theory is one explanation among several of why we disapprove of Congress as an institution.

Chapter 2 provides an account of news-grazing behavior. I first describe news grazers in demographic terms. While grazers are younger than average, they are no less informed or engaged than nongrazers. I next contrast grazing to a related but distinct selective-exposure concept. Grazing includes a sometimes distracted and often inadvertent roaming news-gathering behavior, suggesting that news is not always intentionally selected. The analytical question, "Why graze?" is the focus of the remainder of Chapter 2. I give some contrasting explanations for news-grazing behavior and find support for all of these theories.

One explanation for grazers is a gratification hypothesis, suggesting that grazers are largely in search of entertainment. If they enjoy politics, they may briefly watch the news. If not, perhaps they stop watching the news altogether and instead replace news with entertainment—sports, sitcoms, or reality shows. A gratification view implies that media choice and grazing is widening the gap between a consciously active citizenry and a disengaged public relatively disinterested in the news. My results indicated some support for this gratification hypothesis.

A second explanation, a partisan selective-exposure hypothesis, suggests that grazers may be actively searching for and selecting news that fits with their predisposed political views (Stroud 2008). Partisan selective exposure assumes that people prefer and remember news that they already agree with. Most Americans claim in surveys that they do not prefer like-minded news. However, if Americans generally still express a preference for objective news and analysis, why do we gather news in ways that promote partisan news stratification? My results indicate some support for the contention that partisans search for and stay tuned longer at like-minded news outlets.

Finally, I offered a third hypothesis implying that grazers are not largely moving away from the news, nor are they searching for like-minded news.

Instead, they are increasingly expecting news that engages them. Grazers prefer news that both informs and entertains. This new media explanation implies that grazers sample from a broad range of media platforms and program formats. News must engage grazers, though, to hold their attention. This new media explanation implies that media consumers with low political interest are not wholly divesting from the news, as a uses and gratification explanation would predict. These Americans are still collecting some news, albeit in a different form. Additionally, I argue that the way they are collecting news, grazing, affects what and how news is produced.

It is this latter point that I explore in Chapter 3 on commentary news. I make the case that media choice has transformed information economics. Hard-news reporting, I argue, is becoming a public good for which news agencies have weakening economic incentives to provide. Growing media choice increasingly turns headline news into a commodity, a product that is largely undifferentiated across suppliers.

In response to changing information economics, the news is increasingly customized to match both our political and entertainment interests. News makers and producers are adapting to our changing news-gathering habits. Expanding media choice has led news makers to generate stories and information that anticipate media producers' demand to hold a news audience while also advancing news makers' political goals. I evaluated concepts of the permanent campaign, direct communications, and message politics—all communications strategies to help copartisans achieve political goals.

News producers, likewise, are crafting news stories to achieve their goal of engaging and retaining a fickle news audience. One way of achieving this goal is with more commentary news formats. Opinion, urgency, and entertainment are integrated with straight news to retain grazers' attention. I report evidence that commentary news formats are filling a greater share of the news hole across cable and online news platforms. Other news media platforms—newspapers and network news—have not adapted to commentary news as much. These platforms have a smaller and older audience share over time. In summary, I argue in Part I—Chapters 1, 2, and 3—that media choice has transformed our news habits, which, consequently, is resulting in fundamental changes in what and how news is reported.

In Part II, I explore the effects of commentary news formats on attitudes toward political institutions, particularly Congress. Chapters 4 through 7 describe and evaluate commentary news formats. I describe the audience composition and news content of commentary formats laden in urgency, opinion, and entertainment. Each chapter includes analysis of experimental and survey evidence indicating that commentary news promotes political distrust independent of viewers' self-selection of the media choices.

I analyze partisan news formats in Chapter 4 by exploring the prevalence and effects of political talk shows. Like earlier studies, I find that opinion-based news promotes partisan selective exposure. Partisan news hosts attract an audience of politically like-minded viewers. I also find that partisan news viewers have high levels of political interest. The news content of partisan news varies by audience makeup; however, the common feature is stories and guests that trigger negative assessments of opposing parties or groups. My experimental results generally show that partisan news can promote hostility toward what we call *out-groups*, individuals or organizations that have opposing views from the partisan news host. Higher rates of anger are reflected in partisan news, which triggers negative stereotyping, viewers' agreement with general labels, and criticisms of the political opposition. Anger and distrust are triggered with loud, interrupted exchanges between hosts and the "guests" from the opposing side. These uncivil, partisan-charged formats are intended to grab the attention of potential viewers, as well as hold the interest of those who selectively expose themselves to the program.

I next analyze news urgency in Chapter 5 by exploring the growth and effects of breaking-news and conflict-ridden news programs. Media coverage of the 2013 government shutdown, for instance, presented a case of how extended breaking news may affect perceptions of Congress. News urgency broadly is media format that intentionally elevates immediacy of a story and correspondingly viewers' engagement toward the event. Cable and online producers have increased the amount of "breaking news" or "news alerts," often repeating and extending coverage of stories that have strong visual appeal and trigger viewers' emotions. Breaking-news coverage related to Congress often presents partisan conflict, obstruction, or scandal. The analysis of news urgency found that breaking-news exposure led to greater anxiety toward news and Congress.

Finally, the behavior effects of fake or satirical news is assessed. I discussed the broad concept of fake news, particularly in the 2016 election, before focusing on political satire as a source for fake news. Humor has always had a place in politics; however, media choice has expanded its appeal for distracted news grazers. I argue that satire broadly can have a powerful impact on selective exposure and retention of news. Compared with straight news, satirical news requires higher levels of cognitive engagement to "get the joke." This engagement elevates the persuasive effects of the satirical news format. Satire can have positive effects on viewers by increasing their political interest and news retention. In this way, fake news can broaden the news audience. However, I also found that fake-news exposure results in more cynical views toward Congress, reinforcing negative stereotypes of opposing partisans.

Evaluating the evidence overall, a new media explanation for news grazing is a compelling model for changing news-gathering habits. Commentary news formats affect public attitudes toward Congress and the media in negative ways. My analysis supports the other partisan selective-exposure and gratification explanations as well. However, the commentary news theory, though, includes a broader explanation of changing relationships among news consumers, producers, and makers. The growing competition between news outlets leads media outlets to produce news that engages us beyond mere news content. News producers have increasingly used a mixture of news and commentary to retain an increasingly distracted, disloyal news audience. Opinion, urgency, conflict, or entertainment may be the sugar that makes the news medicine go down. I find that news grazing is indirectly affecting how we see the news and perceive our political institutions. The residual effect of our media choices is a heightened public perception of distrust toward Congress and a polarization of political actors.

While news grazing is allowing us greater freedom to control what and how much news we choose to consume, it is also creating incentives for news makers and producers to frame news stories in ways that will engage or activate us. These news frames may be unintentionally promoting civic disharmony. In this concluding chapter, I explore some broader implications of the news-grazing thesis, returning to the question of the political impacts of congressional disapproval.

An Overexposed Congress: Does It Matter?

Public distrust of Congress has been a lasting trait of our national politics. Since the advent of scientific polling, a large majority of Americans have expressed disapproval of Congress's job performance. Still, the degree and intensity of dissatisfaction has grown in the last few decades. Academics have proposed alternative explanations for congressional distrust, which I reviewed in Chapter 1. My analysis of commentary news does not discount any of these varied explanations for congressional distrust. Congressional disapproval is often a self-inflicted wound triggered by members' incivility, partisanship, or scandal. I argue, though, that public perceptions of these institutional excesses have only been strengthened by media choice and news grazing. Commentary news formats place a typically critical, sometimes warped, lens on Congress. Greater exposure to news urgency contributes to a growing public agitation toward public affairs generally. Greater exposure to conflict-oriented coverage contributes to a growing public distrust toward opposing sides. Finally, greater exposure to fake news leads to public cynicism toward the institution.

In the next sections, I expand my overexposure thesis by evaluating how low institutional trust affects voters, Congress, and the media. For voters, I assess how growing public cynicism toward Congress affects congressional elections, as well as voters' attitudes toward individual members and Congress generally. Recent scholarship indicates a relationship between congressional disapproval and incumbents' reelection vote share. Is low congressional approval related to individual members' reelection and electoral polarization? For Congress, I assess whether congressional approval has any effect on how Congress works. Is Congress's performance of its constitutional roles hampered by its low public regard? Finally, I evaluate the implications for the media of low institutional approval. Ultimately, does it matter that most Americans do not trust the news media? Previewing our answer to all these questions, I think congressional and media disapproval affect the nature of how well we achieve or move toward our democratic ideals.

Overexposure and Congressional Elections

Does public disapproval of Congress alter election voting patterns? That is, do voters assess institutional performance when casting their ballot for district- or state-level congressional candidates? The conventional wisdom gleaned by pundits of congressional elections has been that, for at least House elections, "all politics is local." In other words, low institutional approval has not significantly affected individual congressional elections. The electoral power of incumbency swamped voters' negative national assessments of Congress. Voters generally did not hold their individual member accountable for their dissatisfaction with the institution. Congressional critics have long lamented the lack of institutional accountability that resulted from this individualistic, "all politics is local" logic (Farrier 2015; Fiorina 1980; Mayer and Canon 1999). Following this logic, members were free to shirk or obstruct institutional duties and then merely blame the collective Congress for the unpopular outcome.

The 1994 midterm election deviated from this "all politics is local" logic, resulting in a fifty-four House seat swing from Democrats to

Republicans and establishing a new Republican House majority party. In all, thirty-four incumbents (all Democrats) were defeated in the 1994 House midterm election including Speaker Tom Foley, D-Wash.; Ways and Means Committee chair Dan Rostenkowski, D-Ill.; and Judiciary Committee chair Jack Brooks, D-Texas. Hypothetically, a cohesive majority party coalition in the House could achieve institutional accountability. The House majority party took greater control and, correspondingly, electoral responsibility for House outcomes.

Congressional scholars continue to debate the extent to which institutional or majority party assessments affect individual congressional elections. Jones and McDermott (2009) argue that contemporary congressional voters punish House majority party members for poor institutional performance. Congressional disapproval lowers House majority party members' electoral vote share while increasing minority partisans' vote share. Jones and McDermott argue that the importance of institutional performance on voters' electoral decisions has grown as party polarization has increased. Jones (2014) extends the argument, showing that passage of the Affordable Care Act led to diverging institutional assessments between partisan voters. These different institutional assessments solidified both electoral party bases in the 2010 midterm elections.

The degree to which institutional assessments matter to election outcomes is still unresolved. However, there is growing evidence from House election results that *not* all politics is local. Congressional disapproval appears to be affecting candidate entry and some voters' election choices in the last few decades, as indicated by growing electoral volatility in incumbent reelection rates and House seat change. Harbridge and Malhotra (2011) find that partisan institutional conflict affects weak partisan and independent voters more than strong. As congressional party polarization grows, voters assume the House and Senate majority parties are responsible for setting a floor agenda and managing vote outcomes. Consequently, a dysfunctional Congress reflects poorly on the majority party. Lower congressional job performance depresses the majority party's incumbent party vote share.

This majority party referendum hypothesis of congressional approval has troubling implications for bipartisanship and civility in the House. The argument that majority partisans are rewarded and punished for institutional performance suggests minority partisans may intentionally disrupt and even sabotage floor activities for minority party electoral gain. By actively promoting institutional stalemate, the minority party can advance their party's electoral gains. In practice, this minority party obstruction has diverging political consequences between the House and Senate.

For the House of Representatives, this minority recalcitrance may lead to uncivil debate at times but also to what Roberts (2012) calls "a procedural arms race" that provides the House majority party with "a full arsenal of tools to deploy in order to gain passage of preferred legislation" (123). House party conflict is managed by the majority party's procedural control of floor rules. The House majority party may simply frame majority floor coalitions within their party caucus. The so-called "Hastert Rule" has been an informal norm among House Republicans in which the Speaker will not schedule a floor vote on any bill that does not have majority support within the majority party caucus, even if a bipartisan majority of House members would vote to pass it. Speaker John Boehner's violation of the unwritten rule on so-called "fiscal cliff" tax bill in 2012 and to raise the debt ceiling in 2013 contributed to his declining support within the House Republican Conference.

For the U.S. Senate, the majority party referendum hypothesis implies truly perverse outcomes for democratic accountability. Minority partisanship typically leads to floor gridlock given that Senate floor prerogatives advantage individual senators rather than the majority party. Frances Lee (2009) finds that contemporary Senate majority party leaders structure—or at least try to structure—floor agendas and floor voting more than in past decades. Ideological differences between congressional partisans alone do not account for the degree of partisan floor division. In fact, she concludes that 44 percent of partisan floor votes are on issues that have no clear ideological consequence. Senators divide by party not only because of principle but also politics, to frustrate an opposing party's procedural influence, or to burnish their own party label. In sum, punishing the majority party for unpopular congressional outcomes does not promote democratic accountability in the Senate. A majority party referendum explanation for low congressional approval implies minority party disruption and results in a growing bicameral dysfunction.

Jones and McDermott's majority party referendum hypothesis of congressional disapproval presumes that voters do not blame minority partisans for institutional gridlock. An alternative hypothesis, a party leadership explanation, is that voters' congressional disapproval largely is a proxy for their dissatisfaction toward the opposing party leadership. That is, voters largely attribute blame for congressional dysfunction to the other party, not their own party. Voters project their institutional disfavor particularly on the opposing party leaders as embodying all that is wrong with the institution.

This party leadership hypothesis of congressional disapproval implies that Democratic voters project institutional disfavor on the congressional

Republican leaders while Republican voters project on Democratic leaders. As voters' assessment of congressional job performance drops, their willingness to support an opposing party incumbent declines. Voters' congressional disapproval decreases their party ticket-splitting behavior—their willingness to vote implicitly for the other party's leadership. This effect would be greatest among voters who are strong partisans.

The party leadership hypothesis of congressional disapproval also has troubling implications for bipartisanship, though different from the majority party referendum explanation. In this case, the electoral importance of institutional disapproval has grown as congressional partisanship has strengthened. Voters reasonably infer that their member's performance follows their party's performance as party voting rates have increased. Members' electoral fates are more affected by their party's public reputation. Greater institutional partisanship begets greater electoral partisanship. As the party effect has grown, the political value of compromise has lessened. The consequent legislative stalemate results in greater congressional disapproval, which again begets greater electoral partisanship. A cycle of institutional and electoral partisanship has left recent Congresses with sustained, record-low approval rates, as well as public perceptions that the legislative process cannot resolve a broad range of policy challenges. Both the party leadership explanation and the majority party referendum explanation of congressional disapproval imply that bipartisanship is less likely.

The party leadership explanation of congressional disapproval differs from a majority party referendum explanation in important ways, though. Particularly, the electoral effects of congressional disapproval are not felt by all members equally. The majority party referendum model implies that all majority party members are electorally hurt by a dysfunctional, unpopular Congress. In contrast, the party leadership explanation implies that members from marginal districts are disadvantaged. In marginal districts, ones with a closer mix of Republicans and Democrats, congressional disapproval may place these incumbents at greater electoral risk. Members from these electorally marginal districts are at greater electoral risk as congressional disapproval drives swing voters back toward their party.

Following the party leadership explanation, incumbents from electorally safe districts in which one party dominates elections actually may benefit from congressional disapproval. Congressional disapproval does not pose an electoral threat to incumbents in safe districts composed of strong partisan voters; in fact, low approval reflects the incumbent's partisan fidelity in opposition to unpopular opposing party leaders. In this case of high institutional disapproval, members from safe districts can stick with their party on closely divided votes without threatening electoral defeat. However, moderate members can expect less cross-party electoral support from swing voters in a general election with low congressional approval. These swing voters blame the opposing party leadership for institutional problems and may identify the incumbent from that opposing party as supporting these leaders.

These moderates from marginal districts may oppose their party leadership on a salient floor vote to distance themselves from unpopular party leaders and positions. Still, a party defection on highly salient floor vote may risk the member's reputation among House copartisans and could lead to a contested primary. From this perspective, the party defection does not win the electoral support of potential swing voters. Generally, moderate members from marginal seats are at greater electoral risk during times of high institutional polarization.

Figure 7.1 summarizes the two explanations of how congressional disapproval affects voters' electoral assessments. The two models offer contending answers to who is blamed for low institutional performance and why institutional conflict persists. According to the party leadership explanation, moderate members from marginal districts are at greatest electoral risk from congressional disapproval. The partisan electoral tide rolls away those who are least supportive of their party. In this regard, high rates of congressional disapproval may heighten electoral and institutional party polarization.

The 1994, 2006, and 2010 midterm elections present cases for evaluating both models of congressional disapproval. These recent congressional midterm elections resulted in perhaps a counterintuitive combination of greater electoral party partisanship and greater electoral volatility. One might think that greater rates of electoral party loyalty may correspond with lower seat turnover for the majority party. However, these midterm election years saw both greater rates of congressional seat turnover and stronger

Figure 7.1 Contrasting Models for Congressional Disapproval		
	Majority Party Referendum	**Party Leadership**
Blame Attribution	Majority Party	Opposing Party
Democratic Outcomes	Senate Gridlock	Party Polarization

Source: Created by the author.

voter party loyalty. All three recent "wave" elections not only saw a tsunami-like voting surge toward the minority party (and away from the president's party) but also resulted in the chambers becoming more polarized.

The disquieting effect of institutional distrust may be that it does not affect all incumbent members the same. The electoral consequences of institutional disapproval may depend also on the electoral competitiveness of a congressional district and the incumbent's partisanship. Strongly partisan members from electorally safe districts may actually benefit from (or at least be immune to) an unpopular Congress, as implied by the opposing party leadership model. These disapproving electorates that blame the opposing party only strengthen the partisan incumbents' electoral base. On the other hand, less partisan members from electorally marginal districts may have a greater electoral threat from an unpopular Congress than from strong partisans. These members may lose electoral share from an unpopular Congress, as implied by the majority party referendum model. Independent and moderate voters punish the majority party for poor institutional performance. As a result, congressional disapproval may promote both majority party volatility and party polarization.

The most recent 2010 election is an example of how low congressional approval affects elections. Congress's approval rating in the spring leading up to the 2010 congressional elections was down to 22.2 percent, a significantly lower rate than the average approval rating, 34.9 percent, since 1974. Jones and McDermott (2011) report statistical evidence that supports the party referendum model. They demonstrate that low congressional approval helps to predict majority party seat loss. House Democrats lost sixty-three seats in the 2010 midterm election (the biggest electoral loss by any party since 1948) losing majority control of the chamber. At the same time, low institutional approval triggered electoral polarization. Strong partisans mobilized against the opposing party leadership. Notably, a fiscally focused Tea Party movement became a vocal force in mobilizing voters for conservative Republican candidates and against Speaker Nancy Pelosi.

In summary, congressional disapproval leads to greater electoral party volatility and lower incumbency voting for weak partisan members. Recent scholarship supports both majority party referendum and party leadership models of how congressional disapproval affects voting behavior. This scholarship and these models counter the traditional view that members are insulated from collective responsibility for legislative outcomes. All politics is no longer local. Both models imply that congressional disapproval promotes electoral and institutional polarization. This congressional disapproval matters electorally as congressional parties become more ideologically homogenous but also polarized. An overexposed Congress reinforces these electoral trends and polarization. Media coverage of congressional actions tends to inflame partisan emotions. The next section extends the overexposure thesis by assessing the internal operations of Congress itself.

Overexposure and the Congressional Process

An overexposed Congress affects the institution as well. Ramirez (2009) finds that higher rates of partisan conflict tend to result in lower congressional approval over time. Low public approval toward Congress correlates with periods of partisan gridlock—the inability of the congressional process to induce bipartisan compromise. Congressional elections, however, are not necessarily self-correcting in this case. As discussed, the electoral effects of low congressional approval do not necessarily lead to institutional change that promotes bipartisan compromise. The opposing party leadership model suggests that partisan voters blame the opposing party for low congressional job approval. From this perspective, partisan voters believe that the solution to a dysfunctional Congress is to further strengthen their party's institutional powers.

Mann and Ornstein (2006, 2016) analyze recent congressional dysfunction and the growing importance of party organization within the House and Senate. They argue broadly that our congressional institutions are in decline as current members no longer follow earlier norms of institutional patriotism and civility, the unwritten practices among former members to loyally protect the institutional powers and public image of Congress. Throughout the post–World War II era of Congress, these institutional norms encouraged legislators to identify themselves as Congress members first, not as partisans. Mann and Ornstein argue that this loss of institutional identity and an indifference to institutional reform among contemporary members have followed from the growing intraparty homogeneity and interparty polarization described earlier. According to scholars, congressional partisanship is killing off old norms of institutional patriotism and civility. Members' identity is increasingly with their party caucus, not the institution as a whole. The norms and institutional structures of today's partisan Congress have supplanted the ones that existed in earlier congressional eras in which parties did not matter as much.

I argue that an overexposed Congress lessens institutional effectiveness by further weakening processes that have traditionally served to frame bipartisan compromise in Congress: standing committees and conference committees. An overexposed Congress lessens the prospects for members to work outside of the media glare to negotiate privately between partisans. Additionally, an unpopular Congress has lessened members' confidence in advancing institutional reforms that strengthen the governing capacities of Congress. Distrusting partisans are skeptical of institutional reforms to strengthen committees. The net effect of an overexposed Congress is increasing institutional weakness. There is compelling evidence to support this overexposure argument.

An overexposed Congress first contributes to a weakened committee system. Congress scholars have worked to address why members would ever willingly give up power over legislation by devolving authority to a committee. Giving up power seems counter to legislators' immediate self-interest. Scholars have advanced three alternative explanations for why legislators would willingly delegate power to strong committees: distributive, informational, and partisan theories for committee organization.

The distributive theory perhaps cynically suggests that congressional committees exist so that members can "bring home the bacon." That is, members can serve their local constituencies' particular economic or social interests by sorting themselves onto congressional committees that have narrow policy jurisdictions built around these parochial interests (Adler and Lapinski 1997; Alvarez and Saving 1997). For instance, Iowa members may serve on the Agriculture Committees, members from New York City may serve on the Transportation Committee, and Wyoming members may serve on the Natural Resources Committee. Because members self-select which committee to serve on, committees become composed of *preference outliers*, a group of members with similar economic interests who demand high levels of service in this select policy area. In this case, committees frame chamber agreement and compromise by allowing factions of members to win legislative battles in policy areas that their district cares most about.

An alternative explanation of committees—an informational theory—implies that the purpose of congressional committees instead is to promote policy expertise, the degree to which committee members specialize in a narrow topic like transportation, tax, or energy policy. Devolution of policy-making authority to committees empowers those members and induces them to concentrate on their committee work. Ways and Means Committee members become tax experts, Financial Services members become banking experts, and Armed Services Committee members become defense policy experts.

From these distributive and informational perspectives, the committee system has existed independent of party leaders. In fact, from these views, committees act as a competitor to parties for power and influence within Congress. The committee system induces members to form geographically and ideologically diverse coalitions to pass legislation out of a committee. Committees, from distributive and informational perspectives, may promote compromise.

In contrast, a final theory of committee organization suggests that committees serve as the tools of the majority party. This partisan theory implies that majority party leaders largely hold sway over the membership, rules, and legislative output of congressional committees. The partisan view of committees presumes the purpose of committee system is to protect the electoral value of the majority party's label—Republican or Democrat. Strong committees empower the majority party to advance their policy agenda, thus improving their electoral chances of holding the majority. Committees controlled by the majority party can intentionally prevent bills from reaching the floor that might divide majority partisans. Correspondingly, these committees can intentionally advance bills that are strongly supported within the majority party caucus.

Aldrich and Rohde (2000) argue persuasively that committee partisanship has strengthened since the 1990s. Their "conditional party government" theory predicts that as preference homogeneity within the majority party increases, majority party members will be progressively more willing to cede strong institutional powers to leaders and to support the exercise of those leadership powers. The "condition" in this theory is that growing preference homogeneity within congressional parties and a widening ideological divide between the congressional parties together drive congressional parties to take greater political control of the committee system.

As preference homogeneity has grown, House majority party leaders have strengthened their institutional powers to control which bills reach floor consideration. After the 1994 election, a newly empowered Republican majority elected Newt Gingrich as Speaker. Speaker Gingrich led a "Republican Revolution" to centralize committee authority to the party leadership. The goal was to enhance their party's floor control and, correspondingly, to frustrate the minority party. Committees shifted from institutional tools for compromise to partisan tools for strengthening agenda control. Speaker Gingrich ignored traditions of seniority in making committee leadership appointments, bypassing the more senior Republicans on the Appropriations, Commerce, and Judiciary Committees (Aldrich and Rohde 1997). The House Republican Conference also reduced the number of standing committees, reduced the number of committee appointments, reduced committee staff by a third, and limited the terms of committee and subcommittee chairs. In all, the Republican Revolution propelled an institutional path toward the subordination of committees to parties.

Since the 104th Congress, both House Republican and Democratic majorities have kept to this path of partisan committees. In 2003, House Republicans altered their party rules to require Appropriations subcommittee chairs to be approved by their party Steering Committee. House Democrats, led by Speaker Pelosi, followed a similar path to centralize party control over committee leadership and agendas. Taking back the majority in 2010, House Republicans and the Tea Party faction, continued the practice of framing legislation within the party conference as opposed to the standing committees. Today's overexposed Congress, in which media messaging has become a part of forming floor support, has subjugated the committee process to largely address the majority party's legislative priorities.

Similar to weakening the committee system, an overexposed Congress lessens the effectiveness of the conference committee process for resolving interchamber differences. The parity (in size) and polarization of the Republican and Democratic party caucuses over time has promoted an active, ongoing media effort by both parties to undermine the opposition's political messages. *Message politics*—the contentious communications battle of contending press releases, talking points, and media spokespersons between congressional parties—have weakened conference committees' capacity to forge bipartisan and interchamber agreement.

Congressional conference committees have historically met in secret to quietly negotiate the differences between House and Senate versions of a bill. Oleszek (2014) underscores the obscurity of the conference committee process relative to the more public, plenary floor stage. Traditionally, the House and Senate committee leaders originating the legislation tended to serve as the conference committee members, or conferees, for their bills, assuring that they exercised influence at this penultimate legislative stage. Shepsle and Weingast (1987) theorized that this hidden committee power, conferee appointment, functioned as an "ex post veto" for originating committee leaders. By dominating conference committee selection, these committee leaders could discreetly detach unwanted floor amendments from the bill and nudge final legislation back toward the authorizing committee's version.

The contemporary partisan Congress, though, has elevated media strategy as a substitute to quiet conferee negotiation. Lazarus and Monroe (2007) show that House Republican leaders have biased the selection of conference committee members in favor of the majority party. Aldrich and

Rohde (2009) also find that Republican leaders have, at times, blocked Democratic conferees from conference committees. The House majority party has increasingly used its agenda control to pass more partisan bills and to use conference committee selection as a tool for advancing these partisan bills. The net effect has been to weaken the capacity of conference committees to resolve interparty and interchamber differences.

In summary, overexposure of Congress to commentary news has contributed to the weakening of institutional processes that have traditionally promoted legislative compromise. The standing committee system and conference committees have quietly functioned over time to advance cross-party coalitions and policy expertise, alternatives to the influence of party leadership. Party messaging and the influence of congressional party caucuses have diminished this regular order of committee system. Committees are less able to form policy agendas and frame final legislative compromises. These changes have lessened Congress's capacity to resolve internal conflict. Overall, an overexposed Congress—and the consequent decline in congressional trust—is a weakened legislative body.

An Overexposed Media: Does It Matter?

Like Congress, the contemporary news media also is overexposed to negative popular assessments. Overall, Americans' confidence in the news media is greater than trust in Congress and other political institutions. However, confidence in the news media dropped sharply during the 1980s and 1990s. This decline continued during the past few decades. According to Gallup, 54 percent of Americans in 1999 believed that mass media could be trusted "a great deal" or "fair amount," dropping to 40 percent by 2015.

This declining trust in the news media is typically associated with the perceived shortcomings of current news media to a journalistic ideal. That journalistic ideal includes standards of news accuracy, balance, objectivity, civility, and independence from sources. Williams and Delli Carpini (2011) give a historical perspective of news journalism, noting different "media regimes" over time. This progression of media regimes represents periods of stability, each followed by dramatic change. New communication technologies typically trigger transitions in media regimes. They argue that the contemporary media regime is still taking form, largely in response to the Internet. Earlier news media regimes had to adapt to economic, political, cultural, and technological changes, and they argue that the current emerging regime will also adapt.

My focus has been only on these contemporary changes. I have argued that expanded media choice—the growing presences of online, cable, and citizen journalism—has resulted in a loss of professional journalistic control over what and how news is reported. This loss of control results in a more eclectic world of news providers offering more varied and dynamic news. The current news media regime, I argue, has been increasingly responsive to news grazers leveraging the opportunity of new communication technologies. News producers today offer more news, a broader mix of news, and news on demand. However, these changes also contribute to news media deviating from these traditional, professional ideals.

Most troubling, news media today may be less able to frame greater public agreement by informing public opinion, as well as clarifying fact from opinion. This democratic function seems less attainable for today's media. I argue that commentary formats intentionally elevate perceived urgency, intensify viewers' partisan opinions, and promote public cynicism. The news media is increasingly communicating more than just straight news and, as a result, is increasingly exposed to critics. Negative public assessments of the contemporary news media have increased while news media choice has expanded.

To be fair, the decline of media trust is partly a return to a normal state of public skepticism toward journalists. Ladd (2011) challenges the conventional wisdom that a trusted journalistic media establishment is a natural state within a politically diverse culture. He claims that there is no return to a mid-twentieth-century "golden age of journalism" in which news producers projected a more professional, competent, and trusted public image. This transitory "golden age," Ladd argues, was a unique period with low levels of economic competition within media industry and less partisan polarization between our national parties. Media distrust has been the norm for most periods in our democracy. An overexposed media, one that is generally disliked and distrusted, is and will remain the normal condition given media economics and partisan politics.

An overexposed media, nonetheless, has consequences. I analyze two ways that media overexposure affects how well news journalists fulfill their public function of informing citizens. First, news credibility has declined as a result of an overexposed news media. Ladd reports evidence that media distrust heightens viewers' resistance to new information that counters these viewers' political predispositions. The credibility of the news has declined partly because viewers assume that commentary formats are less than wholly objective. I argue that this news media distrust contributes to electoral party polarization.

A second effect of news media overexposure is its impact on the public's news interest. An unpopular, overexposed media accelerates changes in our news-viewing habits and interest. The decay of routinized news-gathering habits, along with an overexposed news media, results in a growing divergence among the public in the amount and nature of news accessed. News grazers, who are distrustful toward contemporary news media, are empowered increasingly to target their specific news consumption or to avoid news altogether. I assess how citizens' levels of news interest are contributing to a widening separation in news consumption rates.

Overexposure and News Credibility

It is not a great leap to infer that an unpopular news media affects the public's perceptions of news credibility. Logically, we are less trusting of news received from less trusted sources. News credibility—how much you believe the news stories you consume—has steadily declined in the past decade. The Pew Research Center reports that 71 percent of Americans in 2002 stated that they believed the news that they received. By 2012, 56 percent reported a positive score on the news believability scale. During the 2002 to 2012 period, every news media outlet's believability rating suffered a double-digit drop, except for local daily newspapers and local TV news.

This decline in news credibility is greatest for news received from cable news and online sources. These less trusted news media institutions are contributing to a decline in news credibility overall. The rise of commentary news, in particular, negatively affects news credibility. I argue that news credibility is linked partly to commentary news through these formats' agenda-setting influence, their affective response on viewers, and their spillover onto "old-media" news.

First, commentary news affects the political agenda—the stories that are reported and reach public discourse. My analyses of partisan news, breaking-news, and fake-news formats underscore that these commentary formats are stylistically different from straight, hard news. Commentary news formats also report on a different mix of news stories. Opinion news stories are clearly slanted toward the partisan bend of their host. They present a greater share of news critical of the opposition party. Their news content also has greater rates of stories critical of other media outlets, particularly opposing opinion news programs. The breaking-news format also influences agenda setting. As discussed in Chapter 5, breaking news increases the share of stories on legal controversies, disasters, and scandal.

Visual and emerging stories receive extended news coverage and analysis. The entertainment-based, fake-news formats also alter the news agenda. Broadly, entertainment-based news moves the news agenda away from "hard-news" stories strictly about national politics or international affairs. The political satire format, though, mixes news and humor. As discussed in the previous chapter, political satire tends to frame news events in terms of some action of a political leader or party. The satire genre can be a politically powerful means of framing issues and, by personalizing news events, extends the political agenda.

The broader news agenda resulting from commentary formats contributes to declining news credibility. Commentary news formats select stories that often appeal to a selective viewership while sometimes repelling others. The opinion news format, for instance, strongly promotes ideological sorting. My experiments confirm earlier studies that the opinion format attracts viewers that share the host's political views while driving away viewers with opposing views. The Pew Research Center finds that the percentage of Democrats who respond positively to the news credibility of the Fox News Channel declined from 67 percent in 2002 to 37 percent in 2012. Likewise, Pew reports that the percentage of Republicans responding positively to the news credibility of MSNBC declined from 70 percent in 2002 to 32 percent in 2012. Ideological sorting affects news credibility. Political satire can have a similar effect. Formats that promote ideological sorting invite viewers to question the credibility, the accuracy or objectivity, of other news sources. For instance, "We report, you decide," implies to Fox News viewers that other news sources are biased and that their news, thus, is not to be believed.

Extending this argument, a different news agenda resulting from the breaking-news format also may lessen news credibility. In this case, though, viewers may doubt the credibility of breaking news since it elevates the immediacy of the news over all journalistic standards. Other standards like thoroughness, balance, and accuracy are all subjugated as news values in the case of breaking news to ensure that viewers are given real-time information. The breaking-news format, in some cases, invites speculation by reporters and, even worse, has resulted in misinformation being given by reporters.

A second mechanism in which an overexposed media hurts news credibility relates to the emotional or affective responses of commentary news formats. My experiments discussed in earlier chapters assessed these affective responses of news grazers, the emotional reactions that attracted and retained their attention to commentary news formats. These affective responses included negative stereotyping toward out-groups, anxiousness toward emerging events, and cynicism toward elites and institutions.

I found that the partisan news format had a negative affect response on viewers that impacts news credibility. Along with earlier studies, my experiment found that partisan news strongly promotes ideological sorting, in which regular viewers overwhelmingly share the host's views. I also found that viewers of partisan news were more likely to agree to negative stereotypes of out-groups, individuals or political parties that opposed the host's ideological perspective. Overall, partisan news tends to attract copartisans and promote their affective polarization. In addition to energizing and mobilizing copartisans, opinion-based news fuels its viewers' distrust toward other news sources.

This finding fits with other studies of affective polarization. Some scholars argue that Americans have become more polarized on political issues in the last several decades (Abramowitz 2010; Abramowitz and Saunders 2008). Partisan voters, over time, have become increasingly ideologically sorted, with fewer conservative Democrats and liberal Republicans. An opposing perspective is that most Americans remain moderates in their issue positions even though political elites have polarized (Fiorina 2013; Fiorina and Abrams 2012). Separate from this question of voters' issue evaluations, voters generally have become more polarized in their emotional appeal toward opposing parties. Iyengar, Sood, and Lelkes (2012) and Abramowitz (2014) find affective evaluations of our two political parties have become increasingly polarized. The basis of this partisan polarization is not necessarily grounded in ideological beliefs as it is emotion. Comparing the electorate in 2012 with the electorate in 1978, Abramowitz finds that partisan voters increasingly express greater dislike toward the opposing party.

I found that partisan news viewers typically are more receptive to negative messages about the opposing party and its candidates than those who choose not to watch. Levendusky (2013) also finds that partisan or opinion news promotes affective polarization. Arceneaux and Johnson (2013) confirm this result but also find that selective exposure, the capacity to change the channel, results in those most likely to be offended by uncivil, partisan news formats avoiding these programs. Opinion or partisan news typically reinforces viewers' political predispositions and activates negative affective responses toward the opposition. This affective opposition increasingly includes viewers' perceptions of opposing partisan media given the tendency for partisan news to report more on the news media itself.

Like partisan news, breaking-news and fake-news formats also promote affective responses that lead viewers to question news credibility. I found that breaking-news viewers were more likely to express anxiety or agitation toward the breaking-news event. The format communicates greater news urgency through reporters' tone, live visual cues, and cross-talk. News urgency leaves viewers more anxious or uncertain about emerging news events.

Likewise, heavy viewers of the political satire format also have affective responses, particularly higher rates of cynicism toward political figures and institutions. Baumgartner and Morris (2006) argue that "fake-news" reports of the political satire format result in stronger negative evaluations of politicians and news media. Overall, formats that mix drama or entertainment with the news may keep an increasingly inattentive news grazer from clicking. However, through this mixture, these formats also lead viewers to question the journalistic balance and accuracy of the news itself, and as a result, these formats suppress news credibility.

A final point is that these agenda-setting and emotional effects of commentary news are spilling over into other news formats. That is, the distribution of reported stories and emotion-laden nature of commentary news formats are affecting the journalistic decisions of traditional print and broadcast news producers. It this way, an overexposed media further contributes to declining news credibility.

Part of this spillover effect is due to consumer pressures. Internet and cable news channels create consumer pressure on traditional print and broadcast news outlets to keep up with viewer expectations for immediacy of news and analysis. These consumer pressures may lead these legacy news providers to forgo fact checking and additional news gathering to keep up with a faster news clock. Baum and Groeling (2008) find evidence that partisan news websites and blogs have a discernable partisan slant to which and how stories are reported compared with traditional newswire stories. Baum and others also note the growing consumer demand for soft-news stories, as opposed to traditional hard news. Generally, news consumers are voting with their remote control and mouse. Traditional print and broadcast news producers must adapt to these consumer preferences for immediacy and entertainment.

In addition to consumer pressures, traditional news media have to adapt to the economic pressures that are the result of an increasingly diverse and competitive new media marketplace. As discussed in Chapter 3, I do not think that traditional news is likely to disappear because of economic competition; however, I expect there will be increased blending or blurring between news formats. Staff and budget reductions in network and print news divisions limit capacities for fact checking and more in-depth reporting. Economic pressures also lead broadcast news producers to rely less on edited, taped news packages and more on live talk to fill the broadcast news hole. Print news producers rely less on beat reporting and more on newswire services. Overall, economic pressures lead some traditional news to mimic cable and online news practices. I expect this spillover effect to further diminish public perceptions of news credibility.

Overexposure and News Interest

Another emerging trend resulting from news media choice is greater political stratification among news audiences. One basis for this audience sorting discussed in earlier chapters has been the role of ideology. The ideological divide between "Fox News conservatives" and "MSNBC liberals" is at least louder, if not wider. About a quarter of Americans prefer news that conforms to their partisan or ideological predispositions compared with other news; about half prefer news that takes a more objective or balanced approach (Pew Research Center 2012b). Stroud (2011) points out that this estimate is most likely low since respondents may be reluctant to admit that they favor like-minded news. They may also have a different understanding of what constitutes "like-minded" news compared to the majority view. Some conservative viewers of Fox News, for instance, may not identify their viewing as a "like-minded" preference; they may perceive Fox News as "balanced" while other hostile, biased news sources attract "like-minded" viewers.

Beyond ideology, though, another basis for audience sorting has been news interest. Cable and online news outlets are increasingly drawing viewers with high news interest. These high-news-interest viewers are disproportionately ones with strong partisan and ideological views. In other words, the ideological divide between cable news providers masks a more perceptible divide in rates of news consumption. Americans with low news interest are increasingly turned off by an overexposed, unpopular media. In contrast, strong partisans with high news interest are increasingly energized by drama-laden news. Media choice and commentary news are contributing to an emerging informational divide. I evaluate both ends of this divide in news consumption rates.

The first end of the emerging informational divide is among Americans with low news interest. Pew Research Center measures news interest by individuals' response to how much they enjoy keeping up with the news.

Generally, about half of Americans report that they enjoy keeping up with the news "a lot." However, according to Pew, the percentage of Americans who respond "not much" or "not at all" for enjoying the news has increased over time, doubling from 10 to 20 percent between 2004 and 2012. Furthermore, about a quarter of Americans with low news interest state that they receive no news at all.

Low news interest is most evident among young respondents between eighteen and twenty-nine years old, particularly among young respondents who are news grazers. Only 5 percent of eighteen- to twenty-nine-year-old respondents report following politics and Washington news "very closely," compared with 17 percent among all respondents. The generational gap is also evident in the self-reported amount of time spent in following the news. In a 2012 Pew survey, respondents in their twenties spent on average forty-six minutes a day following the news compared to seventy-seven minutes for respondents between forty-eight and sixty-six years old and eighty-four minutes for those over sixty-seven years of age. Only time will tell whether current young news consumers will increase consumption as they age, implying that this generational difference is largely a function of age. Current young news consumers are different, though, from their seniors in their reliance on the Internet and their preference to news graze. According to the 2012 Pew survey, 71 percent of eighteen- to twenty-nine-year-olds rely on the Internet as their main source of news compared with 38 percent for the fifty to sixty-four age cohort and 18 percent for those sixty-five and older. The changing sources and habits of news consumers imply a persisting gap of news consumption rates between those with high and low news interest.

Along with a decline of news interest, news consumers also have changing preferences for types of news coverage. Boczkowski and Mitchelstein (2013) investigate how news consumers' preferences for information are changing with growing media choice. They find that generally a large proportion of the top stories news media sites disseminate about politics, international relations, and economics are not what news consumers prefer (as evidenced by the most viewed stories). They refer to a "news gap" that persists between the percentage of public affairs news stories and consumers' preferences for accessing news about sports, crime, entertainment, and weather. Public affairs stories are ones that relate to politics, international affairs, and economics.

At the other end of the growing information divide is a news audience with high news interest. These high-interest news consumers have growing access to news, as well as a stronger capacity to sort and screen news that fits their select interests. Those who enjoy following news can now get more news from an expanded set of sources and electronic devices. Markus Prior (2007) discusses the growing informational inequality in a postbroadcast democracy, arguing that this inequality is affecting political polarization and rates of political participation. My analysis does not extend to studying the effects of information inequality. However, I do argue that the current overexposed, distrusted news media in an age of expanded media choice promotes an information divide along news interest. As news-grazing habits become the overwhelming norm of the American electorate, we can expect a growing cohort of hyperinformed news consumers.

Additionally, these hyperinformed news consumers will be disproportionately opinionated. Lawrence, Sides, and Farrell (2010) find that political blog readers are more likely to have strong ideological and partisan attitudes compared with the non–blog readers. Political blog readers also participate more in politics compared with others. This heightened participation, however, does not imply improved deliberation between those with diverse opinions. Lawrence, Sides, and Farrell find that political blogs promote self-segregation, a tendency for left-wing readers to read left-wing blogs and, correspondingly, right-wing readers to read right-wing blogs. Readers of political blogs and online news postings will likely confirm this result. An Internet age of news consumption and grazing is promoting self-segregation of high-news-interest consumers.

Conclusion

This study of news grazing concludes that our changing news-gathering habits are altering the manner and nature of news itself. The rise of commentary news, I argue, is an outgrowth of media choice and our preference for engaging news. These commentary formats are an adaptation to news grazing, and they contribute to the audience receiving different cues about news importance compared with cues framed from mainstream news sources. The partisan news format typically has a confirmatory bias with most of its news audience. The opinion news agenda presents stories that conform to viewers' predispositions and also trigger negative stereotypes of the opposition. The breaking-news format cues to its viewers that news importance corresponds with highly visual and urgent stories. Fake news cues viewers to stories that personalize events to political elites and that simplify complex news events.

Overall, commentary news formats affect viewers' political perceptions about Congress and the news media. Particularly, they inflame affective partisanship, elevate perceptions of news urgency, and promote public cynicism toward both Congress and the media. These viewer perceptions promote a picture of Congress as a more dysfunctional institution than in previous eras; in short, the media lens from which we view Congress is increasingly a critical one. We do not want to be apologists for contemporary congressional delay and partisanship; there are many reasons for the contemporary institutional problems of Congress. We only note that the news media is important and a less understood source of congressional disapproval.

This concluding chapter has made the case that these perceptual effects of commentary news matter to both Congress and the news media. I have argued that Congress and the media are overexposed; they are increasingly susceptible to negative public assessments from the emergence of commentary news formats. This overexposure affects the capacities of both congressional and media institutions in performing their public roles.

For Congress, an increasingly unpopular and polarized Congress has effects on both congressional voters and the institution. Recent research shows that negative congressional assessments are correlated with higher rates of congressional partisanship. I argue that congressional voters' negative institutional assessments lead to strong negative associations with the opposing party leadership. Partisan voters generally blame the opposing party for institutional gridlock or undesired policy actions. Consequently, an overexposed Congress results in heightened party voting in congressional elections. Polarizing media tends to polarize the electorate.

An overexposed Congress also matters in that it affects the governing capacity inside Congress. I argue that the agenda-setting power of standing committees and the amendment control power of conference committees have been weakened over time. This displaced power has been captured by the party leadership. Contemporary party leaders and their caucuses are more attentive to public evaluations and more involved in crafting media messages to affect these evaluations. Today's party leaders spend much more time than earlier generations trying to control media presentation of party positions and responding to other political actors' media actions. Message politics consumes more time and energy of congressional parties than ever; it also limits the ability of committee chairs and conference committees to work toward negotiated, bipartisan agreements. The quiet diplomacy of committees has been supplanted by the public and angry brand of partisan message politics.

For the media, I argue that commenting on the news supplants time and resources dedicated traditionally to reporting on the news. An overexposed news media matters because it is associated with declines in the public's perceptions of news credibility and news interest. First, unpopular news institutions lead to less public confidence in the news itself. News credibility refers to the extent to which the public believes the news they receive. I made the case that commentary formats affect news credibility by their agenda-setting influence, their affective response on viewers, and their spillover onto old-media news. Second, unpopular news institutions promote variance in news interest among Americans. Segments of the American public are repelled by commentary news; other segments are attracted. I argue that this separation in news interest among Americans may have disquieting effects for the democratic ideals of the news media.

An overexposed, unpopular Congress and media evidently matter in important ways. Is it possible for Congress and the media to limit their exposure to negative public assessments? Can the trend toward public disapproval of political institutions be reversed? Unfortunately, I do not foresee much change from current trends. My thesis has been that commentary news is ultimately an outgrowth of—a response to—changing media-viewing habits: news grazing. While popular critics blame the media and Congress for political polarization, it is audiences' news grazing that ultimately has led media and political elites to alter how politics is presented. A larger percentage of citizens, over time, have news habits that promote negative perceptions of Congress and the media. The American news media has and will always respond to consumer, political, and technology forces. These forces currently propel us toward an overexposed news media and show no signs of abating.

We cannot naively wish, hope, or assume that news audiences will become more interested in high-quality news journalism. The demand for "high-journalism" news may indeed grow, but it seems doubtful that it will largely supplant other news formats or occur by empty pleas for a more informed citizenry. Much of what popular critics claim today to be media biases are largely due to viewers' own news and perception biases—our preference to be engaged by the news, not merely informed. News grazers respond to conflict, immediacy, and entertainment. A news media limited to nonpartisan, nonsensational news would not be responding to these consumer preferences.

Additionally, it is highly doubtful that public attitudes toward Congress will change much in the near term. An increasingly critical public is responding to heightened congressional partisanship, and we cannot assume change by berating politicians to be less partisan. The struggle over who sets the congressional agenda has been the principal driver of congressional partisanship since World War II (Rohde, Stiglitz, and

Weingast 2013). Scholars have demonstrated that this growing partisan polarization within Congress is embedded in the institution's electoral and institutional design. Current trends in congressional partisanship will not change short of these institutional processes being changed.

To be clear, my analysis has not been that the news media necessarily promotes mass political polarization; instead, it has been that news grazing is promoting a trend toward commentary news, and these formats promote the negative messages of Congress and the media. Ultimately, the growth of media choice has been the principal driver of the news-grazing phenomenon. From all indications, media choice will only continue to expand with the emergence of new information technologies. Emerging news sources and formats are increasingly diverse partly as a response to these changing media technologies. The current path toward smaller, mobile information technology devices, for instance, will only strengthen consumers' preference for immediacy and their tendency for news grazing. Media choice and news grazing, for the foreseeable future, are propelling a politics of immediacy, a politics that places both Congress and the media in an increasingly negative public light. While we cannot change these social trends, we can be more sensitized to how our news-gathering habits affect our news and, correspondingly, affect how we see Congress.

Breaking-News Experiment

Pretest/Post-Test Script

Pretest Questions

As part of a research project we are conducting a brief survey about political attitudes and the media viewing habits. Please answer the following questions, which should take approximately 5 minutes. Your participation is entirely voluntary and would be greatly appreciated. Your responses are wholly anonymous and confidential.

1. On a scale of 1–10, how do you feel about President Barack Obama? The higher the number, the more favorable you feel toward Barack Obama. The lower the number, the less favorable you feel toward Barack Obama. An answer of 5 would indicate you feel neither favorably nor unfavorably toward Obama. Circle the number that best corresponds to your feelings.

1	2	3	4	5	6	7	8	9	10
Cold				Neutral					Warm

2. On a scale of 1–10, how do you feel about the Republican Party in Congress? The higher the number, the more favorable you feel toward the Republican Party. The lower the number, the less favorable you feel toward the Republican Party. An answer of 5 would indicate you feel neither favorably nor unfavorably toward the Republican Party. Circle the number that best corresponds to your feelings.

1	2	3	4	5	6	7	8	9	10
Cold				Neutral					Warm

3. On a scale of 1–10, how do you feel about the Democratic Party in Congress? The higher the number, the more favorable you feel toward the Democratic Party. The lower the number, the less favorable you feel toward the Democratic Party. An answer of 5 would indicate you feel neither favorably nor unfavorably toward

---

The online experiments were part of earlier research studies completed between 2013 and 2015.

the Democratic Party. Circle the number that best corresponds to your feelings.

1	2	3	4	5	6	7	8	9	10
Cold				Neutral					Warm

4. Generally speaking, do you consider yourself a Republican, a Democrat, an independent, or what?

_____ Strong Democrat

_____ Democrat

_____ Independent leaning Democrat

_____ Independent

_____ Independent leaning Republican

_____ Republican

_____ Strong Republican

_____ Don't know, or apolitical

5. Did you vote in the 2010 Congressional elections?

_____ Yes

_____ No

_____ Don't remember

For each of the following, please indicate if you watch or listen to it regularly, sometimes, hardly ever, or never.

6. Watch the Cable News Network (CNN)

_____ Regularly

_____ Sometimes

_____ Hardly ever

_____ Never

7. Watch the Fox News Channel

_____ Regularly

_____ Sometimes

_____ Hardly ever

_____ Never

8. Watch *The Daily Show With Jon Stewart*

_____ Regularly

_____ Sometimes

_____ Hardly ever

_____ Never

9. Watch the national nightly network news on CBS, ABC, or NBC? This is different from local news shows about the area where you live?

_____ Regularly
_____ Sometimes
_____ Hardly ever
_____ Never

10. Read a daily newspaper (other than the school newspaper)?

_____ Regularly
_____ Sometimes
_____ Hardly ever
_____ Never

Answer each of the following questions to the best of your ability.

11. Who is the speaker of the U.S. House of Representatives?

_____ Harry Reid   _____ John Boehner
_____ Dennis Hastert   _____ Nancy Pelosi
_____ Newt Gingrich   _____ Don't know

12. Do you know which party has a majority in the House and Senate of the U.S. Congress?

_____ Republicans
_____ Democrats
_____ The Democrats control the House, and the Republicans control the Senate.
_____ The Republicans control the House, and the Democrats control the Senate.
_____ Don't know

13. Who is the Chairman of the Federal Reserve Board?

_____ Richard Cheney   _____ Colin Powell
_____ Ben Bernanke   _____ Alan Greenspan
_____ Newt Gingrich   _____ Don't know

14. Which of the following individuals is a Justice on the U.S. Supreme Court?

_____ John Roberts   _____ Harry Reid
_____ Joseph Biden   _____ Condoleezza Rice
_____ Newt Gingrich   _____ Don't know

15. Generally speaking, do you consider yourself a Conservative, a Liberal, middle of the road, or what?

_____ Strong liberal

_____ Liberal

_____ Moderate leaning liberal

_____ Moderate/middle of the road

_____ Moderate leaning conservative

_____ Conservative

_____ Strong conservative

_____ Don't know, or apolitical

16. What is your gender?   _____ Female   _____ Male

17. How old are you? _____

18. What is your race?

_____ Caucasian   _____ Non-white Hispanic

_____ African-American   _____ Asian

_____ Other

Post-Test Questions

Please indicate whether you agree or disagree with the following statements. Check only one response for each statement.

1. The programs I viewed made me feel angry about our political system.

_____ Strongly disagree

_____ Somewhat disagree

_____ Neither agree nor disagree

_____ Somewhat agree

_____ Strongly agree

2. The programs I viewed made me feel nervous about the nation's future.

_____ Strongly disagree

_____ Somewhat disagree

_____ Neither agree nor disagree

_____ Somewhat agree

_____ Strongly agree

3. The programs I viewed made me feel optimistic about political system.

_____ Strongly disagree
_____ Somewhat disagree
_____ Neither agree nor disagree
_____ Somewhat agree
_____ Strongly agree

4. Generally, current Congress members hold themselves to high standards of ethical conduct.

_____ Strongly disagree
_____ Somewhat disagree
_____ Neither agree nor disagree
_____ Somewhat agree
_____ Strongly agree

5. Generally, do you agree or disagree that the delays in Congress are due to legitimate policy differences over issues?

_____ Strongly disagree
_____ Somewhat disagree
_____ Neither agree nor disagree
_____ Somewhat agree
_____ Strongly agree

6. Generally, do you agree or disagree that the delays in Congress are due to political bickering and scoring political points?

_____ Strongly disagree
_____ Somewhat disagree
_____ Neither agree nor disagree
_____ Somewhat agree
_____ Strongly agree

7. Overall, do you approve or disapprove of the way Congress is handling its job?

_____ Strongly approve
_____ Somewhat approve
_____ Neither approve nor disapprove
_____ Somewhat disapprove
_____ Strongly disapprove

8. Overall, the current Congress works to resolve key issues facing the country.

_____ Strongly approve

_____ Somewhat approve

_____ Neither approve nor disapprove

_____ Somewhat disapprove

_____ Strongly disapprove

9. I trust the Congress to act in the public interest.

_____ Strongly disagree

_____ Somewhat disagree

_____ Neither agree nor disagree

_____ Somewhat agree

_____ Strongly agree

Thank you very much for your participation in our survey. In accordance with University of Mississippi guidelines, we would like to assure you that your participation will be kept strictly confidential. If you are interested in the results of this survey, you may call or e-mail Dr. Richard Forgette.

Please do not write your name anywhere on the survey.
It is designed to be completely anonymous and confidential.

Satirical News Experiment

Pretest/Post-Test Script

"Political Attitudes" Survey Instrument Pretest Questions

As part of a research project we are conducting a brief survey about political attitudes and the media viewing habits. We ask that you answer the following questions, which should take approximately 5 minutes. Your participation is entirely voluntary and would be greatly appreciated. Your responses are wholly anonymous and confidential.

On a scale of 1–10, how do you feel about President Barack Obama? The higher the number, the more favorable you feel toward Barack Obama. The lower the number, the less favorable you feel toward Barack Obama. An answer of 5 would indicate you feel neither favorably nor unfavorably toward Obama. Circle the number that best corresponds to your feelings.

1	2	3	4	5	6	7	8	9	10
Cold				Neutral					Warm

On a scale of 1–10, how do you feel about the Republican Party in Congress? The higher the number, the more favorable you feel toward the Republican Party. The lower the number, the less favorable you feel toward the Republican Party. An answer of 5 would indicate you feel neither favorably nor unfavorably toward the Republican Party. Circle the number that best corresponds to your feelings.

1	2	3	4	5	6	7	8	9	10
Cold				Neutral					Warm

On a scale of 1–10, how do you feel about the Democratic Party in Congress? The higher the number, the more favorable you feel toward the Democratic Party. The lower the number, the less favorable you feel toward the Democratic Party. An answer of 5 would indicate you feel

---

The online experiments were part of earlier research studies completed between 2013 and 2015.

neither favorably nor unfavorably toward the Democratic Party. Circle the number that best corresponds to your feelings.

1	2	3	4	5	6	7	8	9	10
Cold				Neutral					Warm

Generally speaking, do you consider yourself a Republican, a Democrat, an independent, or what?

_____ Strong Republican

_____ Republican

_____ Independent leaning Republican

_____ Independent

_____ Independent leaning Democrat

_____ Democrat

_____ Strong Democrat

_____ Don't know, or apolitical

Answer each of the following questions to the best of your ability.

Who is the speaker of the U.S. House of Representatives?

_____ Harry Reid   _____ John Boehner

_____ Dennis Hastert   _____ Nancy Pelosi

_____ Newt Gingrich   _____ Don't know

Do you know which party has a majority in the House and Senate of the U.S. Congress?

_____ Republicans

_____ Democrats

_____ The Democrats control the House, and the Republicans control the Senate.

_____ The Republicans control the House, and the Democrats control the Senate.

_____ Don't know

Who is the Chairman of the Federal Reserve Board?

_____ Richard Cheney   _____ Colin Powell

_____ Ben Bernanke   _____ Alan Greenspan

_____ Newt Gingrich   _____ Don't know

Which of the following individuals is a Justice on the U.S. Supreme Court?

_____ John Roberts   _____ Harry Reid

_____ Joseph Biden   _____ Condoleezza Rice

_____ Newt Gingrich   _____ Don't know

What is your gender?   _____ Female   _____ Male

How old are you? _____

What is your race?

_____ Caucasian   _____ Non-white Hispanic

_____ African-American   _____ Asian

_____ Other

"Political Attitudes" Post-Test Questions

Please tell me how much *confidence* you, yourself, have in each institution in American society—a great deal, quite a lot, some, or very little.

The military

_____ A great deal   _____ Very little

_____ Quite a lot   _____ None

_____ Some

The U.S. Supreme Court

_____ A great deal   _____ Very little

_____ Quite a lot   _____ None

_____ Some

The Obama administration

_____ A great deal   _____ Very little

_____ Quite a lot   _____ None

_____ Some

The U.S. Congress

_____ A great deal   _____ Very little

_____ Quite a lot   _____ None

_____ Some

The news media

_____ A great deal   _____ Very little

_____ Quite a lot   _____ None

_____ Some

Please indicate whether you agree or disagree with the following statements. Check only one response for each statement.

Most politicians are competent people who know what they are doing.

_____ Strongly disagree

_____ Somewhat disagree

_____ Neither agree nor disagree

_____ Somewhat agree

_____ Strongly agree

Politicians put their own interests ahead of the public's interest.

_____ Strongly disagree

_____ Somewhat disagree

_____ Neither agree nor disagree

_____ Somewhat agree

_____ Strongly agree

Politicians are out of touch with life in the real world.

_____ Strongly disagree

_____ Somewhat disagree

_____ Neither agree nor disagree

_____ Somewhat agree

_____ Strongly agree

I believe that the Republicans and Democrats in Washington can put aside their party interests to do what is best for America.

_____ Strongly disagree

_____ Somewhat disagree

_____ Neither agree nor disagree

_____ Somewhat agree

_____ Strongly agree

The Democrats in Washington don't seem willing to work with the Republicans.

_____ Strongly disagree

_____ Somewhat disagree

_____ Neither agree nor disagree

_____ Somewhat agree

_____ Strongly agree

The Republicans in Washington don't seem willing to work with the Democrats.

_____ Strongly disagree
_____ Somewhat disagree
_____ Neither agree nor disagree
_____ Somewhat agree
_____ Strongly agree

I would like to see a major third party develop in America.

_____ Strongly disagree
_____ Somewhat disagree
_____ Neither agree nor disagree
_____ Somewhat agree
_____ Strongly agree

The news media have a liberal bias.

_____ Strongly disagree
_____ Somewhat disagree
_____ Neither agree nor disagree
_____ Somewhat agree
_____ Strongly agree

The news media have a conservative bias.

_____ Strongly disagree
_____ Somewhat disagree
_____ Neither agree nor disagree
_____ Somewhat agree
_____ Strongly agree

I trust the media to cover political events fairly and accurately.

_____ Strongly disagree
_____ Somewhat disagree
_____ Neither agree nor disagree
_____ Somewhat agree
_____ Strongly agree

References

Abramowitz, Alan. 2010. *The Disappearing Center: Engaged Citizens, Polarization, and American Democracy.* New Haven, Conn.: Yale University Press.

———. 2014. "Partisan Nation: The Rise of Affective Partisanship in the American Electorate." In *The State of the Parties: The Changing Role of Contemporary American Parties,* edited by John C. Green, Daniel J. Coffey, and David B. Cohen, 21–36. Lanham, Md.: Rowman & Littlefield.

Abramowitz, Alan I., and Kyle L. Saunders. 2008. "Is Polarization a Myth?" *Journal of Politics* 70 (2): 542–55.

Abramowitz, Alan I., and Steven Webster. 2016. "The Rise of Negative Partisanship and the Nationalization of U.S. Elections in the 21st Century." *Electoral Studies* 41: 12–22.

Aday, Sean. 2010. "Leading the Charge: Media, Elites, and the Use of Emotion in Stimulating Rally Effects in Wartime." *Journal of Communication* 60 (3): 440–65.

Adler, E. Scott, and John S. Lapinski. 1997. "Demand-Side Theory and Congressional Committee Composition: A Constituency Characteristics Approach." *American Journal of Political Science* 41 (3): 895–918.

Alden, Dana L., Ashesh Mukherjee, and Wayne D. Hoyer. 2000. "The Effects of Incongruity, Surprise and Positive Moderators on Perceived Humor in Television Advertising." *Journal of Advertising* 29 (2): 1–15.

Aldrich, John H., and David W. Rohde. 1997. "The Transition to Republican Rule in the House: Implications for Theories of Congressional Politics." *Political Science Quarterly* 112 (4): 541–67.

———. 2000. "The Consequences of Party Organization in the House: The Role of the Majority and Minority Parties in Conditional Party Government." In *Polarized Politics: Congress and the President in a Partisan Era,* edited by Jon R. Bond and Richard Fleischer, 31–72. Washington, D.C.: CQ Press.

———. 2009. "Congressional Committees in a Continuing Partisan Era." In *Congress Reconsidered* (Vol. 9), edited by Lawrence C. Dodd and Bruce Oppenheimer, 217–240. Washington, D.C.: CQ Press.

Allcott, Hunt, and Matthew Gentzkow. 2017. "Social Media and Fake News in the 2016 Election." *Journal of Economic Perspectives* 31 (2): 211–36.

Althaus, Scott L. 2002. "American News Consumption During Times of National Crisis." *PS: Political Science & Politics* 35 (3): 517–21.

Alvarez, R. Michael, and Jason L. Saving. 1997. "Deficits, Democrats, and Distributive Benefits: Congressional Elections and the Pork Barrel in the 1980s." *Political Research Quarterly* 50 (4): 809–31.

Anderson, Daniel R., and John Burns. 1991. "Paying Attention to Television." In *Responding to the Screen: Reception and Reaction Processes,* edited by Jennings Bryant and Dolf Zillmann, 3–25. Hillsdale, N.J.: Erlbaum.

Ansolabehere, Stephen, Roy Behr, and Shanto Iyengar. 1993. *The Media Game: American Politics in the Television Age.* New York: Macmillan.

Arceneaux, Kevin. 2012. "Cognitive Biases and the Strength of Political Arguments." *American Journal of Political Science* 56 (2): 271–85.

Arceneaux, Kevin, and Martin Johnson. 2013. *Changing Minds or Changing Channels? Partisan News in an Age of Choice.* Chicago: University of Chicago Press.

Arceneaux, Kevin, Martin Johnson, René Lindstädt, and Ryan J. Vander Wielen. 2016. "The Influence of News Media on Political Elites: Investigating Strategic Responsiveness in Congress." *American Journal of Political Science* 60 (1): 5–29.

Arceneaux, Kevin, Martin Johnson, and Chad Murphy. 2012. "Polarized Political Communication, Oppositional Media Hostility, and Selective Exposure." *Journal of Politics* 74 (1): 174–86.

Auxier, Richard C. 2010. "Congress in a Wordle." Pew Research Center, March 22. http://www.pewresearch.org/2010/03/22/congress-in-a-wordle.

Barker, David C. 2002. *Rushed to Judgment: Talk Radio, Persuasion, and American Political Behavior.* New York: Columbia University Press.

Barthel, Michael, and Amy Mitchell. 2017. "Americans' Attitudes About the News Media Deeply Divided Along Partisan Lines." Pew Research Center, May 10. http://www.journalism.org/2017/05/10/americans-attitudes-about-the-news-media-deeply-divided-along-partisan-lines.

Baum, Matthew A. 2003. *Soft News Goes to War: Public Opinion and American Foreign Policy in the New Media Age.* Princeton, N.J.: Princeton University Press.

———. 2005. "Talking the Vote: Why Presidential Candidates Hit the Talk Show Circuit." *American Journal of Political Science* 49 (2): 213–34.

Baum, Matthew A., and Tim Groeling. 2008. "New Media and the Polarization of American Political Discourse." *Political Communication* 25 (4): 345–65.

Baum, Matthew A., and Samuel Kernell. 1999. "Has Cable Ended the Golden Age of Presidential Television?" *American Political Science Review* 93 (1): 99–114.

Baumgartner, Frank R., Jeffrey M. Berry, Marie Hojnacki, David C. Kimball, and Beth L. Leech. 2009. *Lobbying and Policy Change: Who Wins, Who Loses, and Why.* Chicago: University of Chicago Press.

Baumgartner, Jody C., and Jonathan S. Morris. 2006. "*The Daily Show* Effect: Candidate Evaluations, Efficacy, and the American Youth." *American Politics Research* 34: 341–67.

———, eds. 2012. *Laughing Matters: Humor and American Politics in the Media Age.* New York: Routledge.

Baym, Geoffrey. 2005. "'The Daily Show': Discursive Integration and the Reinvention of Political Journalism." *Political Communication* 22: 259–76.

———. 2008. "Serious Comedy: Expanding the Boundaries of Political Discourse." In *Laughing Matters: Humor and American Politics in the Media Age*, edited by Jody C. Baumgartner and Jonathan S. Morris, 21–38. New York: Routledge.

———. 2010. *From Cronkite to Colbert: The Evolution of Broadcast News.* Boulder, Colo.: Paradigm Publishers.

Baym, Geoffrey, and Jeffrey P. Jones, eds. 2013. *News Parody and Political Satire Across the Globe.* New York: Routledge.

Bellamy, Robert V., and James R. Walker. 1996. *Television and the Remote Control: Grazing the Vast Wasteland.* New York: Guilford.

Bennett, W. Lance. 1990. "Toward a Theory of Press–State Relations in the United States." *Journal of Communication* 40 (2): 103–27.

———. 2016. *News: The Politics of Illusion*. 10th ed. New York: Pearson Longman.

Bennett, W. Lance, and Shanto Iyengar. 2008. "A New Era of Minimal Effects? The Changing Foundations of Political Communication." *Journal of Communication* 58: 707–31.

Bennett, W. Lance, Regina G. Lawrence, and Steven Livingston. 2008. *When the Press Fails: Political Power and the News Media From Iraq to Katrina*. Chicago: University of Chicago Press.

Blumenthal, Sidney. 1982. *The Permanent Campaign*. New York: Simon & Schuster.

Boczkowski, Pablo J., and Eugenia Mitchelstein. 2013. *The News Gap: When the Information Preferences of the Media and the Public Diverge*. Cambridge, Mass.: MIT Press.

Bolls, Paul D., Annie Lang, and Robert F. Potter. 2001. "The Effects of Message Valence and Listener Arousal on Attention, Memory, and Facial Muscular Responses to Radio Advertisements." *Communication Research* 28 (5): 627–51.

Brewer, Paul R., and Xiaoxia Cao. 2006. "Candidate Appearances on Soft News Shows and Public Knowledge About Primary Campaigns." *Journal of Broadcasting and Electronic Media* 50: 18–35.

Brock, David, and Ari Rabin-Havt. 2012. *The Fox Effect: How Roger Ailes Turned a Network Into a Propaganda Machine*. New York: Anchor.

Butler, Daniel M., Christopher F. Karpowitz, and Jeremy C. Pope. 2012. "A Field Experiment on Legislators' Home Styles: Service Versus Policy." *Journal of Politics* 74 (2): 474–86.

Cantor, Paul A. 1999. "*The Simpsons*: Atomistic Politics and the Nuclear Family." *Political Theory* 27: 734–49.

Cao, Xiaoxia. 2008. "Political Comedy Shows and Knowledge About Primary Campaigns: The Moderating Effects of Age and Education." *Mass Communication and Society* 11: 43–61.

Cao, Xiaoxia, and Paul R. Brewer. 2008. "Political Comedy Shows and Public Participation in Politics." *International Journal of Public Opinion Research* 20 (1): 90–99.

Cappella, Joseph N., and Kathleen Hall Jamieson. 1997. *Spiral of Cynicism: The Press and the Public Good*. New York: Oxford University Press.

Carr, Steven A. 1992. "On the Edge of Tastelessness: CBS, the Smothers Brothers, and the Struggle for Control." *Cinema Journal* 31 (4): 3–24.

Caumont, Andrea. 2013. "12 Trends Shaping Digital News." Pew Research Center, October 16. http://www.pewresearch.org/fact-tank/2013/10/16/12-trends-shaping-digital-news.

Cho, Chang-Hoan, and Hongsik John Cheon. 2004. "Why Do People Avoid Advertising on the Internet?" *Journal of Advertising* 33 (4): 89–97.

Clinton, Joshua D., and Ted Enamorado. 2014. "The National News Media's Effect on Congress: How Fox News Affected Elites in Congress." *Journal of Politics* 76 (4): 928–43.

Compton, Josh. 2008. "More Than Laughing? Survey of Political Humor Effects Research." In *Laughing Matters:*

Humor and American Politics in the Media Age, edited by Jody Baumgartner and Jonathan S. Morris, 39–65. New York: Routledge.

Cook, Timothy E. 1998. *Governing With the News: The News Media as a Political Institution*. Chicago: University of Chicago Press.

Dalton, Russell J., Paul A. Beck, and Robert Huckfeldt. 1998. "Partisan Cues and the Media: Information Flows in the 1992 Presidential Election." *American Political Science Review* 92: 111–26.

Dautrich, Kenneth, and Thomas H. Hartley. 1999. *How the News Media Fail American Voters: Causes, Consequences, and Remedies*. New York: Columbia University Press.

Davis, Richard, and Diana Owen. 1998. *New Media and American Politics*. New York: Oxford University Press.

Deery, June. 2004. "Reality TV as Advertainment." *Popular Communication* 2 (1): 1–20.

Delli Carpini, Michael X., and Scott Keeter. 1996. *What Americans Know About Politics and Why It Matters*. New Haven, Conn.: Yale University Press.

Dimitrova, Daniela V., Adam Shehata, Jesper Strömbäck, and Lars W. Nord. 2014. "The Effects of Digital Media on Political Knowledge and Participation in Election Campaigns: Evidence From Panel Data." *Communication Research* 41 (1): 95–118.

Downie, Leonard, Jr., and Michael Schudson. 2009. "The Reconstruction of American Journalism." *Columbia Journalism Review* (November/December). http://www.cjr.org/reconstruction/the_reconstruction_of_american.php.

Druckman, James N., Donald P. Green, James H. Kuklinski, and Arthur Lupia. 2006. "The Growth and Development of Experimental Research in Political Science." *American Political Science Review* 100 (4): 627–35.

Durr, Robert H., John B. Gilmour, and Christina Wolbrecht. 1997. "Explaining Congressional Approval." *American Journal of Political Science* 41: 175–207.

Edwards, Carol, and Diane Williams. 2006. *The Arbitron Cable Television Study: Exploring the Consumer's Relationship With Cable TV*. New York: Arbitron.

Edwards, III, George C., and Stephen J. Wayne. 2013. *Presidential Leadership: Politics and Policy Making*. Boston: Cengage Learning.

Elving, Ronald D. 1996. "Accentuate the Negative: Contemporary Congressional Campaigns." *PS: Political Science & Politics* 29 (3): 440–46.

Entman, Robert M. 2003. "Cascading Activation: Contesting the White House's Frame After 9/11." *Political Communication* 20 (4): 415–32.

Esterling, Kevin M., David M. J. Lazer, and Michael A. Neblo. 2013. "Connecting to Constituents: The Diffusion of Representation Practices Among Congressional Websites." *Political Research Quarterly* 66 (1): 102–14.

Evans, C. Lawrence, and Mark J. Oleszek. 2001. "Message Politics and Partisan Theories of Congress." Paper presented at the Annual Meeting of the Midwest Political Science Association.

Farhi, Paul. 2002. "Going Live." *American Journalism Review* 24 (9): 28–33.

Farrar-Myers, Victoria A., and Justin S. Vaughn, eds. 2015. *Controlling the Message:*

New Media in American Political Campaigns. New York: NYU Press.

Farrier, Jasmine. 2015. *Passing the Buck: Congress, the Budget, and Deficits*. Lexington: University Press of Kentucky.

Feldman, Lauren. 2011. "Partisan Differences in Opinionated News Perceptions: A Test of the Hostile Media Effect." *Political Behavior* 33 (3): 407–32.

Fenno, Richard. 1975. "If as Ralph Nader Says, Congress is 'The Broken Branch,' How Come We Love Our Congressmen So Much?" In *Congress in Change: Evolution and Reform*, edited by Norman Ornstein, 277–87. New York: Praeger Press.

———. 1978. *Home Style: House Members in Their Districts*. New York: HarperCollins.

———. 2010. *Learning to Govern: An Institutional View of the 104th Congress*. Washington, D.C.: Brookings Institution Press.

Ferguson, Douglas A. 1994. "Measurement of Mundane TV Behaviors: Remote Control Device Flipping Frequency." *Journal of Broadcasting and Electronic Media* 38: 35–47.

Fiorina, Morris P. 1980. "The Decline of Collective Responsibility in American Politics." *Daedalus* (Summer): 25–45.

———. 2013. "America's Polarized Politics: Causes and Solutions." *Perspectives on Politics* 11 (3): 852–59.

Fiorina, Morris P., and Samuel J. Abrams. 2012. *Disconnect: The Breakdown of Representation in American Politics*. Norman: University of Oklahoma Press.

Forgette, Richard, and Jonathan S. Morris. 2006. "High Conflict Television News and Public Opinion." *Political Research Quarterly* 59: 447–56.

Frantzich, Stephen E. 2015. *Congress, the Media, and the Public: Who Reveals What, When, and How?* New York: Routledge.

Fox, Julia, Annie Lang, Yongkuk Chung, Seungwhan Lee, Nancy Schwartz, and Deborah Potter. 2004. "Picture This: Effects of Graphics on the Processing of Television News." *Journal of Broadcasting and Electronic Media* 48 (4): 646–74.

Gallup. 2016. "Congress and the Public." http://www.gallup.com/poll/1600/congress-public.aspx.

Goel, Vinod, and Raymond J. Dolan. 2001. "The Functional Anatomy of Humor: Segregating Cognitive and Affective Components." *Nature Neuroscience* 4 (3): 237–38.

Goldberg, Bernard. 2002. *Bias: A CBS Insider Exposes How the Media Distort the News*. Washington, DC: Regnery.

Gottfried, Jeffrey, and Monica Anderson. 2014. "For Some, the Satiric 'Colbert Report' Is a Trusted Source of Political News." Pew Research Center, December 12. http://www.pewresearch.org/fact-tank/2014/12/12/for-some-the-satiric-colbert-report-is-a-trusted-source-of-political-news.

Graber, Doris A. 2001. *Processing Politics: Learning From Television in the Internet Age*. Chicago: University of Chicago Press.

———. 2006. *Mass Media and American Politics*. 7th ed. Washington, D.C.: CQ Press.

Graber, Doris A., and Johanna Dunaway. 2014. *Mass Media and American Politics*. 9th ed. Washington, D.C.: CQ Press.

Gray, Jonathan, Jeffrey P. Jones, and Ethan Thompson, eds. 2009. *Satire TV: Politics and Comedy in the Post-Network Era*. New York: NYU Press.

Gupta, Pola B., and Kenneth R. Lord. 1998. "Product Placement in Movies: The Effect of Prominence and Mode on Audience Recall." *Journal of Current Issues & Research in Advertising* 20 (1): 47–59.

Gutmann, Amy, and Dennis Thompson. 1996. *Democracy and Disagreement*. Cambridge, Mass.: Harvard University Press.

Haiman, John. 1998. *Talk Is Cheap: Sarcasm, Alienation, and the Evolution of Language*. New York: Oxford University Press.

Hamilton, James T. 2004. *All the News That's Fit to Sell: How the Market Transforms Information Into News*. Princeton, N.J.: Princeton University Press.

Hannity, Sean. 2002. *Let Freedom Ring: Winning the War of Liberty Over Liberalism*. New York: Regan Books.

Harbridge, Laurel, and Neil Malhotra. 2011. "Electoral Incentives and Partisan Conflict in Congress: Evidence From Survey Experiments." *American Journal of Political Science* 55 (3): 494–510.

Hardin, Russell. 2015. *Collective Action*. New York: Routledge.

Hart, Roderick. 1994. *Seducing America: How Television Charms the Modern Voter*. New York: Oxford University Press.

Heclo, Hugh. 2002. "Perfecting the Permanent Campaign." *The World & I* 16 (7): 32.

Heeter, Carrie, and Bradley S. Greenberg. 1988. "Profiling the Zappers." In *Cableviewing*, edited by Carrie Heeter and Bradley S. Greenberg, 67–73. Norwood, N.J.: Ablex.

Hetherington, Marc J., and Thomas J. Rudolph. 2015. *Why Washington Won't Work: Polarization, Political Trust, and the Governing Crisis*. Chicago: University of Chicago Press.

Hibbing, John R., and Elizabeth Theiss-Morse. 1995. *Congress as Public Enemy: Public Attitudes Toward American Political Institutions*. New York: Cambridge University Press.

———. 1998. "The Media's Role in Public Negativity Toward Congress: Distinguishing Emotional Reactions and Cognitive Evaluations." *American Journal of Political Science* 42: 475–98.

Hoffman, Lindsay H., and Tiffany L. Thomson. 2009. "The Effect of Television Viewing on Adolescents' Civic Participation: Political Efficacy as a Mediating Mechanism." *Journal of Broadcasting & Electronic Media* 53 (1): 3–21.

Holbrook, R. Andrew, and Timothy G. Hill. 2005. "Agenda-Setting and Priming in Prime Time Television: Crime Dramas as Political Cues." *Political Communication* 22 (3): 277–95.

Iyengar, Shanto, and Kyu S. Hahn. 2009. "Red Media, Blue Media: Evidence of Ideological Selectivity in Media Use." *Journal of Communication* 59 (1): 19–39.

Iyengar, Shanto, and Donald R. Kinder. 1987. *News That Matters: Television and American Opinion*. Chicago: University of Chicago Press.

Iyengar, Shanto, and Jennifer A. McGrady. 2007. *Media Politics: A Citizen's Guide*. New York: W. W. Norton.

Iyengar, Shanto, Mark D. Peters, and Donald R. Kinder. 1982. "Experimental Demonstrations of the 'Not-So-Minimal' Consequences of Television News Programs." *American Political Science Review* 76 (4): 848–58.

Iyengar, Shanto, Gaurav Sood, and Yphtach Lelkes. 2012. "Affect, Not Ideology: A Social Identity Perspective on Polarization." *Public Opinion Quarterly* 76 (3): 405–31.

Jacobson, Gary C. 2007. "Referendum: The 2006 Midterm Congressional Elections." *Political Science Quarterly* 122 (1): 1–24.

———. 2017. "The Triumph of Polarized Partisanship in 2016: Donald Trump's Improbable Victory." *Political Science Quarterly* 132 (1): 9–41.

Jamieson, Kathleen Hall, and Joseph N. Cappella. 2008. *Echo Chamber: Rush Limbaugh and the Conservative Media Establishment.* New York: Oxford University Press.

Jenkins, Henry. 2006. *Convergence Culture: Where Old and New Media Collide.* New York: NYU Press.

Johnson, Justin P. 2013. "Targeted Advertising and Advertising Avoidance." *RAND Journal of Economics* 44 (1): 128–44.

Jones, David R. 2014. "A More Responsible Two-Party System? Accountability for Majority and Minority Party Performance in a Polarized Congress." *Polity* 46 (3): 470–92.

Jones, David R., and Monika L. McDermott. 2009. *Americans, Congress, and Democratic Responsiveness: Public Evaluations of Congress and Electoral Consequences.* Ann Arbor: University of Michigan Press.

———. 2011. "The Salience of the Democratic Congress and the 2010 Elections." *PS: Political Science & Politics* 44 (2): 297–301.

Jones, Jeffrey P. 2005. *Entertaining Politics: News Political Television and Civic Culture.* Lanham, Md.: Rowman and Littlefield.

———. 2010. *Entertaining Politics: Satiric Television and Political Engagement.* Lanham, Md.: Rowman & Littlefield.

Kakutani, Michiko. 2008. "Is Jon Stewart the Most Trusted Man in America?" *New York Times*, August 17.

Kernell, Samuel. 2006. *Going Public: New Strategies of Presidential Leadership.* Washington, D.C.: CQ Press.

Khan, Huma. 2010. "Stephen Colbert's Super PAC Takes on the NBA." http:// abcnews.go.com/blogs/politics/2011/10/ stephen-colberts-super-pac-takes-on-the-nba.

Kinder, Donald R., and Thomas R. Palfrey, eds. 1993. *Experimental Foundations of Political Science.* Ann Arbor: University of Michigan Press.

Kitman, Marvin. 2012. "The Fox News Effect." *The Nation*, March 7. https://www .thenation.com/article/fox-news-effect.

Kohut, Andy. 2013. "Pew Surveys of Audience Habits Suggest Perilous Future for News." Poynter, October 4. http:// www.poynter.org/2013/pew-surveys-of-audience-habits-suggest-perilous-future-for-news/225139.

Ladd, Jonathan M. 2011. *Why Americans Hate the Media and How It Matters.* Princeton, N.J.: Princeton University Press.

LaFave, Lawrence, Jay Haddad, and William A. Maesen. 1996. "Superiority, Enhanced Self-Esteem, and Perceived Incongruity Humor Theory." In *Humor and Laughter: Theory Research and Applications*, edited by Antony J. Chapman & Hugh C. Foot, 63–91. New Brunswick, N.J.: Transaction.

LaFerle, Carrie, and Steven M. Edwards. 2006. "Product Placement: How Brands Appear on Television." *Journal of Advertising* 35 (4): 65–86.

Lang, Annie. 2000. "The Limited Capacity Model of Mediated Message

Processing." *Journal of Communication* 50 (1): 46–70.

Lang, Annie, Paul Bolls, Robert F. Potter, and Karlynn Kawahara. 1999. "The Effects of Production Pacing and Arousing Content on the Information Processing of Television Messages." *Journal of Broadcasting & Electronic Media* 43 (4): 451–75.

Lang, Annie, Jennifer Borse, Kevin Wise, and Prabu David. 2002. "Captured by the World Wide Web: Orienting to Structural and Content Features of Computer-Presented Information." *Communication Research* 29: 215–45.

Lang, Annie, Kulijinder Dhillon, and Qingwen Dong. 1995. "The Effects of Emotional Arousal and Valence on Television Viewers' Cognitive Capacity and Memory." *Journal of Broadcasting & Electronic Media* 39 (3): 313–27.

Lang, Annie, Mija Shin, Samuel D. Bradley, Zheng Wang, Seungjo Lee, and Deborah Potter. 2005. "Wait! Don't Turn That Dial! More Excitement to Come! The Effects of Story Length and Production Pacing in Local Television News on Channel Changing Behavior and Information Processing in a Free Choice Environment." *Journal of Broadcasting and Electronic Media* 49 (1): 3–22.

Laufer, Peter. 1995. *Inside Talk Radio: America's Voice or Just Hot Air?* Seacaucus, N.J.: Carol Publishing Group.

Lawrence, Eric, John Sides, and Henry Farrell. 2010. "Self-Segregation or Deliberation? Blog Readership, Participation, and Polarization in American Politics." *Perspectives on Politics* 8 (1): 141–57.

Lazarsfeld, Paul Felix, Bernard Berelson, and Hazel Gaudet. 1948. *The People's Choice: How the Voter Makes Up His Mind in a Presidential Campaign.* New York: Columbia University Press.

Lazarus, Jeffrey, and Nathan W. Monroe. 2007. "The Speaker's Discretion: Conference Committee Appointments in the 97th through 106th Congresses." *Political Research Quarterly* 60 (4): 593–606.

Lee, Frances E. 2009. *Beyond Ideology: Politics, Principles, and Partisanship in the US Senate.* Chicago: University of Chicago Press.

Lee, Hoon, and Nojin Kwak. 2014. "The Affect Effect of Political Satire: Sarcastic Humor, Negative Emotions, and Political Participation." *Mass Communication and Society* 17 (3): 307–28.

Leighley, Jan E. 2003. *Mass Media and Politics: A Social Science Perspective.* Boston: Houghton Mifflin.

Levendusky, Matthew. 2009. *The Partisan Sort: How Liberals Became Democrats and Conservatives Became Republicans.* Chicago: University of Chicago Press.

———. 2013. "Why Do Partisan Media Polarize Viewers?" *American Journal of Political Science* 57 (3): 611–23.

Lichter, S. Robert, Jody C. Baumgartner, and Jonathan S. Morris. 2014. *Politics Is a Joke!: How TV Comedians Are Remaking Political Life.* Boulder, Colo.: Westview Press.

Lichter, S. Robert, and Richard Noyes. 1996. *Good Intentions Make Bad News: Why Americans Hate Campaign Journalism.* Lanham, Md.: Rowman & Littlefield.

Limbaugh, Rush. 1993. *The Way Things Ought to Be.* New York: Pocket Books.

———. 1994. *See, I Told You So.* New York: Pocket Books.

Livingston, Steven. 1997. *Clarifying the CNN Effect: An Examination of Media*

Effects According to Type of Military Intervention. Cambridge, Mass.: Shorenstein Center, Harvard University.

Lodge, Milton, and Ruth Hamill. 1986. "A Partisan Schema for Political Information Processing." *American Political Science Review* 80: 505–19.

Lodge, Milton, Kathleen M. McGraw, and Patrick Stroh. 1989. "An Impression-Driven Model of Candidate Evaluation." *American Political Science Review* 83 (2): 399–419.

Lodge, Milton, Marco R. Steenbergen, and Shawn Brau. 1995. "The Responsive Voter: Campaign Information and the Dynamics of Candidate Evaluation." *American Political Science Review* 89 (2): 309–26.

Luskin, Robert. 1990. "Explaining Political Sophistication." *Political Behavior* 12 (4): 331–61.

Madden, Thomas J., and Marc G. Weinberger. 1982. "The Effects of Humor on Attention in Magazine Advertising." *Journal of Advertising* 11 (3): 8–14.

Maestas, Cherie D., Lonna Rae Atkeson, Thomas Croom, and Lisa A. Bryant. 2008. "Shifting the Blame: Federalism, Media, and Public Assignment of Blame Following Hurricane Katrina." *Publius: The Journal of Federalism* 38 (4): 609–32.

Malecha, Gary Lee, and Daniel J. Reagan. 2012. *The Public Congress: Congressional Deliberation in a New Media Age.* New York: Routledge.

Mann, Thomas E., and Norman J. Ornstein. 2006. *The Broken Branch: How Congress Is Failing America and How to Get It Back on Track.* New York: Oxford University Press.

———. 2016. *It's Even Worse Than It Looks: How the American Constitutional System Collided With the New Politics of Extremism.* New York: Basic Books.

Martinelli, Diana Knott. 2012. "Strategic Communication Planning." In *The Practice of Government Public Relations*, edited by Mordecai Lee, Grant Lee, and Kendra Stewart, 143–156. Boca Raton, Fla.: CRC Press.

Mayer, Kenneth R., and David T. Canon. 1999. *The Dysfunctional Congress?: The Individual Roots of an Institutional Dilemma.* Boulder, Colo.: Westview Press.

McChesney, Robert W., and John Nichols. 2010. *The Life and Death of American Journalism: The Media Revolution That Will Begin the World Again.* New York: Nation Books.

Mellman, Mark. 2015. "The Young and the Newsless." *The Hill*, January 27.

Miller, Andrea, and Glenn Leshner. 2007. "How Viewers Process Live, Breaking, and Emotional Television News." *Media Psychology* 10: 23–40.

Miller, Arthur H., Edie N. Goldenberg, and Lutz Erbring. 1979. "Type-Set Politics: Impact of Newspapers on Public Confidence." *American Political Science Review* 73 (1): 67–84.

Mitchell, Amy, Jeffrey Gottfried, Michael Barthel, and Elisa Shearer. 2016. "The Modern News Consumer." Pew Research Center, July 7.

Mitchell, Amy, Jeffrey Gottfried, Jocelyn Kiley, and Katerina Matsa. 2014. "Political Polarization & Media Habits." October 21. http://www.journalism.org/2014/10/21/political-polarization-media-habits.

Mitchell, Amy, and Dana Page. 2015. *State of the News Media 2015.* Washington, D.C.: Pew Research Center.

Mobbs, Dean, Michael D. Greicius, Eiman Abdel-Azim, Vinod Menon, and

Allan L. Reiss. 2003. "Humor Modulates the Mesolimbic Reward Centers." *Neuron* 40 (5): 1041–48.

Morone, James A. 1998. *The Democratic Wish: Popular Participation and the Limits of American Government*. New Haven, Conn.: Yale University Press.

Morris, Jonathan S. 2005. "The Fox News Factor." *Harvard International Journal of Press/Politics* 10 (3): 56–79.

———. 2006. "Car Crashes and Soap Operas: Melodramatic Narrative on Cable News." In *Americana: Readings in American Popular Culture*, edited by Leslie Wilson, 99–104. Hollywood, Calif.: Press Americana.

———. 2007. "Slanted Objectivity? Perceived Media Bias, Cable News Exposure, and Political Attitudes." *Social Science Quarterly* 88 (3): 707–28.

Moy, Patricia, Michael A. Xenos, and Verena K. Hess. 2006. "Priming Effects of Late-Night Comedy." *International Journal of Public Opinion Research* 18: 198–210.

Munson, Wayne. 1993. *All Talk: The Talkshow in Media Culture*. Philadelphia: Temple University Press.

Mutz, Diana C. 2006. *Hearing the Other Side: Deliberative Versus Participatory Democracy*. New York: Cambridge University Press.

———. 2015. *In-Your-Face Politics: The Consequences of Uncivil Media*. Princeton, N.J.: Princeton University Press.

Mutz, Diana C., and Byron Reeves. 2005. "The New Videomalaise: Effects of Televised Incivility on Political Trust." *American Political Science Review* 99: 1–15.

Napoli, Philip. 2003. *Audience Economics: Media Institutions and the Audience Marketplace*. New York: Columbia University Press.

———. 2012. "Audience Evolution and the Future of Audience Research." *International Journal on Media Management* 14 (2): 79–97.

National Public Radio. 2012. "Re-Becoming the Nation We Always Were." http://www.npr.org/templates/transcript/transcript.php?storyId=162304439.

Newhagen, John E., and Byron Reeves. 1992. "The Evening's Bad News: Effects of Compelling Negative Television News Images on Memory." *Journal of Communication* 42 (2): 25–41.

Niven, David. 2002. *Tilt?: The Search for Media Bias*. Westport, Conn.: Praeger.

———. 2003. "Objective Evidence on Media Bias: Newspaper Coverage of Congressional Party Switchers." *Journalism & Mass Communication Quarterly* 80 (2): 311–26.

Niven, David, S. Robert Lichter, and Daniel Amundson. 2003. "The Political Content of Late Night Comedy." *Harvard International Journal of Press/Politics* 8: 118–33.

Oleszek, Walter J. 2014. *Congressional Procedures and the Policy Process*. Thousand Oaks, Calif.: Sage.

Olson, Mancur. 1965. *The Logic of Collective Action: Public Goods and the Theory of Groups*. Cambridge, Mass.: Harvard University Press.

O'Reilly, Bill. 2006. *Culture Warrior*. New York: Broadway Books.

Ornstein, Norman J., and Thomas E. Mann. 2000. *The Permanent Campaign and Its Future*. Washington, D.C.: American Enterprise Institute.

Owen, Diana. 2017. "Tipping the Balance of Power in Elections? Voters' Engagement in the Digital Campaign." In *The Internet and the 2016 Presidential*

Campaign, edited by Jody C. Baumgartner and Terri L. Towner, 151–178. Lanham, Md.: Lexington Books.

Page, Benjamin I., Robert Y. Shapiro, and Glenn R. Dempsey. 1987. "What Moves Public Opinion?" *American Political Science Review* 81 (1): 23-43.

Parkin, Michael. 2010. "Taking Late Night Comedy Seriously: How Candidate Appearances on Late Night Can Engage Viewers." *Political Research Quarterly* 63 (1): 3–15.

Parsons, Patrick R. 2008. *Blue Skies: A History of Cable Television*. Philadelphia: Temple University Press.

Patterson, Thomas E. 1993. *Out of Order: How the Decline of the Political Parties and the Growing Power of the News Media Undermine the American Way of Electing Presidents*. New York: Alfred Knopf.

———. 2000. "Doing Well and Doing Good." Faculty Research Working Paper Series, John F. Kennedy School of Government. Cambridge, Mass.: Harvard University.

———. 2016. "News Coverage of the 2016 Presidential Primaries: Horse Race Reporting Has Consequences." Shorenstein Center. http://shorensteincenter.org/news-coverage-2016-presidential-primaries.

Patterson, Thomas E., and Wolfgang Donsbach. 1996. "News Decisions: Journalists as Partisan Actors." *Political Communication* 13 (4): 455–68.

Patterson, Thomas E., and Robert D. McClure. 1976. *The Unseeing Eye: The Myth of Television Power in National Politics*. New York: Putnam.

Perloff, Richard M. 2015. "A Three-Decade Retrospective on the Hostile Media Effect." *Mass Communication and Society* 18 (6): 701–29.

Peterson, Russell L. 2008. *Strange Bedfellows: How Late-Night Comedy Turns Democracy Into a Joke*. New Brunswick, N.J.: Rutgers University Press.

Petrocik, John R. 1996. "Issue Ownership in Presidential Elections, With a 1980 Case Study." *American Journal of Political Science* 40: 825–50.

Pew Research Center. 2005. "Reporting Katrina." September 11. http://www.journalism.org/2005/09/11/reporting-katrina.

———. 2008. *Audience Segments in a Changing News Environment: Key News Audiences Now Blend Online and Traditional Sources*. August 17. https://web.archive.org/web/20080918160513/http://people-press.org/reports/pdf/444.pdf.

———. 2010. "Americans Spending More Time Following the News." September 12. http://www.people-press.org/2010/09/12/americans-spending-more-time-following-the-news.

———. 2012a. "In Changing News Landscape, Even Television Is Vulnerable." September 27. http://www.people-press.org/2012/09/27/in-changing-news-landscape-even-television-is-vulnerable.

———. 2012b. *Trends in News Consumption: 1991–2012*. http://www.people-press.org/2012/09/27/section-4-demographics-and-political-views-of-news-audiences.

———. 2016. "Newspapers: Daily Readership by Age." *The State of the News Media, 2016*. http://www.journalism.org/media-indicators/newspapers-daily-readership-by-age.

Pika, Joseph A., John A. Maltese, and Andrew Rudalevige. 2016. *The Politics of the Presidency*. Washington, D.C.: CQ Press.

Prior, Markus. 2003. "Any Good News in Soft News? The Impact of Soft News Preferences on Political Knowledge." *Political Communication* 20: 149–71.

———. 2005. "News vs. Entertainment: How Increasing Media Choice Widens Gaps in Political Knowledge and Turnout." *American Journal of Political Science* 49 (3): 577–92.

———. 2007. *Post-Broadcast Democracy: How Media Choice Increases Inequality in Political Involvement and Polarizes Elections.* New York: Cambridge University Press.

———. 2010. "You've Either Got It or You Don't? The Stability of Political Interest Over the Life Cycle." *Journal of Politics* 72 (3): 747–66.

———. 2013. "Media and Political Polarization." *Annual Review of Political Science* 16: 101–27.

Project for Excellence in Journalism. 2012. *The State of the News Media 2012.* http://www.pewresearch.org/2012/03/19/state-of-the-news-media-2012.

Rahn, Wendy M., John H. Aldrich, and Eugene Borgida. 1994. "Individual and Contextual Variations in Political Candidate Appraisal." *American Political Science Review* 88 (1): 193–99.

Ramirez, Mark D. 2009. "The Dynamics of Partisan Conflict on Congressional Approval." *American Journal of Political Science* 53 (3): 681–94.

Reinemann, Carsten, James Stanyer, Sebastian Scherr, and Guido Legnante. 2012. "Hard and Soft News: A Review of Concepts, Operationalizations, and Key Findings." *Journalism* 13 (2): 221–39.

Roberts, Jason M. 2012. "House Rules and Procedure: A Procedural Arms Race." In *New Directions in Congressional Politics*, edited by Jaime L. Carson, 111–25. New York: Routledge.

Robinson, Michael J. 1974. "The Impact of the Televised Watergate Hearings." *Journal of Communication* 24 (2): 17–30.

Rohde, David W., Edward H. Stiglitz, and Barry R. Weingast. 2013. "Dynamic Theory of Congressional Organization." Unpublished manuscript. https://web.stanford.edu/group/mcnollgast/cgi-bin/wordpress/wp-content/uploads/2013/10/rsw_dynamics_1302171.pdf.

Rosenstiel, Tom. 2008. "The How vs. Where of News Consumption." Pew Research Center, August 20. http://www.journalism.org/2008/08/20/the-how-vs-where-of-news-consumption.

Sabato, Larry. 2000. *Feeding Frenzy: Attack Journalism and American Politics.* Baltimore: Lanahan Publishers.

Schaffner, Brian F., and Patrick J. Sellers, eds. 2009. *Winning With Words: The Origins and Impact of Political Framing.* New York: Routledge.

Schmitt, Kathleen M., Albert C. Gunther, and Janice L. Liebhart. 2004. "Why Partisans See Mass Media as Biased." *Communication Research* 31 (6): 623–41.

Sears, David O. 1986. "College Sophomores in the Laboratory: Influence of a Narrow Data Base on Social Psychology's View of Human Nature." *Journal of Personality and Social Psychology* 51: 515–30.

Sellers, Patrick. 2009. *Cycles of Spin: Strategic Communication in the U.S. Congress.* New York: Cambridge University Press.

Sheppard, Si. 2007. *The Partisan Press: A History of Media Bias in the United States.* Jefferson, N.C.: McFarland.

Shepsle, Kenneth A., and Barry R. Weingast. 1987. "The Institutional Foundations of Committee Power." *American Political Science Review* 81 (1): 85–104.

Speck, Paul S., and Michael T. Elliot. 1997. "Predictors of Advertising Avoidance in Print and Broadcast Media." *Journal of Advertising* 26 (3): 61–76.

Stroud, Natalie J. 2008. "Media Use and Political Predispositions: Revisiting the Concept of Selective Exposure." *Political Behavior* 30: 341–66.

———. 2010. "Polarization and Partisan Selective Exposure." *Journal of Communication* 60 (3), 556–76.

———. 2011. *Niche News: The Politics of News Choice.* New York: Oxford University Press.

Subramanian, Courtney 2012. "Stephen Colbert's Super PAC Satire Lands Him a Peabody." *Time*, April 5. http://newsfeed.time.com/2012/04/05/stephen-colberts-super-pac-satire-lands-him-a-peabody.

Sunstein, Cass. 2001. *Republic.com.* Princeton, N.J.: Princeton University Press.

———. 2009. *Going to Extremes: How Like Minds Unite and Divide.* New York: Oxford University Press.

Taber, Charles S., and Milton Lodge. 2006. "Motivated Skepticism in the Evaluation of Political Beliefs." *American Journal of Political Science* 50 (3): 755–69.

Twain, Mark (Samuel Clemens). 1897. "Pudd'nhead Wilson's New Calendar." In *Following the Equator.* http://www.gutenberg.org/ebooks/2895.

Vallone, Robert P., Lee Ross, and Mark R. Lepper. 1985. "The Hostile Media Phenomenon: Biased Perception and Perceptions of Media Bias in Coverage of the 'Beirut Massacre.'" *Journal of Personality and Social Psychology* 49: 577–85.

Vinson, C. Danielle. 2017. *Congress and the Media: Beyond Institutional Power.* New York: Oxford University Press.

Voth, Ben. 2008. "*Saturday Night Live* and Presidential Elections." In *Laughing Matters: Humor and American Politics in the Media Age*, edited by Jody Baumgartner and Jonathan S. Morris, 229–40. New York: Routledge.

Waldrop, Robert V. 2012. *Will Rogers Views the News: Humorist Ponders Current Events.* Bloomington, Ind.: Abbott Press.

Wanzer, Melissa B., Ann B. Frymier, and Jeffrey Irwin. 2010. "An Explanation of the Relationship Between Instructor Humor and Student Learning: Instructional Humor Processing Theory." *Communication Education* 59 (1): 1–18.

Watts, Mark D., David Domke, Dhavan V. Shah, and David P. Fan. 1999. "Elite Cues and Media Bias in Presidential Campaigns: Explaining Public Perceptions of a Liberal Press." *Communication Research* 26 (2): 144–75.

West, Darrell M., and John M. Orman. 2003. *Celebrity Politics.* Upper Saddle River, N.J.: Prentice Hall.

Widyanto, Laura, and Mark Griffiths. 2006. "Internet Addiction: A Critical Review." *International Journal of Mental Health and Addiction* 4 (1): 31–51.

Williams, Bruce A., and Michael X. Delli Carpini. 2011. *After Broadcast News: Media Regimes, Democracy, and the New Information Environment.* New York: Cambridge University Press.

Winkler, Alexander, Beate Dörsing, Winifried Rief, Yuhui Shen, and Julia A. Glombiewski. 2013. "Treatment of Internet Addiction: A Meta-Analysis." *Clinical Psychology Review* 33 (2): 317–29.

Yarwood, Dean L. 2004. *When Congress Makes a Joke: Congressional Humor Then and Now.* Lanham, Md.: Rowman & Littlefield.

Young, Dannagal Goldthwaite. 2004. "Late-Night Comedy in Election 2000: Its Influence on Candidate Trait Ratings and the Moderating Effects of Political Knowledge and Partisanship." *Journal of Broadcasting & Electronic Media* 48: 1–22.

——. 2006. "Late-Night Comedy and the Salience of the Candidates' Caricatured Traits in the 2000 Election." *Mass Media & Society* 9: 339–66.

——. 2013. "Laughter, Learning, or Enlightenment? Viewing and Avoidance Motivations Behind *The Daily Show* and *The Colbert Report*." *Journal of Broadcasting & Electronic Media* 57 (2): 153–69.

Young, Dannagal G., and Russell M. Tisinger. 2006. "Dispelling Late-Night Myths: News Consumption Among Late-Night Comedy Viewers and the Predictors of Exposure to Various Late-Night Shows." *Harvard International Journal of Press/Politics* 11 (3): 113–34.

Young, Dannagal Goldthwaite, and Sarah E. Esralew. 2011. "Jon Stewart a Heretic? Surely You Jest: Political Participation and Discussion Among Viewers of Late-Night Comedy Programming." In *The Stewart/Colbert Effect: Essays on Real Impacts of Fake News*, edited by Amarnath Amarasingam, 99–115. Jefferson, N.C.: McFarland.

Zaller, John R. 1992. *The Nature and Origins of Mass Opinion*. New York: Cambridge University Press.

Zhang, Yong, and George M. Zinkhan. 2006. "Responses to Humorous Ads: Does Audience Involvement Matter?" *Journal of Advertising* 35 (4): 113–27.

Index

audience size, variability in, 136, 137, 140, 141

bin Laden killing, coverage of, 135, 136, 141

branding trend and, 143

cable/Internet news platforms and, 133, 134–135, 136, 137, 138, 140, 141, 144–145

cable news viewership, surges in, 136, 140, 141

clickbait and, 138

clicking phenomenon and, 146

congressional brinksmanship and, 134–135

congressional elections/proceedings, reporting on, 133–134, 136, 145

congressional trust/approval attitudes and, 135, 145–150, 150 (table)

content analysis, news agenda and, 143–145

crosstalk phenomenon and, 138

debate/roundtable news show format and, 138

debt ceiling crisis and, 133–134, 135, 136, 189

drama-laden news stories and, 136, 137, 138, 141, 143, 146

evolution of, 139–141

foreign policy crises, government decision process and, 140

framing process and, 148

global terrorism, coverage of, 136–137

immediacy/real-time coverage, demand for, 133, 136–137, 141, 142–143, 200

Internet news production techniques and, 138

like-minded news sources and, 142

live/speculative commentary and, 137

mobile news access and, 143

news-grazing habits/attitudes, assessment of, 147–148

news holes, filling of, 91 (figure), 137, 144

news urgency, congressional disapproval/anxiety and, 145–150, 150 (table)

news urgency, description/definition of, 137–139

news urgency, impetus for, 136–137, 139, 146

on-demand news delivery and, 137

partisan/ideological divide and, 142

prevalence of, 136–137

production techniques, implied urgency and, 137–138, 146

social media resources and, 142–143

television network programming and, 140

24/7 all-news channels, 140, 141, 143, 145

uncivil political discourse/political polarization, effects of, 138–139

unfolding/emerging news events and, 137, 140–141

Weiner sexting scandal, coverage of, 135

See also Breaking-news experiment; Commentary news formats; Fake-news genre; Partisan news format

Breitbart News, 26, 86, 106

Brock, D., 25

Bush, G. H. W., 160

Bush, G. W., 161

Butler, D. M., 20

Cable television, 9, 10, 11, 14, 17, 24, 30, 62, 72, 82–83, 87, 88, 90, 104, 105, 106, 133, 134–135, 136, 137, 138, 140, 141, 144–145

Canon, D. T., 19

Cantor, P. A., 167

Carr, S. A., 167

Carson, J., 160

CBS, 9, 36, 37, 51, 52, 53, 54, 111, 116, 118, 141, 163, 167

CBS Evening News, 115, 116, 117, 121

Checkbook journalism, 92

Citizens United v. FEC (2010), 157

Civil rights conflicts, 15

Civil society, ix

Clickbait, 138

Clicking phenomenon, 41, 42, 43, 50, 59, 89, 101, 138, 146, 202

About the Author

Richard Forgette is an associate provost and professor of political science at the University of Mississippi. He also serves as the interim director of the Center for Intelligence and Security Studies at the University of Mississippi. Rich served as the American Political Science Association's Steiger Congressional Fellow in 1996–1997, working in the U.S. House of Representatives and the U.S. Senate.

Rich's research and teaching fields are in the study of legislatures, political reform, and elections. He is the author of two books and numerous journal articles on the U.S. Congress, the federal spending process, legislative parties, legislative elections, voting rights, redistricting, and public budgeting. His research has been funded by the National Science Foundation and Department of Homeland Security. He also led interdisciplinary research teams assessing disaster recovery and security after Hurricane Katrina, creating measures and models of community resilience to withstand large-scale disasters.

Rich received his BA from Pennsylvania State University, an MA degree at the University of North Carolina at Chapel Hill, and an MS in public policy analysis and a PhD in political science at the University of Rochester.